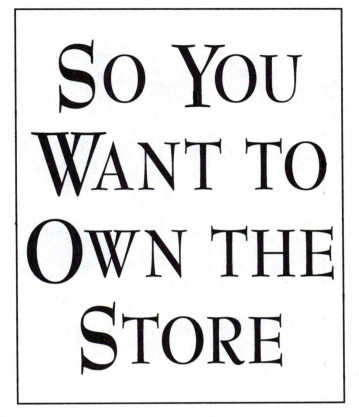

So You Want to Own the Store

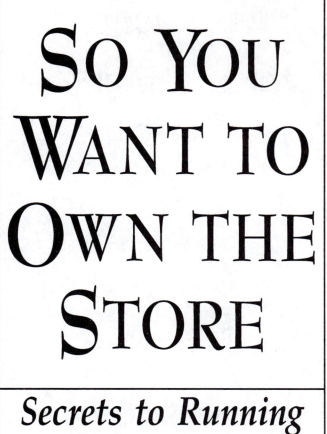

SO YOU WANT TO OWN THE STORE

Secrets to Running a Successful Retail Operation

MORT BROWN AND THOMAS TILLING

CONTEMPORARY BOOKS

Library of Congress Cataloging-in-Publication Data

Brown, Mort.
    So you want to own the store : secrets to running a successful
retail operation / Mort Brown and Thomas Tilling.
        p.   cm.
    Includes index.
    ISBN 0-8092-3236-7
    1. Stores, Retail—United States—Management.   I. Tilling,
Thomas.   II. Title.
HF5429.3.B754   1997
658.8′87—dc21
                                         97-6705
                                       CIP

17   16   15   14   13   12   11   10   9   8   7   6   5   4   3   2   1

To the three women who have influenced my life in the most positive of ways—my daughter, Lisa; my friend Lucy Rucker; and my wife, Ruth—and to my son, Jeffrey Brown, who teaches me life's true lessons every day. I cherish every day that I am fortunate to have him for my son.

Contents

Acknowledgments

Special thanks to Erik Sandberg-Diment, whose vision and intellect brought this book from dream to reality; to Sue, who more than any one person moved the book to a timely and successful conclusion—"when everything was said and done, more was done than said"; and to the millions of entrepreneurs who every day are living proof that the American dream is still alive and well.

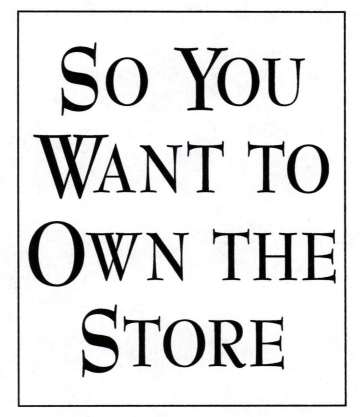

So You Want to Own the Store

1 The Bottom Line Is You

It was a great temptation for me to make the very first words of this book a repeat performance of that shopworn chestnut heard more than ever since the nineties began, "Today is the first day of the rest of your life." After all, it could well be.

Since you picked up this book, I know you're at least reading about—if not quite ready to make—some drastic changes. You're seriously thinking of trading in the eight hours a day you spend in somebody else's business for the twenty-four hours an entrepreneur spends in his or her own, each and every day. Now that's resetting your clock in a big way.

Even more than that, though, it's resetting your lifestyle to one so alien to most normal working folk that you might as well be packing up one fine weekend without warning and moving to China. Retailing can seem like a foreign country. There aren't many good maps of the place, and the going can be treacherous.

Then there's the fear. Let me tell you about the fear.

In 1975 I gave up a lucrative but—need I say it?—frustrating insurance career. When I fired my employer that year, I was making $40,000. In those days, 1975, that was enough to support a comfortable home and lifestyle for my wife and kids, then seven and five years old. In return, I expected to sink my life savings plus $7,000 borrowed from my father-in-law to supplement a bank loan into opening a pet store from which I planned to draw $18,000 a year.

Two weeks after I signed the lease, my father-in-law called to tell me that his son was terribly worried about us all, the store location was all wrong, the economy was terrible, and I was bound to put the whole family out on the street.

My mother thought I'd lost my mind.

I traded in my brand-new Monte Carlo for a Datsun station wagon. The springs squeaked the entire way home from the lot. The window stuck when, waiting at a red light, I tried to crank it down. I stared at the light and thought, Swift move, Mort, swapping $40,000 a year for this plus $1,500 a month and $50,000 worth of debt. Really swift!

The light turned green. Yes, but I'm going to make it on my own, I told myself.

The day the store opened, October 18, 1975, the weather was so bad that the World Series game was canceled, and the Datsun wouldn't start. I was so nervous that I had to ask a friend to drive me to the store. On the way I told him I was going to sell the store as soon as I could and get a real job again.

From the moment the doors opened, the store was mobbed. My emotions went from absolute relief to absolute disbelief.

I haven't looked back since, but every now and then fear slips in like a shadow behind me. I can live with that, and so can you if you're the kind of person cut out to be an independent retailer.

There's a bottom line in retail that is not computed in stock, sales, or even money. In no other commercial enterprise do the persona and mood of the owner so permeate the character of the establishment as they do here. That personality factor is the other, too often ignored bottom line you need to evaluate carefully when you're considering launching a retail venture.

Overcoming the occasional anxiety attack and dealing with the unexpected are only two of the capabilities the retail entrepreneur needs to have. You need to be a self-starter, too. When you're in business for yourself, only you can start and keep the wheels turn-

You Know You're Ready to Go into Business for Yourself When . . .

1. The fear of keeping your job has become greater than the fear of opening your own business.

2. You're humming "Take This Job and Shove It" as you work.

3. People in your personal life—boyfriend, girlfriend, husband, wife—are rooting for you to set out on your own.

4. You perceive that in an era when AT&T lays off 45,000 people at a swoop, risk lies not in working for yourself, but in being a disposable resource in corporate America.

5. You're tired of talking about starting a business and realize it's time to act.

6. You finally accept what you've been suspecting all along, that no matter what the risk, and no matter that the immediate rewards are small, the only person you want to work for is yourself.

ing. There's no one else around to do it for you. This doesn't mean dashing about in random hyperactivity, like a retailer on Ritalin. It means you do—as in execute, perform, accomplish, achieve, complete, conduct your business, work.

Try This Experiment

I have an experiment for you. Here's the hypothesis. Like most hypotheses, it has a couple of preliminary assumptions. The first is that you're serious enough about opening a store to have looked for a book on the subject as a start to some serious research on how to facilitate this objective.

The second assumption is that you found such a book, one that provides a good solid beginning for that research. Its author speaks from many years of successful personal experience in retail and offers practical, real-world advice. You bought the book.

Fine. That brings us to where you are right now.

Now let's say the book suggests that, to find out whether you really have the get-up-and-go needed for the day-to-day operations of a retail business, you do something rather than just read about it. The book suggests that you put the reading aside right now, get in your car, and drive around town until you find two store locations for rent. Note the rental agents' telephone numbers. Call each agent and ask the following questions:

"I noticed you have a vacancy on the corner of Street X and Avenue Y. Is it still available for a retail operation?"

"What's the square footage of the store?"

"What kind of dollars are you looking for?"

You're not intending to actually lease either of these locations, because, as the book will tell you later, choosing the location for your store isn't a step to be taken lightly. The exercise is simply to instill a feel for what embarking on such a retail adventure is like.

Now, are you still sitting in your comfortable chair reading, or are you on your way? Better yet, are you just picking up the book again after having spoken with the leasing agents?

Beyond having a *doing* rather than a *thinking-about-it* personality, the successful store owner is a team player, albeit not the ordinary one. The straight team player goes the corporate route. The entrepreneur, on the other hand, is a team captain, someone who knows that one person can't do everything, knows who can be counted on to do what, and knows how to orchestrate and direct the team he or she recruits. "It's my team and we play my way."

A team captain not only leads, defining the goals and policies of the business, but develops its formative operating strategies, as well as its adaptive, rethinking strategies, for the best of plans go awry. These strategies are carefully mapped out to take the entrepreneur from here to where he or she wants to go.

The goals are always stated, the steps always complete, the means always flexible. There's a certain military precision about the planning of a retail operation, which is why the war analogy is so often used in marketing and business discussions as a whole. This doesn't mean that you must have a militaristic mind-set. You do have to be comfortable in the role of a general, and you do have to do some detailed planning.

Take This Test

1. Given a choice of pets, and expenses being of no concern, you would pick
   a. a cat
   b. a dog
   c. tropical fish
   d. a horse

2. When it comes to a car, you would rather have
   a. a Volvo
   b. a minivan
   c. a Hummer
   d. a pickup truck

3. The philosophy that most closely approximates yours is
   a. "Life is what happens when you're making other plans."—John Lennon
   b. "Opportunity does not come to those who wait. It is captured by those who attack."—General Douglas MacArthur
   c. "Do or do not. There is no try."—Yoda
   d. "The crab instructs its young 'Walk straight ahead—like me.'"—Hindustani proverb

4. You would rather
   a. eat at home in front of the television
   b. go to a church, school, or volunteer fire department picnic
   c. order Chinese takeout
   d. dine leisurely at a French restaurant

5. You discover that the payroll program has been deducting $2 too much from each employee's paycheck for medical insurance, so you
   a. inform the employees and refund all the overwithholding
   b. inform the employees and tell them that you have corrected the problem
   c. don't tell the employees and use the "extra" funds to reduce the company's share of the insurance payments
   d. tell the employees that you have negotiated a better deal with the insurance company and that from now on $2 less will be deducted from their paychecks each week for medical insurance

6. With regard to the telephone, you
   a. like it, chat with friends and relatives often
   b. have call waiting, two telephones (cell phones excluded) or other means of never missing a call
   c. have a cell phone
   d. don't often call people, they call you

7. You subscribe to or regularly read
   a. a newspaper
   b. at least four different magazines
   c. neither of the above, you get your news from the radio and television
   d. a newspaper and at least four different magazines of which at least one is a business publication

8. You still have
   a. your high school yearbook
   b. your birth certificate in a drawer somewhere
   c. your birth certificate in the safety deposit vault
   d. ticket stubs from your first Grateful Dead or other rock concert

9. When it comes to shoveling snow or mowing the lawn, you
   a. use a service
   b. hire a local kid to do the job
   c. get someone in the family to do it for free
   d. do it yourself

10. Come vacation time,
    a. you have a favorite hideaway you go to every year
    b. no matter where you go, you always collect a pile of brochures, even if you never get around to reading them
    c. you don't take vacations
    d. every year is different, and you don't know what you'll be doing this year

Scoring

No.	Points	No.	Points	No.	Points	No.	Points
1a.	2	4a.	0	7a.	2	10a.	2
1b.	4	4b.	5	7b.	3	10b.	5
1c.	0	4c.	2	7c.	0	10c.	0
1d.	5	4d.	0	7d.	5	10d.	4
2a.	3	5a.	4	8a.	2		
2b.	5	5b.	2	8b.	3		
2c.	0	5c.	0	8c.	5		
2d.	4	5d.	5	8d.	1		
3a.	1	6a.	3	9a.	1		
3b.	5	6b.	5	9b.	4		
3c.	5	6c.	2	9c.	4		
3d.	2	6d.	0	9d.	5		

Points Scored	Recommended Course of Action
40–50	Go for the store.
30–40	Opening one is probably a good idea.
20–30	Maybe.
0–20	It's up to you, but I wouldn't.

The Business Plan—Everyone Wants One and Hardly Anyone Understands It

Your first strategic task as a future store owner is to put together your business plan. While this is something the bank will require—and probably not read—it can also be a handy personal tool for surveying the landscape of your venture.

There are scores of books and software packages out there devoted exclusively to cultivating and polishing a business plan. Indeed, the nuts and bolts of such a plan really do require an entire volume to detail. So what I will do here is cover what these books and software packages don't.

First of all, it's very close to impossible to draw up a truly accurate business plan. Think about it a minute. All the highly paid economists in the world haven't been able to come to any agreement in predicting the economic direction in which we'll be headed next year. The powerful politicians in Washington, all of whom depend on low unemployment during their tenure to ensure their reelection, can't arrange for that desirable condition. Renowned old-line department stores with large financial planning staffs go belly-up.

And then you, going into business for probably the first time, are expected to weigh countless variables that can't be divined, much less defined, precisely—labor costs, margins, rents tied to overall earnings that may or may not go up. Then you're supposed to add these ingredients to a merchandise mix that can in no way be predicted because only your future customers could tell you what they'll be buying two years hence. Finally, out of this collection of imponderables, you should come up with a sound five-year business plan?

Well, by all the rules of logic, it's impossible. Yet, amazingly enough, it can happen.

By looking at every aspect of your potential business from every angle, by plugging in numbers that approximate the real world as closely as possible, you can actually achieve a business plan that three years into your venture, against all odds, mirrors fairly accurately what has taken place.

The real world, stripped of any illusions, is where you begin. That's where the numbers need to come from. You gather them the hard way, listening to merchants, your future landlord, potential suppliers, your accountant, and others. That's what makes your business plan different from the musty, unused ones in so many entrepreneurs' file drawers.

Video Game Business Plans

Most software programs that generate business plans make great video games. You can play them for months, tweaking sales and other variables until the results look perfect. Unfortunately, by then those results usually have little to do with reality. Be mindful and wary of false hopes raised by numbers manipulated to create a pleasing picture that's just right for the audience. You need to be real, not just right.

Besides, who's your audience? In all probability nobody but you is going to read the business plan anyhow. Your banker will put the copy you deliver in your loan folder. The eye-catching bar charts might earn a passing glance, but will what you're proposing actually be perused and absorbed by anyone in the bank? Not likely. It has no particular relevance to your loan application; it's just paper that has to be in the folder, along with the net worth statement that's much more interesting to the bank.

So why bother? Well, you bother because, quite apart from needing a business plan to be considered for a loan with which to finance your venture, *writing it down is the first step in making something happen.* Talk about your future business, and it will be washed away on a tide of enthusiasm and tumbled words. Put the ideas down in black and white, and in that plain, stark environment, the illusions will have no place to hide.

A business plan written to define realistically the scope of your enterprise will lend you perspective and a good view of the terrain for the journey you are about to undertake—for a business is a journey, not a destination. The business plan will be your map to follow—more importantly, to change where new ravines have opened up or flash floods washed the road away—enabling you to undertake that journey successfully.

Only if opening day lasts forever can you be assured of ongoing achievement in retail today. Getting as far as opening day is the other half of the equation. The following pages are a guidebook to help you start off on the right foot in navigating that course. It won't guarantee you instant success. It won't magically transform you into a seasoned retailer. Based as it is on thirty-odd years of retail experience, it will give you a realistic perception of and feel for what you're getting into when you step over the lease line.

2 The A Team

Retailing is a people business, start to finish. Your success in the trade will depend as much on the people whose counsel you seek before you even open the doors to the shop—the attorneys, accountants, and insurance agents whose guidance and support you rely on when you're first learning the ropes—as on the staff you eventually choose to help you run the store. These advisers are your A team.

When it comes to engaging professional services, don't shop dollars, shop experience. As a rule, too, stay away from professionals you've dealt with in your previous life. When we are challenged or stressed, we seek the familiar. Don't. Few specialists can be authorities in one field and experts on all, and the very thing that's beyond their ken may be the thing you need to know. However tempting it might be, resist the perfectly normal human impulse to turn for advice to someone you know who happens to have represented your interests before.

Hiring the Wrong Lawyer

The lawyer I hired to help me negotiate my first store lease was the same one I'd consulted when my wife and I bought our first home. Why not? After all, he'd handled other family matters for us satisfactorily. He was quiet, competent, and reasonably efficient, if somewhat unimaginative, but that didn't bother me a great deal.

What did bother me was that when we met to go over the lease about a week after he'd received it, he proceeded to read it to me. Some ten minutes into his presentation, I interrupted the recital. I was quite capable of reading, I reminded him. What I wanted to know was how we could make the terms of the lease more advantageous to me.

"Well," he replied, "basically, they're standard boilerplate. There's not much here the landlord will let us change."

Later I discovered that he hadn't even spoken to the landlord or the leasing representative. Worse yet, he'd never dealt with a commercial lease before. He hadn't the faintest notion that his conclusion should in fact have been his prologue.

In negotiating a lease, the first draft of the document, replete with all those boilerplate clauses landlords insert, is only the starting point. The reason for bringing in an attorney is to help you improve the lease. There will always be things in a lease agreement that the landlord absolutely won't change. These things are known as deal breakers. There will also be things to which you as an aspiring leaseholder would not, could not, or should not agree. These are the tenant's deal breakers. Between these hard pincers of the nutcracker lie the spaces where movement can occur. This is where you and your attorney negotiate the remaining terms of the lease with the landlord and his or her representative.

In the case of my first lease, failing any real help from my compliant attorney and not knowing where else to turn, I went straight to the landlord's leasing agent with my concerns. Foremost among these was that the lease as written was for five years, my bank loan for seven. Theoretically, then, I could end up with a loan and no business, no matter how reassuring the landlord might be about my future. We had to come to some agreement here. Otherwise, we had a real deal breaker on our hands.

What I needed, I explained, was a lease covering at least the period of my note. The leasing agent was perfectly understanding, and the upshot of our talk was that, in the document I eventually signed, the clause covering the term of the lease included a five-year option, considerably enhancing the value of my contract by adding five years of guaranteed space for my store. Meanwhile, the agent told me what her boss was really looking for, what was negotiable, what wasn't, and even how the mall arrived at the terms of its conveyances from a dollar standpoint. That leasing agent was the best real estate teacher I've ever had. Drafted from the opposing team, she became an important member of my first A team.

Maneuvering among the deal breakers, both parties to the negotiation of a lease try to get the best deal possible. This process of give-and-take requires patience and persistence, and that can be wearing for the parties involved. One of your attorney's functions is to bring a fresh, level-headed, dispassionate perspective to the bargaining table. As a vitally interested party, you may be too close to the issues to evaluate them clearly. More removed from those concerns than you are, your attorney is often better able to see the holes through which compromises might wriggle.

On the Shoals of Deal Breakers

Because his background is stuffed with leases, my attorney can deal with landlords or the landlords' representatives using language familiar to them. Going into the negotiations, everyone is comfortable. Everyone knows the deliberations will be on a professional level. No one feels threatened, and no one tries to steamroller a settlement. Being able to set this tone is one of the most valuable skills a good business lawyer brings to the negotiating table. In my capacity as a lease consultant, I've seen far too many merchants' leases threatened as much by the lessee's attorney, or even the merchant's own counsel, as by the frazzling process of negotiation itself.

Several years ago, I helped to negotiate a lease for a jewelry store in a shopping center. The storekeeper and I were negotiating directly with the developer, and in due course we came to an agreement. However, when my client received the actual lease document drawn up for her signature, she found the terms quite different from what we'd agreed upon. Indeed, they were much better for the landlord.

I didn't hear the tale until some weeks after my client had signed the lease. When I asked why on earth she'd accepted such a new and significantly *improved* lease when it was quite contrary to the terms we'd negotiated, she replied that her lawyer had protested, "What can we do? The developer won't close on the deal unless we agree."

Now that, to my mind, is not the kind of advice or support you need from your attorney. As it so happens, I later came to know the particular developer involved in this deal quite well. His word really was his bond. He would have sacrificed his firstborn before knowingly letting anybody's lawyer, his own included, change something to which he had agreed.

What had happened here was something that happens all too often. It's not unusual to find that a deal as it's finally closed is a deal arrived at by two lawyers both of whom have ignored the express wishes of the principals and failed to adhere to the terms acceptable to them.

For this and other reasons, choosing an attorney isn't an easy matter. A lawyer is someone with whom a shopkeeper will share a long professional life. This protracted association virtually requires that you get along personally as well as on a commercial plane. Once you've established the competence and mercantile acumen of a particular attorney, ask yourself, "Is this someone I could enjoy playing poker with every week?"

Determining an attorney's marketplace credentials can be tricky. There may be a bunch of diplomas on the wall and an *Esq.* on the stationery, but how do you know how good a lawyer is?

One factor compounding the problem is the client confidentiality to which an attorney is bound. You can't simply ask, "Now whom in the local business community do you represent?" The answer, were it to include several prominent commercial magnates, would certainly be helpful. Unfortunately, for the attorney to answer the question as posed would be for him or her to jeopardize that client confidentiality several times over.

Instead, suggests Paul Brody, an attorney in private practice whose metier is counseling and representing small- to medium-sized businesses, you could quite legitimately ask, "What local businesses that you represent can you give me as references?" Put this way, the question can be answered with the implied approval of the attorney's clients, posing no risk of any violation of confidentiality.

If an attorney you're considering can't name at least three businesses represented by him or her, ask no more questions. Say your tactful good-byes, and look for another attorney. If the three names are forthcoming, on the other hand, and if they're satisfactory, go on to the next question.

A good business attorney should be able to give you the name of at least one certified public accountant, or CPA, who can attest to the lawyer's savvy from a dollars-and-cents point of view. The accountant is the legal counsel's comrade-in-arms, and no attorney involved in affairs of commerce is without the phone and fax numbers of one such professional associate.

If the attorney passes muster on both these fronts, the next item on the agenda is a frank discussion, right up front, about fees. People don't go to a dentist to have a wisdom tooth extracted without finding out how much it's going to cost. They don't set out to buy a new car and then simply fork over the sticker price, no questions asked. Yet many people fail to ask attorneys what they're getting into financially.

Then, too, not all attorneys take to talking about money graciously. I remember one illustrious blue-blooded legal adviser of whom I inquired about the cost of pursuing a particular endeavor. "Oh, somewhere between $7,000 and $25,000," came back the estimate, intoned in a manner strongly suggesting that gentlemen do not discuss money.

Well, $18,000 is a lot of between, so I persisted in my inquiries. I learned that the gentleman in question billed at $400 an hour. His associate, who could be expected to do most of the work, billed at $125 an hour. I would be charged as well for telephone and copying expenses and, yes, even 32¢ stamps. The between was accelerating rapidly toward its upper reaches in my mind's eye.

You probably won't forget to ask the attorney about that all-important hourly billing rate, but one thing you should remember to ask as well is whether or not you'll be charged for time spent on the phone with you. Some attorneys start the clock with the first ring of the phone. Others don't charge at all for quick telephone advice not requiring any research. They're the ones who believe in preventative law. Mistakes are costly for the client and, accordingly, best avoided. If a client doesn't do well, the lawyer

Four Legal Matters Not to Overlook in Setting Up Shop

1. The lease renewal clause. In negotiating a lease for your store, the renewal terms are often sadly neglected, seeming of little importance compared with other, more immediate concerns. Why should you worry about lease renewal, fifteen years down the pike, before you've even opened the shop doors? If your business is a success, that renewal clause could be worth a small fortune.

2. The name of your store. You can't just pick a name and run with it. You may think you've come up with something absolutely unique to call your store, but you can't be sure of that until it's been cleared by the state. Even then, there may be an establishment with a similar designation somewhere in an adjacent state. Similar is not flattering. One individual opened a store called Pets"Я"Us. To say that Toys"Я"Us was not amused would be an understatement. It costs a lot of money to redo signs, letterheads, and all that, not to mention the fact that your clientele will be very confused by the change in name.

3. A staff manual. Before you start hiring, draw up a detailed employee manual and have your attorney review it. There are more employee suits in retail than there are any other kind of legal problems. Be prepared.

4. A buy/sell partnership agreement. If your business is to take the form of a partnership, such an instrument governing splitting up, in writing, signed and sealed, is a must. It needs to be in force from the very outset of operations. Should you and your partner disagree in the future, it would almost certainly be too late then for you to reach an amicable agreement. Prepare for that eventuality, however unlikely it might seem in the rosy glow and exhilarating aura of the new venture. Another contingency people don't like to think about is the possibility of one partner to a business becoming incapacitated. In that event, the whole store could come to a grinding halt if no buy/sell agreement were in effect, because there would be no pre-established way for the remaining partner to keep the operation running.

will be in demand. If the client is successful, the lawyer will be just as much in demand, but life will be a lot more pleasant.

An attorney's hourly billing and incidental charges are but part of the legal expense of setting up shop. You'll need to ask about the overall costs of creating your new business entity. These costs will include filing fees in addition to the legal fees, and they will vary depending on the nature of the enterprise. Your establishment may take the form of a sole proprietorship, a partnership, a corporation, or a limited liability company, which often goes simply by the acronym LLC. Each of these forms has its own expense structure.

Deciding which legal format best accommodates your venture is likely to be the first bit of business you conduct with the attorney you ultimately retain. The pros and cons of the various legal identities your business could assume are complex issues, so you'll want to explore them thoroughly, taking advantage of all the judicious counsel you can get.

An Accountant You Can Count On

For much the same reason, before you go too far in your deliberations, bring an accountant in on the discussions. You want as many different opinions—provided they're reliable, of course—as you can collect. The perspective and priorities of the accountant will usually be quite different from those of the attorney. The two can effectively counterbalance each other.

In selecting an accountant, as in selecting your attorney, there are a number of questions to be asked. First of all, is the person a certified public accountant or the garden variety? By definition, a certified public accountant must stay abreast of all the latest developments in accounting and tax issues.

Certification doesn't guarantee you a great accountant. I once took on a certified public accountant whose idea of creative retail accounting was to purchase his ledger paper one pad at a time rather than in bulk. What certification does do is to ensure that the accountant is at least aware of the current tax code, accepted accounting practices, and other number-crunching variables that might affect the health of your business. It also assures you that he or she is committed to staying current by taking CPA seminars on the ever-changing laws and regulations of your state.

Ask for names of local retail establishments that the accountant can submit as references. Whom could you call for a recommendation? Rarely—I use the word advisedly, for many of the breed are as dry as they first appear—will an accountant make a sparkling presentation on first encounter. So let experience judge. Clients for whom the accountant has worked over a period of years will be able to assess the person's true abilities. In fact, most likely you'll find your ideal accountant by getting recommendations from successful retailers in your area.

Another consideration is whether or not the accountant has ever been personally involved in a retail operation. While a positive answer to this related question isn't essential, it's a definite plus. Retail experience generates a certain mind-set. If the accountant has it, so much the better.

Last but not least, you need to determine the accountant's fee scale and get a ballpark figure for the annual cost of his or her services to your store. You should also establish a ceiling figure and elicit the accountant's promise to call if it appears that this ceiling will be pierced because of some unusual happenstance. Accountants, as a rule, don't like surprises. They shouldn't give you any, either.

Honesty Is Not Enough

My first accountant was what I call a historian, a breed retailers should definitely avoid. He could, and did, recite everything that had happened in the business during the foregoing year, page and verse. His modus operandi was dependably, fixedly cut-and-dried.

When I told him I was negotiating a new lease, his response was, "Send me a copy of the summary so I can add it to the annual financials." If I asked his advice on how to go about achieving some goal, he never offered a suggestion or proposed an alternative. He only told me what I couldn't do.

He was efficient, honest, and straightforward. A creative entrepreneur and a risk taker he was not. He'd never hurt you, but he wasn't someone you could grow a business with. He was an accountant through and through. Now, twenty years later, he's still a sole practitioner. He's still in the office where he first hung out his shingle, and that's the office from which he'll probably retire.

At the other extreme are the big firms offering a smorgasbord of services. Unfortunately, chances are that a small business such as yours would probably get lost in such a firm. To boot, your account would probably be assigned to a fresh-out-of-college individual lacking the business experience you need in an accountant.

Between these two extremes, there's an accountant for you. That person is one who'll be able to work with you not only on mundane matters of ledger and spreadsheet, but at the managerial level, helping you sort out the pros and cons of the decisions you need to make in terms of how they will affect your business financially.

Your initial conference with an accountant is a good time to ask that person's opinion on the advisable legal model for your store. Usually, he or she will point out that, from an accounting standpoint, a sole proprietorship is far less expensive to set up and maintain than a corporation and that a limited liability company is apt to have higher maintenance costs than the other options. The accountant might suggest starting out with a sole proprietorship and then, if it became necessary because you had accumulated greater exposure and assets, moving up to a corporation or a limited liability company. Meanwhile, an umbrella policy added to your home owner's insurance at a cost of a few hundred dollars would cover you for any off-the-wall liabilities.

Your lawyer may object to that suggestion. The accountant has money on the mind. The attorney is worried about liability. He or she will probably push for the full protection of a corporation or a limited liability company, even though both of these alternatives are more expensive than either a sole proprietorship or a partnership is.

To Sign or Not to Sign

If you are a sole proprietor, you are personally liable for all the debts incurred by your store. In the case of a corporation, on the other hand, should you sign a fifteen-year lease and the store go out of business after two, say, you wouldn't be held liable personally for the next thirteen years' rent. The catch here, of course, is that the land-lord will want you to sign the lease personally anyhow, in spite of the fact that the store is a corporation. You won't get off that hook eas-ily. What you might be able to do, though, is to effect a compromise. You could agree to be held individually responsible for the first five years' lease payments, say, on the condition that those for the next ten become the responsibility solely of the corporation. Your reason-

An Accountant's Six Tips to Starting Right in Retail

1. Borrow more than you think you need and put the extra into a rainy-day fund. Most businesses are undercapitalized, borrowing $30,000 initially, say, when they should have borrowed $50,000. A rainy-day fund lets you take advantage of distributors' and man-ufacturers' overstock and other unexpected buying opportunities.

2. Just because the checkbook shows a healthy balance, don't pay yourself a little extra. Until you know the pulse of your business, which you won't during the first couple of years, it's going to be difficult to tell how much of that generous balance is due to sea-sonal factors and how much to steady growth. Besides, as soon as you take out that little extra, you're almost certain to find you need it to buy more inventory.

3. Stay away from family money. What should be a business deci-sion often becomes fraught with emotion when family funds are involved. You may feel pressured into paying back a family loan sooner than is good for business. At the other extreme is the per-son who feels no compunction about never paying back such a loan, which isn't good for the family.

4. Take out a home equity loan to bolster the business only as a last resort. The reasons are much the same as those for not borrow-ing family money.

5. Keep your financial data entry up-to-date from day one. Particularly, don't put off entering those vendor bills. Being behind on entering data will give you a false picture of your busi-ness's well-being.

6. Monitor the financial picture of your business regularly and often. In retail, you need a full year's cycle of figures to have any meaningful numbers to work with and compare. The more his-torical data you have, the better.

ing would be that the likelihood of your store's failing after being in business that long would be much reduced, and surely its successful track record should merit recognition.

This is exactly the kind of argument your attorney should think of if you don't. Remember that you're collecting information and ideas here. The ability to offer you options is a crucial attribute of all your A team members. Your job is to weigh the advice of the people you've chosen to counsel you in light of what you've learned—largely from their combined experience, perhaps, but always under your own tutelage. You're the one who's going to run the store. The final decisions, from the form it should take to where it should go next, are ones you'll have to make yourself.

Once past the formative stage of setting up shop, you'll probably see your accountant more often than you see your attorney. The nature of shopkeeping is such that there are many more lesser, occasional financial choices to be made than there are large legal issues to be decided.

One of those choices will need to be made at the outset of your actual operations, and that's the option of how the books are going to be kept. The traditional adjunct of the accountant is the bookkeeper. Today, however, you'll probably opt for a software bookkeeper. It's quicker, cheaper, and reasonably flawless—provided you update your records regularly and often.

The particular software package you choose will depend on a number of factors, not the least of which is your accountant's inclination. Another is compatibility with other store operations you might be computerizing. The decision on bookkeeping software is best made in the context of that larger picture (see Chapter 6).

Skip the Payroll

Whichever accounting package you decide on, you'll also have to decide whether or not to use the payroll module. My advice would be not to worry about that particular feature of the software. I wouldn't put off the decision until I'd chosen my electronic bookkeeper. Rather I'd simply open a separate bank account for payroll and engage a payroll service to manage it.

The personal computer is certainly capable of dealing with all the intricacies of payroll taxes, withholding, W-2s, and the constantly changing tax laws, by the simple expedient of gulping down updates as fast as the software company churns them out. My recommendation is based on quite another consideration. I simply class retail payrolls, computer assisted or not, as a pain in the neck.

There are few shopkeeping tasks more onerous than tracking all the loose ends that the payroll entails, largely because it's such an amorphous affair, forever shifting, entailing the entry of new data. Personnel is constantly changing. Employees leave. Seasonal help is taken on. Temporary help is let go again, and so on.

Say, at the moment, you have eight employees, paid weekly. Next week, though, you might have seven employees because one quit. The third week, as it turns out, there are nine people on the payroll. One is a replacement for the employee who left; another is additional staff you've been needing for a while and decided to hire when the perfect person for the job walked in for an interview. In the space of a couple of weeks, then, you've either entered or deleted three entire payroll accounts on your personnel database, considerably altering just the immediate record keeping.

Then there are the quarterly tax forms and the yearly tax forms and the possible audits. All in all, it's a blizzard of paperwork only dimly imaginable until you've actually been snowed under by it. A payroll service can handle the entirety of this clerical drudgery for you, not only taking over the responsibility for its accuracy, but, if need be, defending it for you as well. If you're audited, for example, it's the service's problem to deal with.

The cost of payroll services has come down a lot over the years, and the agencies are highly competitive. Ask for quotes from three of them in your area, and look over the range of services they mention. At this point, don't pay too much attention to the price line. Look at the tasks provided, first.

Payroll service lingo is a little abbreviated in spots. Some of the terms are easy enough to figure out. You'll find your employees multiplied by the number of times a month they're paid and referred to as pays. If some of them want to have their checks deposited directly to their bank accounts, usually the agency will charge a monthly flat fee, as opposed to a per deposit amount, for this service. There will also be a separate pass-through bank charge for the direct deposit, again normally figured on a service rather than a per deposit basis.

If you want the rest of the checks delivered in envelopes, there will be a separate stuffing fee for the labor involved. Don't try to skimp on this feature. Checks arriving without envelopes are an open invitation for everybody to try to sneak a look at everybody else's paycheck. Conversely, checks in sealed envelopes can be dropped off in your absence for each employee to pick up or for your store manager to hand out without launching a scramble for a peek at the contents. The actual delivery to the store will be another separate charge.

Keeping your tax records, preparing the appropriate forms, and taking responsibility for the whole lot are, to my mind, the most wonderful services a payroll agency has to sell. These various services will probably be all lumped together under an unpretentious-looking total tax fee in the estimate an agency gives you. Don't underestimate this modest-sounding item. You'll still have to sign the forms and send them in, but the agency will do all the computations and handle any problems arising from its calculations. These are well-nigh invaluable services.

When you've evaluated the payroll preparation functions you want for your particular operation, circle the agency that best seems to suit your needs and pick up the phone. If the service you're thinking of taking on has all the right features but happens to be more expensive than one of the others on your list, mention that another outfit is offering a better deal. Explain that you'd really like to deal with this one, but you might have to go with the lower bid. Chances are the agency you're after will match the competition's estimate, one way or another.

It may not be by lowering specific charges. It may take the form of a special monthly adjustment of some kind. (See Appendix A for a sample payroll service bill showing the breakdown of charges, including such an adjustment.) Whatever the case, the package price is almost sure to come down. When you look at the final figures, you may find that you can hand your payroll headaches over to the service you'd like to see handling them for something like $2.50 or so per employee per week. If you can do that, my recommendation would definitely be to snap up the bid.

Engaging a payroll service puts protection and support a phone call away in the event of any problems arising in connection with your store's personnel or tax records. These, however, are only two of the fronts where you need protection for your business. In today's litigious world, insurance is as unavoidable as death and taxes.

Insurance, Insurance, and More Insurance

The very lease you're offered, virtually at the outset of your start-up preparations, will dictate certain mandatory insurance provisions. Not only will coverage of the premises be required as one of the conditions of an executed lease, but you will be obliged to carry a specified amount, and the landlord will expect to be named on the policy and notified in the event of its cancellation.

All of this is just the beginning of your insurance obligations. The premises insurance insisted upon by your landlord will cover you for accidents occurring in the store, mishaps such as someone slipping on your floor. A further requirement, usually not stipulated in the lease but imperative all the same, is what's known in the trade as product and completed operations liability insurance. This coverage protects you in the event of a suit over faulty merchandise or an accident caused by defective goods. It's a consideration you'll need to go over point by point with your insurance agent.

There are preestablished policy parameters for almost every conceivable type of retail operation from liquor stores to hardware shops. Every insurance agent has access to these insurance packages delineating the specific perils involved in each enterprise and systematizing its coverage. As a result, your first instinct might be to choose an agent strictly on price.

True enough, there will always be an agent somewhere who can procure for you coverage that's a little cheaper than what you'll find elsewhere. However, you need more than just a bottom-line bargain here. You need an agent who can and will deal with the gray areas halfway up the page.

One of my employees once totaled a delivery van. An indifferent agent might have simply directed the insurance company to send in a claim form. But when I reported the accident to my agent, he inquired about the condition of the truck. I told him that it was an old rattletrap with over 130,000 miles on it, but that it was quite serviceable because I'd just spent $2,000 fixing it up. He asked if I could document these expenses. When I assured him that I could, he commented, "Good. Then we should be able to get more than just book value for the van."

Documentation in hand, we advised the insurance company of the investment I'd made in repairs to the truck. The upshot of our efforts was that the firm shelled out an extra $400 over the book value listed for a van of that year and model. This is the kind of homework you should expect from your agent.

In return, you should be prepared to give the agent you select all your insurance business. This is a bit of a switch from the way most of us buy our personal coverage. It's not unusual for a private citizen to take out life insurance with one company, a home policy with another, and so on. By authorizing your commercial insurance agent to handle all your policy needs, including your personal ones, you enable him or her to send the whole package out to bid.

This takes care of one of your insurance criteria, namely, securing a good price for value received. The other, being able to collect to the maximum on claims, is also enhanced by putting all your insurance apples in one basket. You'll have more leverage when it comes to claims being settled in your favor, because the insurance company will look at the overall picture and realize what's paid out on one policy will be collected in premiums on the others.

Speaking of the overall picture, if you're not familiar with umbrella policies, ask your agent about these insurance instruments. For $300 to $500 a year, you could probably take out an umbrella rider on your regular home owner's policy that would add $1 million to your protection against anything that might go wrong on either the home or the business front. Usually, the cost of such a rider, even though part of your personal insurance, is a business deduction for tax purposes.

The acumen of an insurance agent becomes an important factor indeed when you've put all your apples in his or her basket.

You're relying heavily on this person's advice concerning such potentially all-important matters as that umbrella policy, and you're relying heavily on this person's abilities when it comes to settling claims in your favor.

Bankers Are the B Team

These same qualities of astuteness and competence used to be crucially important attributes to look for in a banker, at one time an indispensable member of your A team. However, in today's depersonalized banking world, your banker, through no fault of his or her own, is no longer a top team member.

You still need the bank's services, obviously, but anyone counting on one of its officers for anything more than the most rudimentary financial operations, performed on a strictly mechanical level, is bound to be disappointed. Don't place any bets on the banking world. Instead, take your A team of attorney, accountant, and agent out there when you go forth to challenge the retail world.

3 Lying to the Bank, and Other Honest Financial Strategies

Once, your banker knew as much about your business affairs as your attorney and your accountant did. He or she also had the discretionary power to lend you up to a given amount, in some instances as much as $50,000, simply on his or her say-so. Unfortunately, that banker is no longer a member of your A team.

I remember one particular banker from those days. He was the president of a small local savings institution—one, I might add, that prospered even throughout the catastrophic eighties, when so many lending institutions were hemorrhaging from failed loans. It wasn't unusual for a self-employed individual I know to approach this gentleman for a $5,000 or $10,000 short-term loan to carry him over some unforeseen cash crisis or other, only to be told, "Here's the money, but we're really busy today, so could you come back next week to fill out the paperwork?"

Now that was a banker who knew his clients, knew their character, knew their business, and knew how to make money for his own establishment. Today, that same bank, though still independent, is busy building fancy new branches around the county. Under the new guard, it takes up to a month of approvals, not to mention the board meeting, to process the same loan, and—you guessed it—the bank is no longer as profitable as it was.

Today's banker seldom if ever has the discretionary authority to grant loans. More significantly, he or she knows your business purely from the standpoint of a financial statement plugged into a computer model. You as a person and your establishment as an operative enterprise doing business in the real world are both unknowns.

Not only is your banker no longer on your A team, but for all intents and purposes he or she is an adversary—and that's all right, too. Adversarial relationships can strengthen your operation, provided they're conducted in a professional, nonabrasive manner. They let you see the negative aspects of your business that you might otherwise overlook.

The last thing I want to do is to denigrate the importance of good banking relations, especially in today's business environment. I borrow from banks all the time, for store expansions and renovations; and I have a healthy regard for both good bank management and capable, congenial bank representatives. I'm simply remarking that banks aren't what they used to be.

Bankers Sell Money

From the standpoint of most of its functions, the bank is a retailer, just as you are. It's merely a retail operation whose goods happen to be money. This means that the bank is eager for good, steady customers. It even has sales like those of any other business establishment: "Special on car loans this week, 1 percent above prime."

It also means that the bank, like any other business, has to make a profit in order to survive. Furthermore, in these days of massive bank consolidation, increasingly it means that the bank must make a megaprofit in order to keep Wall Street happy. Thus, the cordial personal banking relationship of the past has given way to paperwork, projections, and peer decisions, all surrounded by a certain vague aura of paranoia and guarded by extreme circumspection.

The first thing a banker, or anyone else from whom you are seeking financial backing, will want to see is your business plan.

The next one is your personal financial, or net worth, statement. This document will be treated as if it were the Holy Grail, not because it's some magical instrument that will ensure your success and validate the bank's decision to invest in your venture, but because it furnishes a veneer of proof that the bank isn't going to lose money if you go under. The business plan goes beyond that in its attempt to woo the bank.

Most externally driven business plans—those generated for presentation to the financial sector rather than for your own private business projections—endeavor to demonstrate not only that the bank won't lose money, but that the requested loan will generate a comfortable profit for the institution as well. Your business plan, which you'll have in hand by this time, will be a little different from those. Not only will it demonstrate both of these points, but it will accurately and succinctly outline your vision of the retail industry segment you are about to enter and document how that vision has helped to define the essence of your store.

The additional information you supply will probably not better inform the banker, who isn't really interested in such panoramic views, but it will better equip you to do battle in his or her court. Looking at the heft of your document, he or she should be impressed with your business acumen, and certainly with the quantity of detail you've supplied.

Today's bankers—be they customer representatives, loan officers, managers, or vice presidents—are primarily information collectors. Their focus is on facts and formulas, not on the stakes.

Where the Banker Can Really Help

By virtue of being an information collector, the banker is also a gatekeeper. The paperwork you submit must fit the prescribed description, or you won't even get your foot in the door.

Here the banker can be of help. He or she will take your business plan and your personal financial statement and make sure that all the t's are crossed and the i's dotted. Then, when you've filled out the loan application itself, the banker should go over the information with you and, with any luck, help you massage any numbers on the form that might block the door to your loan. Don't be afraid to ask for this help. If you get the loan, it's to the banker's credit—assuming, of course, that your store works out.

Finally, the banker will pursue the references you've supplied and run a credit check. What he or she won't be able to do is to influence the course of your loan application after that. Loan approval is done by committee.

Different banks have different approaches to structuring their loan committees. Generally, however, this committee is composed of the bank's directors. You will not be asked to appear. Your paperwork will speak for you, which is why the business plan is so important.

Of course, most of the committee won't actually read the business plan. What they will look at is the collateral backing the loan. What is your personal net worth? How much will the proposed assets of the contemplated business—the inventory, the equipment you intend to buy with the loan money, and so forth—be worth? What are your projected monthly receivables? In retail, that figure will be about zero, because even credit card sales generate immediate cash. Add these figures together. Cut the total in half. Knock another 10 to 20 percent off for good measure. Now you have the actual loan amount the bank committee might approve in your case if you're lucky.

When it comes to matching cash rather than looking just at your assets, the bank will be more generous, usually lending you 60 to 70 percent if you put up 30 to 40 percent. Say that opening your store is going to require $100,000. If you can come up with $30,000 to $40,000 cash, the bank will give you a $60,000 to $70,000 loan. However, without that personal cash contribution, if the assets listed on your personal financial statement are less than $25,000, don't set your heart on more than a $5,000 to $10,000 loan.

That puts your prospects at the distinctly lower end of retailing. Consider a pushcart.

One of the most important things to weigh in envisioning the venture you're about to launch is its likely fate in the real world. Think big, dream if you will, wish on a star, but don't lose your balance reaching for it. You need your feet on firm ground when you start a business, and your footwork had best be careful and thorough—better a successful pushcart than a failed palatial emporium.

Five Rules for Dealing with Today's Banker and Other Financiers

1. Never rely on what the banker tells you in person. Always get everything in writing. However cordial your banking relationship might be, oral agreements will be discarded in times of difficulty.

2. Don't sign without carefully reading every document, especially those pertaining to a bank loan or your lease. The pressure cooker atmosphere in the loan officer's cubicle or around the closing table works against you. Ask the banker or financier to send the documents for your and your attorney's review in advance of the actual closing.

3. Never sign an arbitration or a jury trial waiver. These waivers are increasingly included in the loan papers. In effect, you are being asked to give up your rights as a citizen.

4. A liability release is a clause also appearing more frequently in present-day loan documentation. The gist of the clause is that if you go under after the loan has been approved, the bank can in no way be held responsible, even when the reason you're broke is that the bank called the loan, leaving you without capital. This is a clause to be avoided at all costs.

5. Always remember that, while a banker may be a pillar of the community and a friend from high school, his or her first allegiance is to the bank. Representatives of that institution are not in the business of lending you money. They're in the business of collecting the bank's money.

Reality and Your Business Plan

Recently, an individual asked my advice on the idea of opening a coffee and sandwich shop in one of the malls where I have a retail operation. The idea seemed a good one. Aside from a Chinese restaurant and a franchised pizza shop, this medium-sized regional mall had no other eating establishments. Store employees alone might form the backbone of his operation.

The gentleman in question didn't want to pay a business consultant once I mentioned that there happened to be two nearby alternative sources for possible advice, both of them free. One was an entrepreneurial center sponsored by a nearby university, the other the regional offices of the Small Business Administration or SBA.

Six months following our conversation, the gentleman stopped by my store to thank me for sending him to the entrepreneurial center. Now here I should protest that I didn't send him there; I merely mentioned that its services were available. Anyhow, with the help of the center, he had put together a neat and persuasive business plan, and the Small Business Administration had told him that it would be interested in guaranteeing a large percentage of his loan. The bank in turn had agreed that the business plan looked fine and suggested that he go ahead and fill out a loan application.

All that having been done, he was now looking for a good attorney. Could I recommend one? I gave him the names of two.

A week later the attorney he had chosen called me. "Mort, you have to help this guy before he shoots himself in the foot. Look at his business plan, will you?"

When I did, the first thing I noticed was that he had projected his food costs at 15 percent of total expenses. Even a big food chain's provisioning expenditures normally run 27 percent of expenses.

The next thing I noticed was the $30,000 he had allocated to his projected annual payroll. Granted, he planned to put in a full week at the sandwich shop. Nevertheless, the establishment would have to keep mall hours, seventy-one of them a week. Cleaning and prepping would bring the actual time someone would have to man the store to 80 hours per week. Even if he himself were there for those 80 hours, $30,000 wouldn't cover two employees, each working a full shift, to back him up.

More amazing was the fact that the future store owner's business plan showed the $50,000 loan he was requesting as an asset—as it should—but made no mention of the debt service that loan would require in the form of regular monthly payments. This omission in one fell swoop increased his break-even point to a completely unworkable level. When you do your business plan, include debt service at 2 to 3 percent above prime, even if what you are putting in is your own money. After all, you deserve a return for the risk as much as any other investor would, and only by including debt service will your business plan show the venture's real break-even point.

A Software Route to Failure

To top off the above would-be entrepreneur's story, the software program used to develop his professional-looking business plan permitted no adjustment of the numbers to reflect seasonal increases in mall traffic, according to him. So the sales projections simply increased by a flat 10 percent annually. Making no allowance for holiday spikes in cash flow is a certified route to failure. You end up having insufficient capital to cover the extra expenses of peak periods, the very times when you should be raking it in.

Above and beyond these considerable flaws, there was no unique marketing focus to the business plan whatsoever. From the would-be entrepreneur's accompanying resumé, I learned that he had never worked in the restaurant trade before, which probably wouldn't help matters. From himself I learned that he did not enjoy waiting on people. That definitely wouldn't help matters. Certainly, the gentleman was sincere in his aspirations, and he was striving for success. All the same, the paperwork and the personality indicated a disaster not waiting to happen, but already in progress.

That notwithstanding, and despite the fact that the business plan itself was a complete collection of misinformation, however unintentional, the bank loved the document, if indeed the committee ever looked beyond the eye-catching graphs. The loan had already been approved by the time I read the proposal.

You might be wondering why.

The answer isn't far away. It's right down the street, in point of fact. The Small Business Administration guaranteed a large share of the loan. The would-be proprietor's personal assets secured the balance threefold. The bank simply acquired a new hireling to fork over a tidy sum of interest every month. When the business owner went under—a foregone conclusion—the bank would get all its money back, guaranteed.

Unfortunately, I suspect the borrowing climate won't improve much within the decade to come. The Small Business Administration, which does not lend money itself, does guarantee some $2 billion to $3 billion in small business loans every year, a circumstance that might be of help in your quest for financial support. And banks do still lend money to small businesses—when the owners have assets to back up the loans. However, there's no denying that the money hurdle is becoming a bigger and bigger hurdle to jump. Increasingly, it calls for ingenuity.

Because banks are constrained by the present-day monetary milieu to make only distinguished profits and take no risks, if you are to succeed in your dealings with them, you need to present yourself as a profitable customer. There are a number of ways to do this.

If It's History, It Helps

One worthwhile strategy is to develop a history. That is to say, as soon as you've started thinking seriously about where you might locate your store, scout the area, interviewing other local retailers, and choose a bank with which you think you'd like to do business. Then take all the cash, CDs, and any other personal liquid assets you have, and deposit them with this bank.

Banks are nearly as enamored of history as they are of money. Even if it takes only six months from the time you begin your market research to the time you open your doors for business—and a year is a much more realistic interval—the bank favored with your patronage will have had the use of your funds for a respectable period. Banks draw interest by lending out their patrons' money. The more of that commodity you have in your account, the more the bank can lend out, and thus the more stature you acquire in its eyes.

Likewise, the more money you borrow, the more money the bank makes, this time at your expense. Who says a bank can't have it both ways?

A bank is perfectly happy to lend you money as long as you don't need any. So open a credit card account with that bank. Take out a short-term personal loan as well, and maybe a second mortgage. Make sure all your payments are punctual. Then pay off the loans, preferably a month or two before you go in for the big one.

Prove You Don't Need Money and the Bank Will Lend You Plenty

Now you're a customer with a history, someone from whom the bank knows it can profit. It's aware of the fact, of course, that since you had money in the bank, you could have drawn on that instead of borrowing for whatever purposes. The point is that you've demonstrated your ability to pay back loans responsibly. Obviously, you didn't blow the borrowed money on a trip to Europe and then fail to pay it back.

Your track record won't guarantee you a loan for a bad business idea, or even a good one. Nevertheless, that history and that impression of profitability will lend you an aura of desirability.

All the same, when you go in to borrow money for your retail venture, the bank will look closely at your net worth. This warrants some creative reflection.

Net worth is a rather flexible concept. Broadly speaking, it's what you own that's worth something minus what you owe. In trying to pin it down more precisely, defining what you owe is the easy part. If you have a mortgage with $93,233.28 of the principal remaining, you owe $93,233.28. It's as simple as that—the kind of figure a banker likes to deal with, precise to the penny.

Something you own, such as your house, is a different matter. One realtor might decide that the house is worth $220,000. Another realtor might appraise it at $195,000. Neither figure represents the price it might fetch if it were put on the market, and even if it were sold at one of these two figures, the realtor would take 6 percent, so your net would be less.

Given such asset flexibility, it's your duty to your future business to inflate the value of your home—not outrageously, but by adding 10 percent to its probable value—when filling out a net worth statement. It's not as if you're really lying to the bank, mind you, because the bank for its part is already prepared to reduce your house's value automatically by 20 percent. The truth lies somewhere between your separate exaggerations.

The same holds true for stocks, bonds, pension funds, and even household furniture. Let's say your stock portfolio is worth

$45,000. On the net worth statement, you list it as $65,000. The bank will call to check the brokerage account and be told, "It's in the middle five figures." However, put down $100,000, and it's a different story.

More Is Not Only Better, It's Absolutely Necessary

There's one thing more to bear in mind when preparing your net worth statement. The bottom lines on the loan application won't match. So don't even try to balance them out. Whatever you do, never adjust your loan requirement down in an attempt to get approval. You should always ask for more money than you think you need, because you'll soon discover that you need more money than you thought you did.

Far too many retail first-timers try, sometimes for admirable reasons, to play the money game conservatively. They borrow the minimum they conclude that they need to start their business. However, this is one place where just putting your toe in the water is not the best policy. *Borrowing is never easy, but it's far easier the first time around.* Go back for a second loan, and the banker may think you didn't know what you were doing to begin with and that your business is in trouble—which by this time, in all probability, it is.

You will go back to the bank, of course, on an almost daily basis once you've opened the doors of your establishment. For one thing, you'll go there to deposit your daily receipts.

If you haven't had occasion to deal with this aspect of commercial bank transactions, you're in for a real shock when you get your bank's first monthly statement. Most of today's banks charge you to make a deposit.

The bank I use for my payroll account currently charges a monthly fee of $13, a deposit fee of 13¢ for each item, plus 65¢ for each deposit ticket. A deposit of ten checks plus the register cash, then, costs me $2.08. In addition to these charges, there's an item-paid fee of 16¢ for each check or *other item paid*. Into this category falls the 16¢ my account is charged when I exchange bills for a couple of rolls of quarters. All in all, unless you're very careful, you can count on a business account costing you about $1,000 a year in deposit charges.

There are ways around some of these charges. Some banks will reduce or eliminate your deposit costs if you keep enough cash in the bank—the old minimum balance trick. One bank I deal with offers business savings accounts, which allow for a more aggressive approach to savings. Unlike its commercial checking accounts, the counterpart savings accounts charge no fee for deposits. Neither are any transfer charges incurred when you move money from one account to another within the bank. Deposit your daily receipts to a savings account, transfer the amounts needed weekly to your payroll account and your general checking account, and you've saved some $20 a week—not a fortune, perhaps, but enough for a good and well-deserved dinner out once a month.

The Perks of Ownership

That dinner out brings to mind a number of small but significant financial matters attendant upon running a small business, matters such as deductible expenses—of which the dinner may or may not be representative—and highly questionable practices, of which stripping the register is an example. These benefits and self-chosen rewards are not to be trifled with, though they might seem insignificant in the context of the total business picture.

To many people, one of the benefits of running a small store is that you can put your hand in the till whenever you want. Well, you can, but in the long run the practice will probably kill your business. If you steal, chances are your employees will steal. Don't ask me how they know. There's an aura about a store whose owner steals, and anyone who works there senses it.

Of course, you can always fire the copycat employee caught stealing. That won't remedy the other problem with stripping the register. When you steal from the store, you never know where your business stands financially. Such fiscal disarray can be as destructive to the operation as shoplifting and pilferage.

Whatever its moral implications, the issue is a plain and pragmatic business one. That said, let me add that there are plenty of ways to use the system and reward yourself for your hard work while still keeping the books straight and following sound business practices. Some of these means may look a lot like stealing, but they have government and social approval.

One of the first anomalies you'll notice in the business world is that conventions and trade shows are rarely held in the obvious places. The biggest trade show in the world, Comdex, the one for personal computer dealers, is held in Las Vegas. Now we all know, don't we, that Las Vegas is the personal computer capital of the States. It just so happens that, in the environs of this exposition, there are all those business-deductible shows and dining opportunities. When my wife, Ruth, and I were running the candy kiosk, we traveled to New Orleans and Orlando and San Francisco every year to check out gourmet gifts and candy trade exhibits. Hey, it was a nice vacation at company expense, and we always picked up new product lines and ideas, too.

Besides such company-paid vacations, you're entitled to a company car, paid life insurance for the company principals, profit-sharing plans, 401(k) retirement plans, and health insurance. Commercial health insurance policies, incidentally, offer some interesting perks and quirks. You always have to offer the coverage to everybody on your payroll if you offer it to anybody, but the extent of the benefit can vary through what's known as discrimination by class. For instance, the company might pay 100 percent of the premiums for managers and above while contributing 50 percent of the expense for assistant managers and 25 percent for employees who have been with the firm for two years or more. Besides providing 100 percent coverage for yourself, such a graduated scale of health benefits becomes a powerful incentive tool for your employees.

Even a security system for your home is a perfectly legitimate deductible expense if you keep the company books and other important papers there. Legitimate business deductions know few surprising bounds.

4 Location, Location, Location—Scouting It Out

Although the story may be apocryphal, the late Sam Walton is said to have picked out new store locations from the air. By flying over an area where he was considering expanding his retail empire, he could watch the traffic flow. He knew that if people had to drive by his store on their way to someplace or other, they were much more likely to drop in to do their shopping than they would be if they had to go out of their way to get there.

Now I'm sure Sam Walton didn't fly over his first location, or his second or third one either for that matter. When you're starting out, you don't have access to that kind of luxury. What I am sure of is that Sam Walton had, then, the same shrewdness that later inspired the notion of doing his scouting by air. He simply applied that shrewdness on a different plane, fitting the puzzle pieces together on a smaller scale.

Even at its most basic, the retail puzzle has many interlocking pieces. Among those that loom large as you survey the puzzle board are location, capitalization, lease arrangements, buying, merchandising, and promotion. Some of the smaller pieces aren't so crucial. If you start out with the wrong product mix, for example, you can readjust the proportions over time as you learn to gauge your customers' wants. If you hire the wrong key personnel, you may get knocked down, but you'll usually be able to get up again.

Put your shop in the wrong place, though, and you'll pay for this mistake for as long as you're in business. There's always the outside chance that by some miracle the demographics might change in your favor, of course. Rescue by that means, however, requires you to believe in miracles—not the soundest way to run a business.

The right location isn't always the best location. Many retailers have profited immensely from deliberately choosing so-called secondary locations. Ames department stores built a fortune in the discount industry by becoming the principal player in noncompetitive, lesser areas such as Ogdensburg in New York State, Rutland in Vermont, and Dayville in Connecticut. Forgoing the allure of bustling large-population locations, the chain concentrated its efforts in rural regions featuring a clearly defined customer base and low overhead. These were the best locations for Ames.

A footnote should be added here, for it puts a period, full stop, in the chain's success story. Ames did so well with its focused strategy that it had the money and credit to buy out ailing Zayres Discount Stores, a chain of retailers situated in first-class locations. Somehow, Ames was under the impression that it could apply the management skills that had led to its success to making Zayres over in its own image. You guessed it. A few years later, Ames was undergoing bankruptcy reorganization.

Your Second Choice May Be the Best Choice

Certain retail operations need the draw of a mall. Others, however, do quite well outside the high-rent district. Look across the street from just about any mall, and you'll see retailers that are not only surviving, but thriving. Toys"Я"Us, Circuit City, The Wiz, Barnes & Noble, even warehouse stores such as BJ's and Sam's are suc-

Six Ways to Make Sure You Pick the Right Mall

1. How does the outside of the shopping center look? A center in need of repair tells a story. A center that's well kept tells quite a different tale—the one you want to hear.

2. Are the stores in the mall well stocked? Besides the shelves being full, is there a lot of variety?

3. If the landlord or developer has other shopping centers, check out his or her track record.

4. How accessible is the center to a main highway? Can cars enter the lot directly from the road, or are a lot of traffic lights and crossovers involved?

5. Grocery stores don't make good anchors. Once you get the groceries, you have to go home before the ice cream melts. Besides, you've just laid out $100, so you're not in the mood to spend.

6. How many stores have come and gone in the mall over the past two years? If the answer is more than three, you'd better find out why.

cessfully following the strategy of living the good life near, but not actually in, large shopping centers positioned to attract customers from a widespread area.

These successes are big, obvious ones. I use them as examples here because they're easily identified. You see them everywhere throughout the land. However, throughout the land isn't where you'll start your business, if indeed you even aspire to end up there. You won't begin your retail venture by opening some mammoth category killer of a store that will obliterate every trace of the competition. Neither are you likely to have the financing to construct a colossal freestanding edifice somewhere to house your inaugural store. Giant oaks from little acorns may grow, but you start with the acorn. So it is that almost anyone's initial venture in retail will be located in somebody else's mall or Main Street edifice, and the first question to be considered in deciding which of these it's to be is, very simply: what kind of store is yours?

Customer Perception Says It All

A retail establishment is most usefully, if rather unromantically, defined in terms of how the customer perceives it. Traditionally, that customer perception has taken one of two forms: a destination or a drop-in emporium.

A destination store, by definition, is one the shopper purposely sets out to visit, in search of very specific wares. High-ticket items and low turnover characterize the typical destination store. Purveyors of durables such as appliances and furniture, goods whose expected life is, say, three years or more, fall into this category. So do grocery stores, which underscores once again that there are no ironclad rules in this business. You might well buy something on impulse at the supermarket, but the reason you're there in the first place is that you have a grocery list and you went to this particular place to procure what's on it.

Contrast the customer bearing a shopping list with the one who decides on the spur of the moment, passing by, to drop in The Sweater Factory because this winter looks like it's going to be a long one and another sweater might be a good idea if there happens to be something nice in an Aran pattern on sale. The Sweater Factory in this instance is not exactly an intentional destination.

A related distinction in retail personae as perceived by the customer is the service store versus the price outlet. Nordstrom's and the warehouse store at exit such and such off such and such a superhighway stand at opposite extremes defined by this distinction. Somewhere between these two poles lie the majority of the smaller shops, more informal and less fixed in their orientation.

Which aspect you focus on, service or price, will place certain limits on your choice of location. A low-price store can rarely support the costly rental charges of a location identified with high-ticket merchandise and extensive customer assistance. On the other hand, a service-oriented store rarely benefits from a bargain-basement location. At best, what's saved on rent in such a situation will be spent on advertising to draw customers to an area they don't associate with the services they're seeking. At worst, the customers simply won't believe they could possibly find what they're looking for in such a place, even after all the money you've spent on promotion.

A service-focused establishment tends to become a destination store as its clientele becomes comfortable there over the years. If it doesn't, the prognosis for its success is usually poor indeed. Establishments selling on price, on the other hand, usually elude facile placement in either category, drop-in or destination. That makes things harder for their owners, for much depends on how their image is promoted and how that projected image is actually viewed by the consumer. We're back to customer perception once more.

If there are stores that don't lend themselves to strict classification as a drop-in or a destination, there are others that don't lend themselves to pigeonholing. Over the course of the past couple of decades, a whole new retail category has come into being. The shops in this genre are what I call access stores.

An access store is not often a destination in the usual, physical sense of the word, and rarely does the buyer impulsively drop by. Peer inside the premises, and there may not be a shopper in sight. Yet, unlike a mail-order operation or television home shopping, the establishment looks like, acts like, and in fact is a real retail enterprise. The shop seems deserted simply because often its clientele shops by phone, fax, or computer.

The prime movers in this innovative shopping trend were the florists, who initiated flowers by wire in the fifties, and takeout/delivery restaurants, which didn't make their appearance until the sixties. In those formative days, the phone calls came on rare and special occasions, happy or sad. The requests were for flowers to be delivered to a sick aunt in the hospital, flowers for a funeral, flowers for a twenty-first birthday or a fiftieth anniversary. Now, however, real-estate agents in ever-increasing numbers call in or fax orders for bunches of country blossoms to be delivered to new home owners, and lawyers treat their clients to blooms as well.

Similarly, businesses call or fax restaurants or take-out counters with lunch delivery requests, no longer for a special catered affair, but simply for convenience. College students order pizza in preference to dining hall fare. In all these instances, the customers could—and might—drop by the premises in person, but they're just as likely to make the transaction by some other means.

If your establishment will be one where access shopping plays a major role, then the location that's right for you could well turn out to be one of the less expensive, less visible sites. Just don't take your clientele for granted if you go that route. People rarely read telephone books for pleasure, and the Yellow Pages isn't very inspiring unless you're hunting down something specific. You'll need to keep your number and location in front of them at all times. Plan to put some extra money into marketing.

Defining your store concept and its conceivable clientele in terms of destination/drop-in/access gives you a generalized heading to list pros and cons under when you're evaluating a potential location. Discovering who those elusive customers really are and where you're going to find them takes time and a fair amount of thought. The process is probably best described in terms of real-life successes and failures, for much will depend on what you're actually selling and the individual circumstances of your venture. All-inclusive rules are hard to come by here. So let's look at a few retail operations that went right and a few that went wrong.

I'll start with the case of the dry cleaner who had never gone fly-fishing. In fly-fishing, the secret of success is to match the hatch. That is to say, you select for your line a fly that is similar in shape, size, and color to whichever insects are hatching out or hanging around the water that day. The fish, having already discovered how much it enjoys these native delicatessen delights, is much more likely to swallow your facsimile, along with the hook, than it would be if the fly looked like last week's appetizer.

The particular dry cleaner whose story I'm about to relate was a former middle-management banker who'd been laid off during the industry's merger mania of the early nineties. He became a dry cleaner after extensively researching the various service trades and selecting dry cleaning as one that he could pursue largely by himself, retaining a lot of control over the business and reducing staffing problems to a minimum. Dry cleaning was considered a steady, stable, dependable operation, offering good, if not spectacular, earnings potential. In fact, a *Wall Street Journal* article published just before he opened his establishment listed dry cleaning as one of the best opportunities for businesspeople interested in a small-scale venture.

The location this gentleman chose for his operation was within commuting distance of Hartford, whose multitudinous insurance employees suited up daily before departing for their cubicles in the city and were thus all potential clients. The product seemed right. The place seemed right. The customer base seemed right.

There were three problems with the picture, he recalled after closing the store. One of those was unforeseeable. Shortly after the dry cleaner opened his doors for business, the insurance industry went into the throes of a megashakeup. By the end of all the multimergers and layoffs, Hartford was the insurance capital of the United States in name only.

The second problem the gentleman should have seen, quite literally. The particular location he chose in the mall where he'd decided to set up shop had no road visibility. When you drove into the shopping center, you never saw the cleaner, stuck in a corner. Out of sight, out of mind.

The third problem that beset the dry cleaner was of the mismatching-the-hatch type. A second, closer scrutiny of his customer base revealed that locally, apart from the Hartford-bound commuters, the disposable income was largely in the hands of a university and college population. "A strictly wash-and-wear crowd," the erstwhile dry cleaner observed mournfully on closing down his shop.

When all was said and done, however, the real reason for his failure, although the dry cleaner himself never thought of it in these terms, was that as a "new kid on the block" he really had nothing new to offer. His establishment had no niche setting it apart from the established competitors in town.

Another failure to fit the puzzle pieces together in selecting the location for a venture occurred when a young couple I know decided to open a Chinese restaurant in a new strip center that was opening up. Here the oversight lay in misinterpreting the future traffic flow on and around the grounds of the complex, a factor related to the habits of tired, hungry shoppers at the end of a buying outing.

The site the couple chose seemed right for them, even though the center rent was high. To keep the monthly charges from overwhelming them, they chose modest premises at one end of the strip and planned to concentrate on takeout. Besides accommodating their concerns about overall expenses, takeout reduced staffing and also eliminated dishes and dishwashing, both space- and time-consuming particulars of any restaurant.

Unfortunately, when the shopping center opened, the traffic pattern that evolved was such that the cars used the driveway nearest to the restaurant as an exit, if at all. Furthermore, the drive veered off toward the main road at just that point where the eyes of the car occupants might otherwise have glanced toward the restaurant. Concentrating on the turn, one tended to zip right past the doors without so much as noticing the sign.

Had the couple looked at the restaurant site through their future customers' windshields, they would have seen that its visibility was very low. Furthermore, while it's true that weary shoppers will often opt for takeout, on impulse, to save themselves the task of cooking, probably half those shoppers would rather not go to even that much effort. They want to collapse on the spot, take the weight off their feet, and have a bite to eat then and there.

Takeout is normally the most profitable part of a Chinese restaurant's business. In this instance, though, focusing on takeout alone eliminated a large number of potential customers. The remaining ones often didn't even discover that the restaurant was there.

The Four "Knows" That Lead to Yes

Know your market, know your customers, know how your customers think, and make every effort to know how your customers will think about you, before you sign on the dotted line for a location. People are the most complex unknown in the puzzle you're trying to piece together. Misgauging your clientele can throw off the most careful location research.

The only way I know to study the market for your store effectively is to spend some time on location, as they say in the movie business. While you're certainly not intending to become a Paul Newman selling spaghetti sauce or a Kenny Rogers selling chicken, and to my knowledge neither of these stars has any intention of opening his own store, never forget that retailers and entertainers are in the same business, namely, show business. You won't make the box office if you can't get your message across, and you won't get your message across if you don't know the first thing about how to reach your audience.

The Toe-in-the-Water Location

A full-fledged store, even one with the best of concepts, may be difficult for an entrepreneur to swing financially the first time around. Then, too, putting your whole life on the line for the sake of such a venture may represent a little more risk tolerance than you're capable or desirous of. In either case, a simple, reasonably uncomplicated pushcart may be what you need.

Looking for new ways to lure shoppers, malls have opened their wide and spacious common areas to a fleet of pushcarts and small freestanding kiosks. For the shopping centers, this means extra rental space and a novel draw. For the would-be retailer, it offers relatively low-price entry to the marketplace. At the same time, the beginner is often in very good company, for pushcarts aren't just for neophytes. Many carts are adjuncts to well-established mall store businesses. Bloomingdale's has a cart at Mall of America, for instance.

The average start-up cost of a cart is somewhere between $5,000 and $10,000. Yet sales may range from $10,000 to as much as $70,000 a month during holiday seasons. In many cases, too, pushcarts can be operated on a seasonal basis alone, providing entry-level retail experience on the side for those just getting their feet wet and not yet willing to give up an existing occupation.

Space for a pushcart can usually be leased for a period of anywhere from three months to a year, or month to month in nonholiday times. Thus, even if you've taken the plunge and left your former job, your whole life and finances aren't tied up in the venture. Call it a retail sabbatical, an opportunity to discover whether or not retailing really will be your dream come true. Do give it your all, though. A halfhearted attempt cushioned by the feeling if you don't make it, well, it was only a temporary fling, will get you nowhere in retail.

From small pushcarts mighty stores can truly grow. Shawna and Randy Heninger left their secure and pension-laden jobs with the IRS to roll out first one and then another mall-based pushcart selling personalized keychains. By the time the *New York Times* chronicled their progress recently, they'd added a real store to their collection of carts, now parked in Florida and Canada as well. Not a huge business, but it's certainly not bad for modern-day peddlers.

Before deciding on the location for my first store, I spent several weeks in and around the shopping center I'd chosen as its potential site. The mall was one recently built in the outlying area of a moderate-sized town, and for anchors it had Caldor's, a solid regional discount store, at one end and Sage Allen, a junior department store, at the other.

What was somewhat unique about this particular mall was that 25 percent of the specialty stores in between these anchors were privately owned. The unusually high percentage of individually held shops was due to the fact that they had been granted government redevelopment money to help them relocate from a rather dilapidated downtown shopping district. Interestingly enough, that downtown hub has since completely collapsed—something to be remembered by way of warning in your location search. The redevelopment turned out to be more destruction than rejuvenation. More than half the Main Street stores are now empty or converted to churches, making for a less than desirable retail location.

The downside of the particular mall I was scrutinizing was that the area in which it was situated had the highest unemployment rate in the state. Counterbalancing this dubious factor in my opinion, however, was the circumstance that two nearby state universities could be counted on to provide a steady influx of customers and cash. Unlike dry cleaning, pets, allowed in the dorms or not, are always in demand by students.

Having decided that the mall had real possibilities, I approached the merchants and store managers already in residence, so to speak, and began asking questions. Starting with the chains, I asked the managers how these mall stores were doing compared with others in the region. I asked the smaller merchants whether they'd encountered any surprises in the customer base. I checked to see what kind of customers the anchor stores attracted—upscale, downscale, what?

Creative Time Wasting

Having gained the answers to those and many other questions, I then spent hours prowling around the premises or just sitting on benches in the mall's common space, "wasting time," watching the activity around me. I was there when the stores opened in the morning. I was there when they closed. I was there in between. I was there on weekends.

I noticed a lot of families shopping and a good mix, considering that this was primarily a college area, of young, middle-aged, and older customers. People seemed to come to the mall for entertainment and socializing, indicating that there would be a lot of impulse buying.

Finally, I decided that this location was indeed the right one for my store. The elusive clues had come together. The pieces of the puzzle fit. I'd grasped a concept and a clientele for my store, and they made sense. The location might not be perfect, but it was good, and I could make it work for me.

The Vision Thing

This perception—the "vision thing" kiddingly in parlance during President Bush's tenure—really does shape your entire retail operation. In the case of site selection, perception is the mood shaper, the impulse that will in large part determine how you view your store's future personality, visualizing it from outside looking in, the shopper's standpoint. Then, too, perhaps because a shopkeeper spends long hours in the store, a pleasant perception of the environs you will be surrounded by so much of the time is nearly a necessity. If you can't elicit that feeling in yourself, don't proceed, because you'll never overcome any feelings of doubt or gloom the environs inspire in you.

Perceptions do change, of course. Rarely do they change for the better, though. A number of years ago, friends of mine were running a successful pet shop in Massachusetts. Eventually, however, a lagging economy and their customers' consequent pessimistic mood convinced them that the retail pet industry in the region was doomed. Persuaded by this new and seemingly appropriate perception, they put the business up for sale.

In due course, the store was sold to the former employee of a competing establishment. What the new owner perceived was a tired shop run by discouraged people. He, on the other hand, felt that there was plenty of room for growth of the enterprise through expansion and the introduction of new merchandise. Under his tutelage, the business blossomed once more, and for the past decade it has been a thriving concern.

And what happened to the discouraged couple who sold out? Well, they found a pet store they really liked in St. Petersburg, Florida, whose owner felt the area was stagnating and wanted to move to the Carolinas, which were undergoing a boom at the time. The Massachusetts couple bought the Florida retail operation, imbued it with a whole new vision, and turned it into one of the most successful pet centers in the region. Perception!

Perception works both ways, remember. How you see the customer and how the customer sees you are interlocking facets of this crucial catalyst of success. That's why selecting a retail operation is like fishing. You learn something about fishing. Then you learn something about the kind of fish you're trying to catch. Meanwhile, the fish has been learning a great deal about fishermen. You'll spend a lot of time casting about for the perfect spot to catch that fish, and even then, you'll have to match the hatch, or you'll come home empty-handed.

5 The All-Important Lease

A commercial lease can be a truly terrifying document when you first see one. We're talking twenty to forty legal-size pages here, all filled with run-on compound sentences that go on for twenty or thirty lines before they finally reach a period. The fact that the opening paragraph often begins with "This indenture . . ." is none too pleasant either. The last time most of us saw that word was in ninth-grade history class, when it was tied to the word *servant,* as in *indentured servant*—not exactly the career track one has in mind when opening a new store. Enforcing the suggestion of bondage, your rights are covered in just one paragraph. The landlord's rights take up the next forty-two pages.

Then too, the landlord, according to the lease, *demises* the premises you hope to turn into a successful store. Now that certainly has a deathly ring to it. A few paragraphs down, furthermore, you discover that if the mall burns to the ground during a nuclear attack after the roof collapsed when both an earthquake

51

and a hurricane struck at the same time, you're still expected to send in your monthly rent check or else.

At this point, you might seriously consider abandoning the whole idea of going into business. I know of one individual who, aspiring to open a bookshop in a mall, simply walked away from the deal after reading the lease clause informing him that he would be responsible for the rent even if the mall closed down because of some natural disaster.

This is an extreme example of how people may react on first viewing a commercial lease. At the other extreme are entrepreneurs so anxious to go into business that they'll sign anything put in front of them if their attorney says it's standard. Between these two needlessly irrational scenarios lies the route to success, the one on which you are about to embark.

Let's say you've done your homework and carefully selected the location for your retail operation. Your next step is to contact the landlord or the landlord's agent, at which point you'll discover that this person isn't particularly anxious to talk to you. You're not Howard Scholz of Starbucks or Sam Walton of Wal-Mart. Chances are you're someone with no track record and limited financial resources.

It's no longer only malls that prefer name brands. Landlords of Main Street retail space, downtown storefronts, and even commercial buildings expect their property to be leased by a division of some large and well-known corporation. If that's what they expect, maybe you're barking up the wrong tree, you conclude. As established proprietors, they must know something you don't. Wrong.

Well-managed specialty shops and hot-concept stores are what give shoppers the variety they're looking for. That's why the boutique business blossomed. Never mind that Williams Sonoma and The Body Shop are now chains found in every mall. Your job is to convince the landlord that the retail operation you have in mind is exactly the right one to fit between megastore one and megastore two in the shopping center, say, or the very shop that's going to be a real traffic stopper in the downtown location you have in mind.

When I was exploring the possibilities for my first store, I asked a shop owner already renting space in the mall where I wanted to locate for an introduction to the landlord's leasing agent. This put me a step ahead of the "I saw your notice about space available" caller. I went from an unidentified hypothetical leaseholder to a successful known entity, simply by association.

Since that first foray of mine into leaseholding, I've initiated dozens of lease negotiations, and the process is always the same. Whenever possible, I contact the actual decision maker, the landlord, directly. If I can't get through to the landlord, then I get as close as I can. Someone negotiating his or her first lease usually reaches, as I did, the leasing agent.

A Lease Is a Legal Document That Won't Be Changed—Unless You Know the Questions to Ask

In pursuing that first lease, once I'd established rapport with the leasing agent, I asked for a meeting with the entrepreneur owner of the complex. We got along really well, and the upshot of the meeting was that some twenty years later, having weathered many

How a Mall Is Leased

Let's say a mall has 250,000 square feet of gross leasable space and the leases are granted on the traditional triple net basis. That is to say, the tenants individually pay all operational costs, everything except the mall mortgage. They pay a prorated share of taxes, insurance, maintenance, and Santa's Christmas call.

Then let's say that the landlord has a mortgage that costs $2.5 million a year to service. To have the requisite cash flow to meet that expense, the landlord needs to collect an average of $10 per square foot in rents for the mall's leasable space ($10 \times 250,000 = 2,500,000$).

This doesn't mean you get to pay $10 a square foot for your store premises. Typically, in a case like this, the large national anchor stores, usually measuring over 30,000 square feet, pay $4 per square foot. Regional chains of the same size pay $6 per square foot. Small national chain stores under 10,000 square feet in size pay $8 per square foot. Regional chain stores in the range of 3,000 to 5,000 square feet pay $10 per square foot. Multistore independents with, say, half a dozen stores throughout the state pay $12 per square foot. One-store independents pay $15 to $20 per square foot—if the landlord will even rent to them.

changes—expansion of the mall, new management, a new leasing agent—my original store is still there.

Granted, it was a lucky opening shot. All the same, you won't get lucky unless you try, and you can't try unless you're equipped to do battle. That entails, first and foremost, knowing what you're getting into.

The first thing a landlord or a leasing agent is going to want to see is your personal financial statement. This will show your assets, your liabilities, and what, in theory, you'd be left with if all your debts were to be paid down to zero. The landlord wants to know these figures because he or she is expecting you to sign your life away in return for an executed lease, and if your life isn't worth much, then even that show of faith on your part isn't going to get you very far.

Most books on starting a small business and most consultants associated with business colleges and local vocational schools will advise you never to sign a lease personally. This is wonderful advice, and it explains why these individuals are teaching rather than doing. Theoretically, I agree with their premise. However, theory and reality, particularly in the world of commerce, rarely coexist. Usually, it's "No signee, no lessee."

Don't panic over signing personally. Just make sure you protect yourself. When I signed my first lease, I did it with a personal guarantee. I'd never do that today. On the other hand, finding a landlord today who will give a first-timer a lease without that personal guarantee is next to impossible.

From the landlord's point of view, signing personally for a lease shows a strong commitment on your part to make the store succeed. From your point of view, it's like having a gun held to your head. The situation need not be quite as terrifying as it seems, though. The trick is to make sure the gun isn't loaded.

Getting Around Signing Personally

There are two ways to unload the gun. One way is to sign the lease, no questions asked, and then transfer all your assets—the house, bank accounts, and whatnot—to your wife's name or that of some other trusted individual not on the lease. This is the question route. While certainly quite feasible, it can lead to numerous complications, not to mention myriad other legal problems. one, landlords, strange creatures that they are, might assume fraud on your part. There have even been instances of faithful spouses selling out and packing up for the Caribbean on their own.

The other, perfectly legitimate way to unload the gun is to agree to sign the lease personally for a given number of years, say the first two or three, with the stipulation that the remainder of the lease period be strictly a corporate obligation. Usually, a landlord will consent to such an arrangement. After all, you may be spending upwards of $100,000 on leasehold improvements, not to mention investing two or three years of your life in the venture, so it's clear that this is no overnight fling. Once you've been in business for a couple of years, you should be entitled to expect your store to be treated as what in fact it is, a respectably established concern.

Besides asking to see your personal financial statement, a landlord is going to want a letter of intent from you. In all probability, he'll send you one ready for your signature. That's fine, because for your purposes a letter of intent simply states that you propose to do something. In this case, you intend to lease space from the landlord. The letter may state a lot of other things, too, such as the proposed lease terms, but you needn't worry about them. This is not a legal document. By the same token, it does not legally entitle you to the premises. Not until the actual lease is signed are you in possession of anything about the place. (See Appendix B for a sample letter of intent drawn up by a rental agent and ready for the lessee's signature. It's fairly typical in the details it covers.)

A letter of intent is not a legally binding document. Still, it's where you should start developing the habit of carefully reading paperwork and then having your attorney check it over before you sign.

In today's overbuilt retail real estate market, neither the letter of intent nor a personal financial statement satisfactory to the landlord should prove to be a major obstacle. Assuming you clear both hurdles, you'll receive a copy of the proposed lease stating the rent the landlord wants to collect and outlining all the other links in the ball and chain you're about to attach to your life. Your job at this stage will be to make the ball and chain as comfortable as it can be for you.

The rent the landlord puts down may be what he'd like to collect—in fact, it's certain to be what he'd like to collect, since he might as well go for the gold. What it's not, just as certainly, is what he needs, expects, or is going to get. *The rent figure as stated in the first drafting of a lease is always open to negotiation.*

While price is something you and the landlord can dicker over, there are other things not open to haggling, issues about which you feel—or should feel—strongly. These are the deal breakers. Here you need to be clear about your concerns, and you need to be clear in reviewing them with your attorney. The negotiating table is not a place where games are played within the safe confines of boilerplate. Negotiating a lease takes resourcefulness and considerable agility. It helps to know what the goalposts look like.

The particular attorney I ask to evaluate the lease I'm considering has twenty years of experience with business deals and knows leasing inside out. The first question he always asks is, "Do you really want to make this deal?"

The question isn't as farfetched as it might seem. It's all too easy to fall in love with a concept and a store location. Love is blind, however, and blind deals can kill a business. So if you've come this far, you really need to step back, take a hard look at the terms of the lease, and say, "All right, I might get this concession here and that modification there. If these are all I get, will I be able to make money or am I just going to be working for the landlord?" Don't sign a lease on a dream.

The second question my attorney asks, once he's established that we're really going ahead, is, "What are the deal breakers?" We take it from there, assessing their impact and looking for legal fallout, particularly personal liability.

A Lease Is Never Long Enough

For me, the duration of a lease can be a real deal breaker. I simply won't sign a lease drawn up for fewer than five years, and I won't sign a lease where I'm not offered at least a three-year renewal option. The option, furthermore, I require to be expressed in dollar amounts, not some ambiguous going-market price or one based on the Consumer Price Index (CPI). The landlord is entitled to a rent increase, but I need the security of knowing the price at which I'm going to be able to extend the lease.

Lease extensions can be a real trap. Recently, the owners of a successful mall sporting goods store whose present long-term lease was coming to an end were offered a new lease with rather good terms except for the apparent technicality that it was a month-to-month conveyance. The owners were inclined to sign on the dotted line, but, worried about the implications of that month-to-month clause, they consulted me for advice.

I had a number of questions to put to them. Were they happy with the location? Was the volume of business good? Did they have any plans to upgrade the store? The answer to all three questions was yes.

I then stressed the same point to them that I now stress to you as a future entrepreneur. *The person who controls the lease controls the business.* In the case of the sporting goods store, no matter how favorable to the tenants the other terms of the agreement might be, if the landlord were permitted to lease the premises on a month-to-month basis, for all intents and purposes he would control the business. The owners would never be able to look past their current month's tenure in their planning. Such traps are to be avoided at all costs.

In this case, we went back to the landlord and explained that the owners were hoping to update the store but that the bank wouldn't finance the modernization with only a monthly lease in place. No consideration would be given to their planned improvements in the absence of a conveyance covering the three-year period that, not coincidentally, equaled the projected duration of the proposed loan. This was an argument any landlord would understand. Besides, upgrading a store in a mall is always good for the entire premises as well.

The landlord understood and sympathized. However, as he now disclosed, two new national anchor stores were about to sign with the mall, and he wanted the flexibility of being able to allocate floor space to those larger tenants as needed.

Fine. Now we knew that the real issue for the landlord was space allocation and store placement, not lease length. We came back offering to give up the existing location of the sporting goods store for an equivalent one elsewhere in the mall if the present space happened to be needed by one of the anchor stores the following year. Since renovation of the sporting goods store was on the drawing boards anyhow, moving would present no major cost obstacle. The renovation could be initiated in the new location. The landlord agreed to a five-year lease, and everyone was happy.

Another potential deal breaker for me is common charges. Let's say a mall lease or one for a strip center calls for your paying a percentage of the common costs, the expenses shared by the mall as a whole, expressed in terms of gross leased space. At the time you sign the lease, your common charges might come to $4 per square foot of leasehold space, an amount representing, say, 1 percent of the total mall costs. That's a typical enough figure nowadays. Now

How Much Is the Rent, Really?

The rent charged for a commercial property is usually expressed as a function of square feet of floor space, and the figure as usually stated is per annum. Thus, for example, given a store measuring 3,000 square feet and a rental figure of $20 per square foot, you as the store owner would be responsible for an annual rent of $60,000, payable in twelve equal installments of $5,000 each.

There are exceptions to this measuring standard, however. Recently, I negotiated a lease on the West Coast for a client who told me that rent was quoted at $1.50 a foot, which seemed ridiculously low. When the actual lease arrived, I found that the rent was $1.50 a foot, all right, but $1.50 a foot per month, not per annum. Well, $1.50 per foot per month multiplied by twelve months comes to $18 per foot per annum, which is the way most leases would have expressed the rate in the first place. Either way, the rent for the 2,000-square-foot store was going to be $36,000 a year.

Another common variation on rental charges is what's known as the percent rent. In effect, this arrangement makes your landlord a partner in your business. Let's say the landlord projects your annual gross sales at $1 million a year. By his or her reckoning, 6 percent of your gross is a reasonable rental charge. So the figure is put at $60,000 per annum on your lease, together with an escalation clause suppose, though, that an anchor store in the mall unexpectedly packs it in two years hence. If the space remains unrented, you might find your common charges suddenly reckoned at $16 per square foot.

What's happened? The mall hasn't changed in size, shape, or form, obviously. The amount of common space remains the same. In fact, that's precisely where the problem lies. Because the anchor is gone, the aggregate amount of store space actually leased and in use has dropped drastically. On the other hand, the amount of leasable space, occupied or no, has remained the same, and you agreed to pay a percentage based on the leasable space. So you and the other remaining tenants have together become answerable for the closed anchor's common charges. Your share of the tab now comes to 4 percent rather than the 1 percent you bargained for.

requiring an additional rent equivalent to 6 percent of any sales above $1 million.

Next year, if your annual sales go to $1.2 million, you'll be expected to add 6 percent of the extra $200,000, or $12,000, to your rent check. Your annual rent just jumped to $72,000. If, the following year, you do a great job of merchandising and your sales hit $1.5 million, then you'll owe the landlord 6 percent of that new $300,000 in sales, or another $18,000, in rent. Now you're up to $90,000 rent.

Now suppose the mall business collapses and your sales decline to a mere $500,000. Your rent declines proportionately, to $30,000, right? Wrong. Dream on. The landlord still gets the full $60,000. You've got a base rate just as if you had a conventional per-foot rate, and the percent rate is added on top of that in good years.

Under a percent rent lease, the landlord will usually want monthly sales figures from you, the right to audit your books will be written into the lease. Any discrepancies will lead to penalties, not to mention your being billed for the audit.

For some merchants, percent rent is a deal breaker. Personally, I build in certain factors, such as rent, as constant costs of my operations. Advertising takes an estimated 3 percent of sales, payroll 20 percent, rent 6 percent, and so on. If profit is expressed as a constant percentage of sales as well, profit will grow splendidly when sales expand even if you're paying a lot more in rent.

Let's say that the new rate you've inherited is going to cost you an extra $24,000 a year in common charges, based on the size of your particular leasehold, which happens to be 2,000 square feet. Do you think the departure of an anchor store is going to increase your sales by the $75,000 or so needed to cover this extra charge? Of course not.

In any lease I'm going to sign, I require that my percentage of common costs be expressed in terms of gross leasable space rather than gross leased space. Oh, what a difference a suffix can make!

A related deal breaker for me as a would-be tenant is capital improvement charges. If a lease in an older mall or center is going to make me responsible for paying a share of roof replacement expenses or similar costs, I'll walk away from it. First of all, as soon as I see a clause about reroofing in a lease, I know the roof is going to need replacing within the first year of my tenancy. Second of all, I know better, period. Capital improvements are the landlord's responsibility even in a triple net lease, where you, the tenant, are required to pay your share of the utilities, taxes, interior maintenance, exterior maintenance, and security.

Something that ought to be a deal breaker for all mall tenants is overlooked by far too many of them, and that's the matter of mall hours—or should I say the lack of them? The failure of a landlord to require uniform, consistent store hours throughout a mall falls into the category of trouble ahead. In a mall or large shopping center setting, if merchants are free to choose their own hours, chaos ensues. People expect the mall to be open from, say, 10:00 A.M. to 9:00 P.M. If they come to a jewelry store at 8:00 in the evening only to find that it closed early, they'll be upset.

Sure, it's bad for business. The jeweler should have known that. One of the basic rules of shopkeeping is to keep consistent hours. However, the repercussions of the incident are what we're addressing here. Irate customers are apt to vent their anger on the whole mall by taking their business elsewhere.

Some anchor stores have the clout to extend their hours beyond those set—or not set, as the case may be—for the rest of the mall. This isn't the same thing as closing early or, say, not opening up shop at all on Sunday when the surrounding shops keep Sunday hours.

Making "Illegal" Lease Clauses Work for You

Lease obligations governing such things as the hours a mall store keeps are perfectly legal restrictive covenants, as these agreements are called. Other restrictive covenants may not be actually sanctioned by law. In any mall lease for a pet shop of mine, I routinely insert a clause giving my store the exclusive right, barring anchors over 50,000 square feet in size, to sell pet-related merchandise in that mall. Now this is probably an unenforceable covenant, as my attorney is the first to remark and the landlord's attorney is the second to point out. However, I've found that the landlord will usually humor me and accede to the clause.

A clause like this works for you in two ways. First, a landlord is reluctant to test the law and tie up a potential tenant in court. Besides, the case could go against the landlord. So he or she will likely let the clause stand and hope it's never put to the test. Second, if the mall management decides that a pet superstore would be a great addition to the complex, such a restrictive clause in your lease might inspire your being approached as the logical person to undertake the venture, essentially becoming your own competition. Now you have both an option and a real bargaining point. If you decide against such an undertaking, you can sell your lease back to the landlord or have the superstore buy it.

Contrast this scenario with another enacted recently in the Northeast. A wave of electronics superstores swept the region. In at least two separate instances, a mall leased space to one of these superstores even though an existing tenant held a long-term lease for a full-line electronics store in the mall. Which situation would suit you better? Would you rather have some extra lease clauses that might or might not be enforceable, just in case they should come in handy someday, or would you prefer to leave yourself wide open to steamrolling by some hulking competitor? Make sure you cover your bets.

When I think I've gotten all the mileage I can out of the lease negotiations in a given situation and the landlord seems to have reached the same conclusion, I say that I'll have my attorney review what we've agreed on. This usually surprises the other side, because the spokesperson feels that all the imaginable concessions have just been made, which is exactly why I like to bring a member of my A team back into the picture. The reason you call an attorney in on lease negotiations to begin with is that he or she knows a thing or two you don't. That's the whole point of having a third party look over a lease. Now you want your attorney to cast a critical eye over the finished negotiations to be sure nothing's been missed in the course of the lengthy deliberations.

A Painless Walk Through the Legalese of a Lease

To give you a feel for what's involved in negotiations like this, let's walk through a real lease, deciphering the major clauses. (For the full text of the lease in question, see Appendix C. Referring to it as you read will help you to familiarize yourself with the legalities. Consider the activity an exercise in page flipping, something you'll be doing a lot of when you're poring over your own future lease. Other leases may have the clauses we're reviewing here shuffled in a different order and worded in a different manner, but they'll be in there somewhere; of that you can be sure.)

1. Premises will be the label usually identifying the first clause in an *Indenture of Lease*. This clause will provide a brief description of the *Demised Premises*, in other words, the location of your proposed store. Sometimes the lawyers will be kind enough to refer to the area more simply as the *Leased Premises*.

The description will be given in square footage, and one thing you want to make sure of here is that the space as designated really is within a foot or two of the actual floor space you intend to lease. *When it comes to leases, a foot is not always a foot.* Slipups in measurements occur even on blueprints, and *approximately* covers a lot of ambiguities you want to avoid if you can. I didn't make an issue of the point in the particular lease discussed here, you'll note, because the shop in question was a freestanding kiosk in a mall's common space.

Quite often there will be a sentence or two describing how the footage was measured, from exterior wall to exterior wall, for example. Here again, for the particular lease we're talking about, no such yardstick definition was specified because of the freestanding nature of the shop. Quite often, too, where the premises are in a mall, a map of the mall layout and facilities highlighting your location will be appended as a separate *Exhibit A*.

2. Term, the label heralding the next clause of the lease, is self-explanatory. The lease term you settle for should be as long as or longer than the period covered by the note you sign for the money borrowed to open the store. Under no circumstances should you sign a lease whose term is shorter than that of your loan. Owing money and having the ground that was generating the wherewithal to pay it back taken out from under you isn't comfortable, much less sensible.

2A. Renewal Option is the cream on your lease. Don't leave the bargaining table without it. Your rent for the option period will probably reflect an increase over what you're agreeing to pay presently. Make sure the adjustment will be based on some reasonable standard established right here, at the outset of your agreement, and talk the arrangements over with your A team. Lest the new figures seem intimidating from your immediate, start-up perspective, though, remember that you'll be operating without the overhead of the bank note, so the business will be far more profitable. That's what makes the renewal option the cream on top.

3. Commencement Date can be a tricky navigation point in your negotiations. Too many first-timers are persuaded by the landlord to view the commencement date as the day when they take possession of the premises they're signing for. Nothing could be further from what you want. The rent meter shouldn't start ticking until 90 to 120 days after the lease is signed by both parties or the day when the store actually opens its doors for business, whichever comes first. Chances are you'll be starting with an empty box of a store. It may not even have interior walls yet, much less fixtures. Several months might be needed to put the premises together and stock the shelves. You can't afford to be paying rent this whole time.

In the lease for my kiosk, the landlord had typed in a commencement date of under a week after signing. His rationale for this date was that there was an established kiosk on the premises in question, so all I had to do was to move in the merchandise, and that shouldn't take more than a few days. My argument was that I couldn't order the merchandise until the lease was signed, and it might take a month after that to arrive. (See the asterisked footnote reflecting the change in this clause, initialed in the margin.)

With the commencement date delayed for a month, my wife and I dashed off to contact the candy distributors we'd approached earlier about doing business with us. We had the kiosk 90 percent stocked in less than a week. As it turned out, it did indeed take almost a month for some of the specialty items to arrive, but we had the shop up and running after that first week, which gave us three rent-free weeks in which to operate.

Rent-free time can make the difference between a real struggle and smooth sailing in a retail operation. It gives you some extra cash flow during that critical opening period when you're first getting a feel for the business. For that reason, it's not uncommon, in an overbuilt real estate market, for an entrepreneur to negotiate two or three or even six months of free rent at the beginning of a lease. The commencement section of the lease is where this bonus goes if you get it. Just remember that you can't get it if you don't ask for it.

4. Use may be referred to in some lease contracts as *Conduct of Business.* Whatever it's called, this clause is where your business, present and/or future, is defined—and where its limits are stated decisively, in very explicit language. This clause will be strictly enforced, particularly if the shop is in a mall and any of the other storekeepers there suspect you might be invading their territory with your merchandise. Be very clear as to the goods you intend to purvey. At the same time, describe them as broadly as possible.

The description of my kiosk wares included *small novelties.* Those two little words took the candy kiosk far beyond the original idea we had in mind when we started. The first small novelties were Christmas stockings, Valentine hearts, and Easter baskets. As time went on, the novelties included mugs, cheese baskets, stuffed animals—hugging lollipops, of course—and the balloons that were to become a huge and highly profitable part of the business.

5. Minimum Rent through *11. Place of Payments* identify the clauses where the actual amount of your rent is finally specified and where the mechanics of it are set forth. Rent increases and taxes will be mentioned, and while they might seem clear enough matters now, in later sections of the lease they will be dissected into myriad bits and pieces strewn with legalese and fraught with disturbing implications. *Additional rent* is another short phrase that may well start alarms going off in your head. You will find it scattered here and there throughout the remainder of the lease, becoming ever more alarming with each appearance, because every time it's alluded to, you can add a little something or maybe a lot of something to your total rent costs. Go over all the clauses where these subjects are mentioned with your accountant as well as your attorney.

In the kiosk lease, two insertions might seem rather startling. *Paragraphs 6, 7 and 8 intentionally omitted* and *Paragraph 12 Intentionally Omitted*, it states. No, the landlord wasn't trying to confuse us here. The text of the lease had passed that number of paragraph breaks long before, which is why I've referred to the various actual sections of the lease as clauses instead. You'll never know what items 6, 7, 8, and 12 were. The notations concerning their absence are made simply so that no one can go back later and say, "Ah, you see? Paragraph 12 is missing. What we really meant here was . . ." or "Paragraph 12 is missing. This contract isn't valid."

13. Construction is another one of those straightforward labels ever so rarely seen in a contract. The activities encompassed by the clause are equally straightforward. In fact, they will be covered in considerable detail in the clauses to follow. What you can do to the premises when you move in, what you can do while you're there, what you can and can't do when you move out—it will all be spelled out.

A subclause x-ed and initialed in my kiosk lease read "(b) the kiosk can be restored to its original condition upon the termination of this Lease." Now the fact of the matter was that the particular kiosk ensconced on the premises at the time didn't really maximize the use of its allocated space. I had in mind either to change it drastically or to replace it altogether. Neither course of action would permit a restoration of it to its present shape or state. The fact that the new kiosk would be vastly improved had nothing to do with the issue in dispute. When you're negotiating a lease, try to think of all the possible future options imaginable, and then try to incorporate as many of them as you can into the lease document.

14. Tenant's Installations and Alterations captions a long list of restrictions on what you can and can't do, inside or out, to alter the appearance and/or functioning of the store. The essential gist here is that you can't do anything without the landlord's express and written approval. On the other hand, the landlord can, with or without your approval, require you to make certain improvements to the premises. You might be directed to spruce up the exterior appearance of your store and introduce new signs, for instance, if the landlord deems it necessary to the overall look of a mall. The clause also makes you responsible for numerous other matters—not to mention expenses—that you might not have taken into consideration yet.

In addition, the clause usually informs you that when you move out or the lease expires, whichever happens first, the landlord will have the right to keep, almost without exception, any and all additions and improvements you've made to the premises. Then again, you might be required to remove certain fixtures and additions upon vacating the premises. Yet you'll be expected to accept the premises *as is.*

15. Operation of Business should warn you that what's coming is no less than a short but to-the-point directive telling you how to run your business. There will be certain standards that the landlord wants maintained, and they'll be spelled out. The choice of inventory for your store might be something that's in your control, for instance, but you can be held responsible for stocking and selling it in such a way as to produce the maximum return—to yourself maybe, to the landlord definitely. *I've actually seen leases where a minimum dollar value was placed on the inventory a store was expected to carry at all times.* Adequate hours, adequate staff, adequate display, adequate repairs, adequate heating, and adequate cleanliness may all be cited requirements. Mezzanine restrictions, advertising restrictions, and competitive restrictions may complete the list.

I negotiated the x-ing out of two stipulations in the kiosk lease. The first was a Sunday closing requirement the landlord had in the contract. At the time, stores in the particular area where the mall was located had just begun opening on Sundays, and I anticipated that mall customers would soon be expecting this service. The second alteration I made to the operations clause was to eliminate a requirement for landlord approval before we could change the name of the kiosk operation. This was my first fling at the candy business, and I had some qualms about the limitations the name we'd chosen for the shop, Chocolate Fantasy, might impose on our image. The landlord agreed to my requested change without a fuss.

16. Compliance with Laws heads another clause defining your responsibilities as a tenant, in this case those having to do with governmental, insurance, and related regulations and requirements. Some leases go into the legal, insurance, and indemnification provisions at great length. Call in your A team.

Your lease, like mine for the kiosk, might specifically prohibit any form of going-out-of-business sale. In that case, you should be advised that while such a restriction is normally aimed at marketeers like those on Broadway in New York who've been having going-out-of-business sales since I was a kid, the clause does in fact eliminate all going-out-of-business sales, even legitimate ones. Of course, you could have a *Lease Terminating* or an *Owner Retiring* sale.

18. Signs, Awnings and Canopies, which in my lease followed another of those intentionally omitted clauses, gives you some idea of how controlling the retail environment has become. Most shopping centers will meticulously define and restrict the type of sign permitted the individual stores. But the unified-look approach is now spreading beyond the malls to downtown shopping areas.

I've been consulting with a couple planning to open a jewelry and gift shop in an exclusive Laguna Beach, California, neighborhood. The local town council is seeking to pass an ordinance that will require its approval of all store signs in the area under its jurisdiction. Not only that, but the ordinance will give the council the right to deny a business license to any store whose merchandise mix doesn't meet its approval. Do note that the inventory referred to is the merchandise mix, not just the merchandise itself—not enough 7-triple-E-size shoes, no license.

The ordinance will probably be challenged on constitutional grounds if and when it's passed, but, from my clients' point of view, it has a certain appeal. Theirs is a very upscale store concept, and there's nothing worse than investing in a Tiffany operation and then seeing T-shirt stalls sprouting all around you.

Whatever the outcome of the Laguna Beach council's quest, it's interesting to note the attempt to impose cohesiveness. *Main Street is beginning to act like a mall.*

19. Assignment refers to a lease provision notable for a number of reasons. It's crucial for you to know that, without the right to sell or assign your lease, you have no business to sell. For this reason, it's of paramount importance that the stipulation *which consent shall not be unreasonably withheld* appear immediately following any clause giving the landlord control over your sale or assignment of the lease by requiring his or her approval of either arrangement.

One very serious warning should be added here. A landlord may retain the right to keep your name on the lease if you sell. Where that's the case, you are guaranteeing the new owner's financial obligations. So if you plan to sell your lease, you'll want to be as sure as possible, before you go ahead with the sale, that the new owner will succeed at the business. You should try to assess his or her chances as carefully and thoroughly as you can. *Taking back a failed store from a buyer is like fishing your prized Porsche out of the river* after you'd invited a fifteen-year-old to take it for as long a joyride as he'd like and just leave it wherever, whenever, afterward.

In the kiosk lease, a reference made in the assignment clause to the landlord's right to terminate the lease upon the sale or transfer of corporate stock to a third party was x-ed out and initialed because no corporation was involved here. The restriction was basically the same as that imposed on the individual tenant, simply recast in corporate terminology.

20. Repairs through *24. Taxes* or some similar tags will mark the lease clauses covering your responsibilities as regards upkeep, maintenance, utilities, and taxes. There's very little flexibility here. You're usually looking at a triple net lease, where, in effect, you're leasing empty space. Everything that makes this space usable, from the interior walls to the sewer services, will be your responsibility, along with your prorated share of the property taxes.

25. Common Mall and Common Parking Area Maintenance through *27. License to Common Areas* are labels that may vary in name from lease to lease but that will all refer to the common space shared by a mall's tenants, the back service halls as well as the parking lot and the pedestrian walkways by which customers enter the stores. For the most part, the clauses will busy themselves with making clear that the landlord is going to do what he wants with this space and that you'll really have no say in the matter.

At the same time, you will be responsible for a monthly prorated contribution, in the form of additional rent, toward the expense of operating and maintaining this space. Reading through the itemization of chores involved, which range from fire protection to planting flowers, is exhausting work. Visualizing the monthly cost of it all, which will begin with the light bulbs and go up from there, may be petrifying.

In the twenty-sixth clause of my kiosk lease, where this contribution was spelled out for me, an initialed x-ed out figure in the text and an asterisked footnote indicating a substitution are worth noting. The original denominator used to determine my share of the maintenance costs was 70,610 square feet. However, the figure was changed to 253,866 square feet for the first five years and 101,835 square feet for the next five years. In using the smaller divisor, 70,610 square feet, the landlord was dropping the anchor stores' footage from the mall common charges. Had I left the clause as it stood, my costs for securities, utilities, and maintenance would have been four times as high as they became with the amended figures.

28. Merchants' Association is a label applied to what, from a landlord's point of view, is a rather clever clause. Most malls and many downtown areas have a tenants' association, the ostensible purposes of which are to promote the area shops and to deal with any communal problems that might arise. Like most organizations, one composed of merchants depends on the individual members for its strength, and so, like most organizations, merchant associations tend to be weak and inefficient. By requiring you to join this association, the landlord neatly unifies the wavering opposition under his own banner.

29. Insurance through *35. Condemnation* identify a bunch of clauses, found in one form or another in every commercial lease, that you should go over with your insurance agent. On the whole, they're fairly standardized in the way they allocate responsibility. A lease will go into incredible detail, though, in specifying the various kinds and amounts of insurance you're obliged to carry. That's why you want your own agent to scrutinize them carefully.

In addition to the lengthy insurance and indemnity provisions, all leases contain a clause called *Destruction.* In the kiosk lease, this happens to be clause 34. The clause is there for the protection of the landlord. What it says, in brief, is that if the mall burns down, or partway down, the landlord has the right to decide whether to repair it, rebuild it, or renege on the venture entirely. You hold your breath and are out of business until he lets you know which it's going to be.

Make sure you have sufficient business interruption coverage in your insurance. You'll probably never use it, but the expense is minimal. Should the need for it arise, it could spell the difference between surviving—with the bonus, perhaps, of an unexpected vacation—and absolute disaster.

35. Condemnation is the name of another contingency that has to be addressed in a lease. In some contracts, this clause may be called *Eminent Domain.* Like destruction and devastation, condemnation for public use is an exceedingly rare occurrence, but it does have to be provided for.

36. Default is a serious flag for a serious offense that your lease will go to great lengths to explain to you. If your rent and other payments are not received within ten days of their due date, you're in default. If they're not received within twenty days, you'll usually be billed for a surcharge or late fee of 3 to 4 percent.

In theory, the default clause also entitles the landlord to demand all the rent due under the lease if you're more than a certain specified number of days late. As unlikely to happen as this might be, it's always best to pay your rent promptly. Even *from the standpoint of cash flow, paying a 3 or 4 percent late fee every month is almost the equivalent of paying a thirteenth month's rent.*

37. Access to Premises and *38. Excavation* or similar phrases in a lease are clues to what you've been suspecting all along, namely, that your home may be your castle, but your store remains the landlord's playground. He or she has the right to enter anytime, anyway, even if it means breaking down the door because you've replaced the lock and the landlord's master key no longer works. Yes, you're the one who will pay for repairs to the door after the break-in.

In the kiosk lease, the landlord injected here the right to put a *To Let* sign in the store window during the last six months of my lease. Personally, I feel that if I'm not allowed to have a going-out-of-business sale, the landlord shouldn't be allowed to so impinge on the last days of my store. The issue wasn't a deal breaker for me, though.

39. Subordination through *55. Limitation of Liability* and similar captions in a lease will bracket an interminable list of extra rights reserved to the landlord, including the right to sell off the whole shebang and retire to a yacht in the Caribbean. All such clauses need to be reviewed by your attorney, for they will cover everything from invasion to rioting in the streets to simple power failures.

From the standpoint of actual store operations, the clause you'll need to scrutinize most closely is the one on rules and regulations. This long, detailed clause will recount how, when, and where you may receive goods, display them, park your car, and use the bathroom. The rules may or may not be enforced, but they're in writing and can be. That's the hook to remember.

So there you have it, the bare bones of a commercial lease outlining your rights and responsibilities and your landlord's rights and responsibilities. What that lease attempts to do is to resolve all manner of imaginable problems before they can possibly arise. Should they ever indeed arise, know that all the agreements set forth in the lease can be enforced and probably will be—to your possible sorrow if you haven't been careful about what you sign. That's why, when you think you've scrutinized, weighed, and negotiated every single detail in a lease, you take it back to your attorney for a final review.

Go for the Extras

This is also a good time to go for a few last little extras. Leave it to your attorney to direct the last round of negotiations. At this juncture, there should be no last-minute deal breakers. However, your attorney might suggest that he or she would like to see a right of refusal for space adjoining your store, for instance, or some opening money in the form of an extra sixty days' rent free initially because it's going to cost more than originally expected to do a really nice storefront. The landlord may or may not go along with these last small concessions, but it's always worth trying for them.

Whether or not you're granted these final concessions, you're ready to affix your John Hancock to the document. All five copies of it go back to the landlord by registered mail. In turn, you'll be sent two copies signed by him or her. You are now on location.

Changing the Unchangeable

A lease signed, sealed, and delivered is still not a document writ in stone, although many people assume just that. Don't be misled by them. Anything is possible if the parties involved agree to it. Twenty-five years of lease negotiations have taught me that, with the right approach and the right documentation, a store owner will be listened to and accommodated by the landlord, particularly if the end result benefits the landlord as well as the shopkeeper.

There are a number of reasons why a landlord is usually willing to renegotiate the terms of a lease where the circumstances warrant a second look at them. The first and most obvious of these reasons is that a landlord doesn't like to lose a tenant, particularly one who has proved honest, reliable, and open with his or her books. This is particularly true where a shopping center or neighborhood is experiencing some retailing difficulties.

Then too, an astute landlord will sense opportunities to benefit in the long run from giving tenants some short-term relief. A tenant has a focused perspective, typically defined by beating last month's or last year's sales. The perspective of the landlord, on the other hand, is always long-range. He or she is always trying to figure out how to profit above and beyond his or her thirty-year mortgage on the premises. Viewed with these considerations in mind, renegotiation, assuming it's conducted reasonably and candidly, becomes quite feasible.

When the lease for one of my mall pet stores was up for renewal, I approached the management with a number of concerns. For a number of years, I'd been regaled with glowing reports of the improvements soon to be made to this rather dowdy mall. The supermarket was to triple its floor space and become a twenty-four-hour megastore, while the tired look of the whole mall, a number of whose stores had been vacant for some time, was to be dispelled by several new hot-concept shops.

What the management had failed to mention was that not all the necessary permits had been granted, the superstore hadn't yet signed a new lease, and none of the hot-concept shops had either—nor would they, as it was to turn out, for a long, long time. The mall was located on a floodplain, and environmental considerations altered since construction of the original building had led to difficulties in obtaining the permits. The lack of permits had led to a lack of new leases, which in turn had led to financing problems, and so on.

Six years later, the mall still resembled a cross between benign neglect and a construction zone. Things would be better within a couple more years, but by then I'd be more than three-quarters of the way through my renewed lease.

Legally, this was my problem. However, my feeling was that if I could make a good case for the mall's keeping me happy in order to keep me there, rather than having me move out at the end of my present lease, just when the mall was struggling to get on its feet again, I'd have some good leverage at the bargaining table. So I contacted the mall manager.

Never Complain—Explain

I did so not to grouse and complain about the lack of progress, but to say, "Look, I really want to be at this location. Am I correct in assuming that you want me here as well?" With an affirmative answer to that question, 70 percent of the renegotiation work was done. If the answer had been no, there would have been no point in my pursuing the matter any further.

Anyhow, I opened up my books, which showed that my gross sales had held steady throughout the fiasco so far. However, the books also showed that my expenses were up and my markup was down. In effect I'd bought customers by lowering prices and over-stocking merchandise. In other words, I was demonstrating my willingness to sacrifice profitability to keeping customers happy during a difficult time. Trying to win them back once the mall was looking good again could be a lot harder.

The manager was both understanding and sympathetic, since she could see that my reasoning made good business sense. My next task was to convince her that I wasn't suffering from pig's disease, a common ailment among negotiators manifested by the obsessive requesting of a little more and then just a little more. Instead of requesting a rent abatement for the entire length of my lease renewal, I asked for one only for the duration of the construction.

After reviewing the store's books with my accountant, the landlord granted me a 50 percent rent reduction until the mall renovation was completed.

The epilogue to the story is that in the period between the time I renegotiated my lease and the time when the last of the construction workers packed it in, four other tenants left the mall. Each of them, when asked their reason, said that there'd been no use talking things over with management because once you signed a lease you had to live with it. During that same period, on the other hand, the pet store witnessed the best twelve months' volume of sales in its twenty-year history.

6

The Computer You Don't Want, Software Not to Get, and Other Contrarian Wisdom

A hundred years ago, a merchant kept his daily cash in a cigar box. Then came the cash register. Ten years ago, the electronic cash register became de rigueur. Today, you need a personal computer and a laser printer—or do you? *The personal computer can be a boon to any business, but it can also lead you down the road to failure if you're not careful.*

On the boon side, there's the matter of bookkeeping. You'll probably opt for an accounting package to do the job. Such software is often quicker, and definitely cheaper, than the traditional bookkeeper. While it's quite accurate, however, it presents one peril. The bookkeeper is by nature methodical; if you use accounting software instead, you must be methodical as well.

A number of software packages will take care of your bookkeeping needs. Among them are M.Y.O.B. Accounting, One-Write Plus, PeachTree Accounting, and QuickBooks. Any one of these programs will enable you to enter your store's daily transactions, track invoices, pay bills, as well as generate a host of reports, from comparative month-to-month sales by department and category to accounts payable and projected cash flow.

In choosing between the various packages available, your accountant's preference should feature prominently in your considerations. There are still accountants who cut their teeth professionally in a world of pens and pencils and One-Write, the original checkbook accounting system. These accountants naturally tend to steer their clients toward the electronic equivalent of that system, One-Write Plus. Other accountants will have a different siren song. My CPA likes the instant update and the question-and-answer access that QuickBooks provides via the Internet.

Both because my accountant uses this software package and because it's so easily followed by those of us who aren't computer types, my own choice is QuickBooks. Choosing a computer program for accounting purposes is much like choosing a car. It's largely a matter of personal preferences—money, what options you want, and your driving style. QuickBooks is the Volkswagen Beetle of accounting systems, but maybe you need four-wheel drive or prefer Cadillacs.

Whatever program you choose, remember that there is one mantra you must recite daily: *"Back up, back up, back up." If you don't, you'll live to regret ever doing business with a computer.*

That said, if you're going to entrust a computer with your books, it would seem to make sense to add an automated sales and inventory package to your software library as well. After all, why not start off altogether in the twenty-first century?

Well, things are seldom what they seem.

Don't Let the Computer Run Your Business

Automated point-of-purchase sales software tends to perform best where it's very merchandise specific. When it is, it can transform the industry for which it was designed. However, a very specialized focus isn't the best thing that can happen to a start-up retail operation. Even the pros who've been zeroing in on the right product mix for a long time warn against drawing facile conclusions from a computer printout.

The proprietor of a package store in a mall near mine uses Saltware, a program devoted exclusively to liquor retailing. On first hearing the name of the product, I imagined that the appellation had something to do with old tavern custom, carried through to this day, of serving free lunches or very salty tidbits to encourage patrons to drink more. It turns out, though, that Salt is the name of the program's developer.

Saltware, which costs about $3,500 per station, or individual computer, employs a bar code scanner to ring up each sale on the register. There are 5,200 SKUs, or stock-keeping units, in the package store's inventory, and as each sale is recorded, the unit is also deducted from the stock.

The software also generates a host of reports at the user's request. For instance, the sales history of any given item can be called up to show its monthly sales over the past year or two. In addition, the software will make ordering suggestions based on historical sales. "I don't follow the suggestions, but I do use them as a guide," says Roger Gagne, the store owner.

The guarded reservation expressed in the first part of Mr. Gagne's statement points up the importance of not becoming too dependent on the computer for your merchandising strategy. It's all too easy to let the machine decide; and if there's one thing the machine can't do, it's empathize. The computer doesn't know your customers. It can't fathom their human, idiosyncratic predilections and penchants.

This is why I can't emphasize strongly enough that you should *by all means get a computer to handle your books, but keep your hands on the merchandise itself, at least for the first couple of years you're in business.* Otherwise, you'll never develop that magic feel for the pulse of your store, the intuitive perception that makes a venture truly a success rather than merely an also-ran.

Keep your hands on the register, too. A fully computerized system for a bookstore, say, including WordStock software, bar code capabilities, and inventory control, typically costs between $20,000 and $30,000. Totally networked, such a system could link a couple of registers, a couple of information stations, back office stations, and a receiving station. It's something you'd expect to find in a bookstore doing sales of $1 million plus a year. Less ambitiously, for $10,000 to $15,000, you could get a single register linked to an information station and a back office station, again complete with software, stock control, and all the other bells and whistles attendant upon basic retail operations.

Leasing the smaller system instead of buying it outright would entail a monthly layout of only $400 to $500 a month, including maintenance charges. Extend the lease term or simplify the system, and you could perhaps reduce the payments to $300 a month. The automated system would provide good electronic customer service support and make possible those myriad computer reports on your store's performance that are so much in vogue in today's business environment.

However, you're selling merchandise, not fancy computer-generated reports. The more good merchandise you carry, the more likely you are to get the sale. That rock-bottom $300 a month that the lease for a low-end computerized system would cost could buy $3,600 worth of stock over the course of a year. Given a 50 percent retail markup, that's $7,200 in sales. If you turn over your stock four times a year, you're sacrificing a possible $28,800 in sales for the point-of-purchase register system.

A good plain-vanilla electronic register, on the other hand, can be bought for about the equivalent of a single lease payment for the point-of-purchase register. It will cost you somewhere between $300 and $600.

Registering Your Sales

Don't get more register than you need. What you want is a basic register supplied with both a customer receipt tape and a detail tape. The detail tape, which stays in the machine until you total your take, provides a record of all the store's sales transactions, including the time of each one. Anytime the cash drawer is opened, even when no customer purchase is involved, that occurrence is noted.

The register should feature at least four and preferably more departments, or category breakdowns, enabling you to classify the merchandise purchased by type as each complete sale is rung up. The classification should be as discrete as the type of inventory you carry allows.

My pet store registers assign purchases to fish and aquarium supplies, dogs and canine accessories, birds and bird supplies, small animal supplies, and a special department. I use the special department category to monitor a new line or a discount item from one of my distributors. I also use it for promotional lines or special items picked up at shows. Generally, the department tracks such an item for four to six weeks.

Over the years, this running categorization will furnish you with a chronicle of trends invaluable in analyzing and evaluating where your business is going. The commentary won't be as detailed as that generated by the fancier computerized point-of-purchase systems, nor will the machine be as flexible a diagnostic tool. Because you have to assess the trends yourself, however, working with the more modest breakdown the plain register tape monitors will imbue you with a greater feel for the business.

Once you have that, you'll be able to appreciate the more glamorous computer-generated reports churned out by the automated sales software, undistracted by their superficial gloss and well aware that, while they might be acceptable guidelines on paper, you can't live by them. By that time, too, you'll be better able to judge which of the many computerized systems available would be most appropriate and productive in your particular operation. Then is the time to get an automated sales and inventory package.

Meanwhile, make your plain-vanilla register work for you. Use those tapes it issues. Particularly when you're first assessing your product mix, the trends it monitors will be a priceless learning tool.

Can't Live Without Plastic

Besides the register, and sitting near it, you'll need a credit card verification system because, today, retailing without accepting credit cards is not an option. Go with the swipe-the-card electronic model rather than the manual imprinter, for two reasons. First, the card-scanning version greatly reduces errors and eliminates lost paperwork. Second, charges recorded that way are credited immediately to your account, whereas imprinted slips entail a processing delay of a week or more. Instant crediting makes card sales almost as good as cash, the *almost* alluding to the credit card companies' take, of course. Debit card billing and check verification, both definite pluses, are available with some of the newer machines.

A lot of merchants accept MasterCard and Visa only, snubbing American Express because its take is up to 4 percent rather than the 1½ to 2½ percent of the other two services. My own experience has been that aggregate American Express charges run 50 percent higher, on the average, than those of either of the other two cards. I welcome all three and then some. The best advice is probably to accept them all and see which ones draw best for you.

Of course, this entails opening an account for each of the cards. You'll deal directly with American Express, but you'll need separate bank accounts for MasterCard and Visa. Open them initially with the bank that gave you your loan, where you probably have your other accounts. At some point, though, you'll want to ask your accountant what banks other clients use and check out those institutions' processing charges, which can vary by a considerable amount and come right off your bottom line. These charges are on top of the percentage-of-sale charge the cards take.

Shoot That Price

While we're still on the subject of costs, there's one other item that's practically a necessity these days, and that's a pricing gun. It's still possible to pen the price of an article on its package or on an unobtrusive tag. In the antique trade, a small, neatly handwritten price label adds charm. Elsewhere, the shopper sees it as unprofessional.

Pricing guns come in a wide range of models, and, once again, choosing among them will be largely a matter of personal preference. Whichever you buy, pick up four to twelve different colored price tags with which to load the device. Switch colors monthly or quarterly, and you'll have a visual dating system for your stock. As you walk through the store, you'll be able to see at a glance older merchandise that needs to be pulled toward the front of a display.

The color coding will make you subconsciously aware of the general rate of stock turnover as well.

A price gun is best used in the stockroom. Avoid pricing merchandise out front as you shelve it if you possibly can. Blocking the aisles isn't conducive to relaxed shopping.

The price gun just about completes the list of utilitarian accoutrements you need out front. The rest of the floor furnishings, including the window display, are a statement of your store's personality and style (see Chapter 10). Meanwhile, a few more necessities still are needed for the back room.

Back in the Nerve Center

The back room—which may not be in back at all, but which we'll call that anyway because it's removed from the front, or display area, of your store—is where your office is housed. There will repose the computer, the telephone, the answering machine, and the now obligatory fax machine, which, incidentally, should have its own separate phone line.

I don't include a coffeemaker in the list, you'll notice. Quite apart from the fact that nobody ever cleans an office coffeepot, I find it far better for employees to get out of the shop on a break than to sit in the back room. Make a deal with a local coffee shop to keep a running tab for your employees. With luck you'll get a discount on the weekly bill for sending the shop all that business.

Because it's all too easy to lose track of time when you're on a coffee break, inside the store or out, a time clock completes the furnishings in the back room of each of my stores. Yes, I know, time clocks have a certain Simon Legree air about them. All the same, it's amazing how people round off an arrival time of 10:05 to 10:00 in a logbook or sign out at 5:15 when they leave at 5:08. It's just human nature. A time clock, representing an investment of $300, leaves no doubt in either your mind or those of your employees about when something did or didn't happen. This is a matter not of trust or mistrust but of simple operational efficiency.

One of the most efficient small pieces of hardware you can buy for your shop, an accessory item, really, but one I highly recommend, is a counterfeit bill pen. It costs less than $5, and to use it all you do is draw a small mark on the questionable bill. If the mark stays yellow, the money's OK. If the mark turns black, the bill is bogus.

A cashier at a busy discount store of which I was manager at the time once called me over because she'd just used such a pen and discovered a bogus $50 bill. When I inquired who had passed the bill, she replied, "The blond just heading out to the parking lot."

I asked her to call the police and located the uniformed security guard who patrolled the store. We charged out to the lot looking for the blond. The city police and the Secret Service showed up in less than fifteen minutes. Unfortunately, I was looking for a blond woman. The sales cashier had meant a blond man.

Perception is everywhere. But sometimes you need a pen to see.

7 The Magic of Opening Orders

Everybody loves a sale. This is doubly true of the successful merchant, who profits not only from the extra customers a sale at the retail level attracts to his establishment, but from manufacturers' and jobbers' sales discounts, price reductions, and extra dating.

"Goods well bought are goods half sold" goes an old saying in the storekeeper's trade. The aphorism is as true today as it ever was, and nowhere is it more important than in opening orders, the very first ones you place with a manufacturer or a distributor. Yielding special discounts, opening orders also set the tone for future deals. This is a consideration never to be underestimated, for *buying right is half the battle in marketing*.

Your buying should begin as early in the game as possible. Even before you sign your lease, sign up for the trade shows for your industry. All you usually need to get in the door is a business card. There's nothing like a trade show for making contacts in the industry and for seeing what's new.

Suppliers Who Come to You

At the outset of operations, you'll probably deal with no more than half a dozen suppliers for the bulk of your inventory. Expect them to come to you before you're even finished setting up shop. They'll want to see the store while the fixtures are still being installed. As they casually drop off a credit application, they'll size up your approach to the business. If you're putting in wire display racks and a small formica checkout counter, the credit line you'll be offered will be small, too.

Distributors look for evidence that your investment is bigger than theirs. While they look at your bank references, they will also try to sense whether your shop will have the ambience suggesting high inventory turnover. Mood plays important background music here. Be at your most optimistic when first dealing with reps, and they will become your biggest advocates in dealing with the home office.

There's always the possibility that, surveying the surroundings, a jobber will decide not to supply the merchandise at all. This might sound strange at first. After all, who would turn down a chance to make a sale? In actual fact, however, plenty of people will do just that. Lacking confidence in your success, they might feel they'd be risking their stock. They might question your ability to pay for the goods.

If your creditworthiness is being challenged, the only means of surmounting this hurdle may be cash on delivery. Paying COD is the very nemesis of good business. Not only are you laying out the cash before you've had a chance to sell the merchandise, but you're incurring COD charges as well. Typically, these run from $4.25 per UPS shipment to around 1 percent of the shipment invoice for trucking firms, and the cost comes right off the top of your profit. All the same, there may be no way to avoid CODs initially. If that's the case, accept the situation gracefully. Do, however, make sure that you still get your opening discounts, along with any special promotional deals available. Discounts and CODs have nothing to do with each other.

There's another reason why a jobber may not want to sell to you, and that's exclusivity. *All the merchandise on the shelves of a store can be replaced by similar products except those that can't be.* Crest toothpaste, Quaker oats, and Godiva chocolates represent instances where people "buy the box." Godiva in a plain brown wrapper simply isn't the article in the gold imprinted box. Of course, it's the same, but it's not the *same.*

The Seven Most Common Stocking Mistakes

1. Buying what you like, not what the customer wants.

2. Failing to keep detailed sales records, not only of what's selling, but of the price range, sizes, and colors that are moving well.

3. Offering too much selection. The almost inevitable corollary is that you can afford to stock only limited quantities of it. This is known in the trade as having too much breadth and not enough depth. Customers always find something they want, but it's never in the model, style, size, or color they need.

4. Carrying lots of trendy hot hits and not enough of the basics. Sure, the sizzle sells, but the overall profit lies in the basics. They've stood the test of time.

5. Stocking too much of one line on opening the store. When you do that, you've effectively committed your future to moving this one line. Your available cash is tied up in it. What if you guessed wrong? Remember that if you display a broad inventory and one line takes off, you can always reorder.

6. Not securing sufficient dating for seasonal merchandise. If Christmas stock is shipped in August and the invoice is due in thirty days, your company is in jeopardy. It's your responsibility as a buyer to obtain dating on extended terms or other compensation for early shipment. You're helping the supplier by ordering and taking delivery early, so you should be able to negotiate the interim use of money that would otherwise not be due the supplier for some time to come.

7. Failing to ask about discounts. This is probably the single most costly buying mistake retailers make. Always try to find a way to make a little more on each sale by increasing the discount to you. Ask the sales rep how much more of an item you'd have to buy to gain an additional quantity discount. Ask when you might be entitled to prepaid freight. Ask if there's any co-op advertising available. Just keep asking.

The tougher a product is to buy, the more in demand it's apt to be. Both customers and other stores will be vying for it. It follows that you as the new kid on the block may not have the clout to get it outright. However, there's more than one way around this hurdle.

At one time, I had a candy kiosk in an eastern Connecticut mall. It was successful and innovative, featuring a lot of eye-catching candy packaging before Easter and Valentine's Day and introducing frozen yogurt fruit drinks in the summertime to offset the seasonal decline in chocolate sales. What the store lacked, though, was a premier line like Godiva.

Frankly, Godiva wasn't interested in the kiosk. In fact, Godiva wasn't interested in this whole half of the state. Connecticut is divided into the wealthy west and the rural, blue-collar east. Now Godiva isn't a working-class chocolate, which is precisely why it held such appeal for me. We retailers are, after all, selling dreams.

The solution to this problem came to me while I was attending a trade show in New York City. Stationing myself by the Godiva booth, I watched the various buyers placing their orders and made a point of chatting with them later on the floor. So it was that I found a buyer willing to resell to me at 10 percent over cost. I had my premier chocolates, something to add a bit of sizzle to the display and act as a marketing magnet. As for the buyer, he increased the volume of his order quite effortlessly, probably receiving a quantity discount from Godiva in the bargain.

Discounts, Discounts, Discounts

Quantity discounts are but one of the many price breaks with which you should familiarize yourself. Among the others are trade discounts, promotional discounts, seasonal discounts, and cash discounts. There are also myriad variations in invoice dating, shipping terms, and return privileges, all of which translate into dollars on somebody's bottom line. What you want is for that bottom line to be yours.

Dealing with vendors involves active and continuous negotiation. Occasionally, a sales representative will mention a special deal, say two free widgets for every dump—one of those freestanding temporary displays such as bookstores often exhibit—that you take. For instance, a publisher is offering to toss in two free copies of a book if you'll stand a boxed display of that title by your register. The extra copies are yours to sell, keeping 100 percent of the take. Maybe your store would be awfully crowded with a display like that, though. You express your doubts to the rep, who suggests that perhaps three free books would alleviate the crowding. You say it's a five-book crowd and finally settle for four.

While the subject of specials or price reductions may be brought up by a good sales rep, as often as not you'll have to fish for such discounts. If you as a buyer don't broach the topic, the vendor may choose to do business as an innocent order taker, never saying a word about any inducements that might be available.

The discount most perplexing to the uninitiated is the trade discount. It is offered by a vendor in exchange for some service, real or imaginary, performed by the buyer. Originally, the trade discount was a way for the seller to circumvent certain antitrust considerations. Today, it's no more than an incentive to buy.

What makes the trade discount complex is the chain concept it so often involves. While the proffered reduction may be simply a straight percentage off the list price, say 20 or 30 percent, it's just as likely to be a stepped discount, where perhaps 20 percent is taken off the list price, 10 percent off the subsequent balance, and another 5 percent off that balance. In effect, then, you're getting a 31.5 percent discount, which is nothing to sneeze at, but you can't just add up the three discounts and think you're getting 35 percent off.

By comparison with the rather complicated trade discount, the quantity discount is simplicity itself, being exactly what the name implies. The more you buy, the less you pay per item—within reason, of course.

The quantity in question may be cumulative or noncumulative. In the first case, you receive a discount based on how many widgets you buy over a given period, say six months. In the second instance, the discount is based on the quantity of a single purchase.

Free merchandise, although it doesn't represent a strictly proportional price reduction, is normally just another form of quantity discount. Taking the guise of the medieval baker's dozen, this form of discounting is probably the oldest on record. A free roll with every twelve, three extras if you buy a case, two for the price of one—these are all quantity discounts.

Free merchandise may also feature in promotional discounts, the price reductions offered in exchange for in-store promotions, local advertising on the part of the retailer, or other area publicity that helps to sell the product. Where promotional discounts don't take the form of free merchandise, they usually consist of paying a certain percentage of the publicity costs. "If you feature our jeans in your newspaper ads for July," goes the typical bargaining ploy, "we'll reimburse you for 50 percent of your advertising costs up to $1,000."

Seasonal sales and seasonal discounts affect some retail operations far more than others. Not surprisingly, ice fishing equipment is usually available to sporting goods stores at a seasonal discount in late spring or early summer. September wholesale price reductions on bathing suits are not uncommon in the rag trade.

Seasonal discounts permit manufacturers to smooth out their production curve and reduce warehousing costs by shipping merchandise that would otherwise sit biding its time.

Seasonal discounts might be offered in a number of ways. You might get a straight 5 or 10 percent off the wholesale price. You might get four articles but be billed for only three, or the vendor might simply not send you a bill until the goods are in season. Let's say you take delivery on summer dresses in January. Both you and the manufacturer know they won't sell until April or so. The bill is dated May 1.

The most common discount of all is the cash, or payment, discount. Its appeal is based simply on the availability—or perhaps I should say unavailability—of money. Few businesses, be they manufacturing, wholesale, or retail, have enough of this commodity. Whether to compensate for the shortage or simply to take advantage of a good opportunity, everybody likes to use other people's money.

A cash discount is a reward for prompt payment. Over the years, payment of a bill in full within thirty days became the expected norm. The inflation of the eighties and the last recession drove this norm to forty-five days in some businesses, even sixty in others. However, it would behoove you as a new entrepreneur to pay all your bills within thirty days of the invoice date to build up your credit rating. If you can take what's known in the trade as the *2%/10*, the discount for paying early, so much the better.

Many invoices are billed *2%/10 net 30*, which means that if you pay within ten days of the invoice date, you can deduct 2 percent from the net total due. For a manufacturer buying raw materials, the cash discount may be as low as 0.5 percent, which really doesn't make sense, since it's so insignificant.

The cash discount is so attractive and so tempting a feature that many businesses take the 2 percent even when they pay in thirty days rather than ten. Department stores in particular are prone to take the deduction on payments made in sixty or even ninety days. They're buying in enough volume to force the issue. As a small-scale retailer, you won't be in a position to do that. Also, in response to this lax reading of their terms, some vendors have in turn eliminated the cash discount.

Wherever a cash discount is indeed available, bear in mind that what it's offering you is the equivalent of an annualized 24 percent tax-free return on your money. That's an absolutely unbeatable return if you have the funds on hand to spend in this fashion. Just don't squeeze your cash flow by trying to grab the discount when what you really need to do is to use the money owed the manufacturer or the distributor to increase your inventory. You are, after all, in the retail business, not the banking sector.

The 2 percent discount is automatically expanded even past the technically indicated ten days when a supplier offers end-of-the-month or receipt-of-goods dating. In either case, the date of the shipment itself has no real bearing on when payment must be made in order for the recipient of the bill to take advantage of the cash discount.

In end-of-the-month dating, the invoice is automatically dated the first day of the month following shipment. If the goods are shipped on May 7, the invoice is dated June 1. To take legitimate advantage of the 2 percent discount, then, you should pay the bill by June 10. Receipt-of-goods dating moves the due date of a bill for discount purpose from the date printed on the invoice to the day on which you actually take delivery of the goods.

The effect of these provisions is to give you a full ten days or more in which to sell the merchandise, pay the vendor for it, and pocket your profit, all without technically having laid out a penny of your own money. When available, these are both excellent ways to expand your inventory with other people's money. However, don't put yourself in a bind by assuming that the merchandise will always walk out the door in time. You always need a cash reserve to pay your bills.

Speaking of delivery, *when you write out an order, you're all too apt to make the assumption that the vendor has what you're asking for. In the real world, this is sometimes not the case.* It may not happen too often, but certainly the predicament will arise frequently enough to cause you grief if you're not prepared for the eventuality. Should you order two gross of chocolate Santas, and should the manufacturer send you one gross in November and the second, back ordered, in January, you'll be eating a lot of chocolate.

Rubber Stamps to the Rescue

To avoid this kind of predicament, buy a rubber stamp. Rubber stamps are some of the best desk toys ever devised. They're far better than those flip-flop sand sculptures or clicking steel balls that swing back and forth when primed. Rubber stamps really do something besides providing an outlet for nervous energy. In this case, a "No back orders without prior written authorization" stamp keeps you from being stuck with a shelfful of unsalable goods. Use it on every purchase order you send out. Eventually, your proviso will be noted in the suppliers' computers, but keep on stamping. You have nothing to lose but unwanted back orders.

What about purchase orders telephoned in, you wonder. That's fair enough. A lot of orders are a quick phone call away. Even when you order by phone, though, you should fill out a purchase order and, initially at least, mail it off to the vendor by way of confirmation. After you've dealt with a supplier for a while, you may not bother to mail it anymore, but you still want that written record.

Whether it originates the transaction or simply records terms agreed upon verbally, every purchase order should identify the requested article or articles as thoroughly as possible, indicating any pertinent inventory or catalog designations and specifying style, description, size, color, and so on. List the quantity and unit price of each item ordered as well as the total charge. Don't forget the ship-by date, especially when you are ordering seasonal merchandise. You have the right to return any merchandise shipped late. The purchase order is a legally binding contract. Specify your terms while you're in control.

Failing a written purchase order, a supplier may deliver a surprise along with the goods. There may have been a price change since you placed your order, and the merchandise is shipped at the new rate without your being told in advance of the markup, for instance.

Then again, the surprise may lie in the goods themselves. In comes a shipment of eight blue vases, six red candy dishes, twelve wooden wind chimes, six metal wind chimes, fourteen concrete lawn frogs, two birdbaths, and sixteen birdhouses. As you unpack, you look at the rather warty frogs. Interesting, but not really that attractive. Why did you ever order so many of them?

Well, the truth of the matter is that you didn't. It was six frogs and fourteen metal wind chimes that you ordered. Your purchase order verifies it.

In addition to matching your purchase order, the merchandise should fit the packing slip. Make sure that whoever does the receiving literally counts the wares and verifies that all the items and quantities listed on the packing slip truly are in the boxes. The packing slip will be the basis of your bill. If it shows merchandise not actually received, you'll still pay.

As to those eight extra frogs, since you have a copy of the purchase order, returning them for credit shouldn't be a problem. They'll cost you time and freight, but nothing else.

Not all returns are that easy, though. So you should determine a distributor's return policy at the outset of doing business. Basically, you shouldn't be selling anything you can't return. There are exceptions to this rule, of course. Dead tropical fish, on the whole, are not returnable. Such exceptions, however, are few and far between.

Returns can be handled in a number of ways. A customer came into one of my pet shops with a bedraggled $6 chew toy. No good, he insisted. From the appearance of the chew toy, it was obvious that his dog had thought it a very fine chew toy indeed. However, the dog was the end user, not the customer.

The customer explained that the toy simply hadn't lasted. Now it could have been that the dog had teeth like Dracula's, or that the animal was a spring-jawed Doberman, or that the chew toy had kept him busy for half a day while the owner was away. That the toy was defective, however, I sincerely doubted.

Did I tell the customer that? No. Being right would have gotten me nowhere except out a customer. I accepted the return, and the customer took his $6 refund and ended up buying $12 worth of merchandise.

I saved the chew toy until the rep who'd sold me on it came by. He took the overchewed toy out to his car and came back with half a dozen chew toys in brand-new colors for the shop to try. Now that's what I call a felicitous return policy.

A good sales rep is one of your best allies in retailing. He or she may call thirty times a year or only three. Either way, at the end of each visit, you'll know what's selling in a line, what would be really good for you to stock, and what's new that would be worth your trying. Treat a salesperson as just an order taker, and you'll get service, no more, no less. Work with your sales rep, and you'll gain the winning edge.

8 Let's Have a Sale

Think retail, and the first thing that comes to mind is usually the word *sale*. Shopper and shopkeeper alike, we've become a nation of bargain hunters. This mentality not only fueled the rise of the discount store and the consequent fall of many historical retail giants, but vastly altered the way we do business. In our consumer society, people want many more things than they really need. So, as a retailer, persuading the customer to want something is a vital part of your business.

As necessity ebbs and wishes take the spotlight, shopping becomes much more selective. Discretionary income is channeled into maximizing purchasing power. "How much can I stretch the wad, or the credit card, to buy?" Thus it happens that shopping becomes almost compulsively price-driven.

At the same time, increasingly, another desire haunts the consumer. The higher the shopping outlets' aisles are stacked with goods upon goods upon yet more goods, the more the isolated customer yearns for service, for the comfort of being waited upon, for shopping to be a pleasant experience again.

It is this ritual of service, as it were, that the independent store owner is uniquely positioned to provide. True, a few major chains still succeed in charming their clientele with service. Of these, Nordstrom's comes first to mind. However, most national and regional chains are so bottom-line-oriented that they can pay lip service at best to the concept of the helpful turn not directly tied to the sale of a commodity.

Anybody can sell a product, and the smaller the markup the easier the widget is to sell. But by slashing prices to draw customers you set a clear tone for your store. You become a player in the price game, and that's a high-stakes game indeed. In this arena, the small-change bidder simply can't compete. With only a modest-sized store and modest inventory for leverage, you'll never be able to sell your wares cheaply enough to rival the superstores and category killers, whose buying power you simply can't match.

If you're not selling on price, what are you selling on? As much as the merchandise itself, you're selling service, knowledge, personality—all the attributes you hope to convey in your store image and cultivate in your staff. These things don't come free, though, and neither does the merchandise. So when all is said and done, your all-important consideration as a retailer is still price.

Does it sound as if we're beginning to go round and round in circles here? Well, we are, because in the mercantile world everything revolves around price. That's what commerce is all about—the exchange of goods for goods, goods for money, or even money for money of a different sort. Price is an integral part of any transaction. Your job is to define the price of the merchandise you're planning to sell within the context of what you want to be, the image you're striving to present and the message you're trying to send the customer. Budget prices don't go with a glitzy image any more than high prices go with the bargain-basement picture, and the customer doesn't like to be confused.

When the message your store conveys and the merchandise it displays are unified, you give the might-be buyer a clear alternative. The shopper can take it or leave it, come into your store or pass it by, but at least he or she knows what to expect inside. You've done your part. After that, the ball is in the customer's court. *In the end, the customer determines the price. It's up to you to find out what the customer has decided.*

Such involute considerations may leave you, a newcomer to the intricacies of retailing, with what increasingly seems an overwhelming question: how on earth, then, am I ever to learn how to set a price on anything? So let's tackle that question.

We need to begin with a quick survey of the pricing formulas in use today. There are three of them, and they're quite different, although, interestingly enough, by their separate routes all three usually arrive at a coinciding answer. We'll plug some figures into the formulas once you're familiar with how they work.

Say you're about to open a gift shop carrying a wide range of items, from corporate desk toys to costume jewelry and from fancy glassware to Christmas stocking stuffers. You ask some local merchants for their suggestions on how to establish a selling price. After all, they've been in business for years. They must know.

Markup Versus Margin

The first person you ask, Fred, looks over your merchandise, points to a bud vase that cost you $10, including freight, and says to mark it up two and a half times. Susan, the second person you ask, says you need a markup of 150 percent. The third person, Ted, twirls the vase in his hand, exclaiming that you need a 60 percent margin. At that point, you're probably completely confused, particularly since all three agree that the vase is definitely a $25 item.

Fred's formula, marking your goods up 2.5 times, is the simplest way to set a retail price.

Cost (In Dollars)	Times	Markup	Equals	Retail Price (In Dollars)
10	×	2.5	=	25

The big drawback to a simple multiplier markup as a means of assigning retail value to a product is that the result isn't expressed in percentage form. Your accountant will be less than enamored with this method. The shop's profit and loss statements, for one, will be expressed in percentages, so, from an accounting point of view, it's preferable to look at the difference between your wholesale and your retail price in the same way.

Susan recommends that you think in terms of percent markup in pricing the vase, because once you've established what your expenses will be and what your desired profit above and beyond those expenses is, the percent markup you need to meet that target can be set very accurately. Take the difference between what you're thinking of selling the vase for—at first, this will involve a bit of guesstimation, but such seat-of-the-pants decisions will soon come more easily to you—and what the vase actually cost, divide that figure by the cost, and multiply the result by 100 to determine the percent markup you need.

For purposes of simplifying the example we're using here, we're viewing profit simply as your wholesale cost, shipping included, subtracted from your selling price. In reality, profit is much more complicated than that. So far we haven't taken into account all the overhead expenses of your operation, all the minutiae attendant upon actually selling your wares. We'll deal with those considerations once we have the formulas in hand.

$$\frac{(\text{Selling Price} - \text{Cost})}{\text{Cost}} \times 100 = \text{Percent Markup}$$

$$\frac{25 - 10}{10} \times 100 = \text{Percent Markup}$$

$$1.5 \times 100 = 150$$

Now Ted prefers to calculate the percentages in terms of margins. He works back to that figure from what you'll actually get for the vase, the selling price, just as Susan did, but with a different twist to his formula.

Your percent margin on the vase is determined by taking your profit on it, again defined here as your selling price minus the cost of the vase to you, dividing that by the selling price, and then multiplying the result by 100 to once more express the number as a percent.

$$\frac{(\text{Selling Price} - \text{Cost})}{\text{Selling Price}} \times 100 = \begin{array}{c}\text{Gross Margin}\\ \text{(in Percent)}\end{array}$$

$$\frac{(25 - 10)}{25} \times 100 = \text{Gross Margin}$$

$$.06 \times 100 = 60$$

For your day-to-day operations, your best bet is to envision pricing in terms of percent markup. It's the preferred tool for ticketing your merchandise item by item. The vases, for instance, will likely sell well with a 150 percent markup. They probably wouldn't move very quickly given a higher markup. The stocking stuffers and other inexpensive items, on the other hand, could safely be priced at a 200 percent or even 300 percent markup without impeding sales.

Your percent markup will always be a higher figure than your gross margin is. Gross margin is used primarily in evaluating such reports as your profit and loss statement and analyzing your overall sales. It's for the big picture, the panoramic view of your operations.

As for Fred, who simply marks up his merchandise by a number of times, well, he's doing things in a rather simplistic way. His method doesn't permit him to integrate pricing into his overall financials. So it's not easily worked into a pricing strategy.

In deciding on your general pricing strategy, first off you need to determine what gross margin you're going to require in order for

A Comparison of Times Markup, Percentage Markup, and Gross Margin

Times Markup	Percent Markup	Gross Margin (in Percent)
1.5	50	33
1.8	80	44
2.0	100	50
2.2	120	55
2.5	150	60
2.7	170	63
3.0	200	67

Three different ways of pricing your goods can be used: times markup, percent markup, and gross margin. Here the three are compared to give you a feel for the numbers. As an example, two-times markup is the same as 100 percent markup is the same as 50 percent gross margin. Run these numbers over and over again when you price merchandise until the numbers automatically convert themselves.

your business to succeed. The gross margin will have to cover all your operating expenses, service any business debts, supply your salary, and generate profits.

Salary Is Not Profit

Don't make the mistake of thinking that your salary and profits are one and the same thing. Profits are the flexible dollars left over after everything else has been paid for. There may be times when you're forced to operate without a profit, but you should be able to make up for this drought later. If you can't, you're in trouble, because those extra dollars aren't a tidy little bonus that you take out of the company on top of your salary. They're your company's future.

Profits are what you put aside to spend on improvements, expansion, or simply replacement of outmoded fixtures. Profits are what tide you over difficult times too. Without them, you're just working for the landlord and the bank.

Comparative Turnover and Markup of Various Stores with Sales of $300,000

Type of Store	Inventory Turnover Per Year	Inventory (in Dollars)
Bagel	300	1,000+
Candy	7	42,800
Fashion	2½–3	75,000–100,000
Jewelry	Less than 1	300,000
Newsstand	15	20,000
Produce	50	6,000

This chart demonstrates the relationship between the dollar cost of inventory and the number of times a year that inventory turns over for different types of retail businesses. All are based on $300,000 annual sales. For instance, to open a produce store you would need roughly $6,000 worth of inventory and this would turn over every week—unless you are selling tomatoes for political rallies.

The profit margin your particular store needs will depend to a considerable extent on your inventory turnover, and that varies tremendously from specialty to specialty and store to store. A newsstand might be able to make do with as low a profit margin as 17 percent. A bagel shop, being highly labor-intensive, might require one as high as 900 percent. However, for the moment, let's go back to the assumption that you're running that hypothetical gift shop we were talking about.

Suppose you've determined that your rent is going to be 8 percent of your cost, salaries 18 percent, advertising 3 percent, and so on. Taking all those factors into account, you've determined that you'll need a gross profit of 48 percent to have 15 percent left to service your debt and grow a bit. As you've undoubtedly noticed, expressing your sales in terms of times markup wouldn't give you a clue to the margin you'll have to make. You'll need a 48 percent margin.

Now if that's the case—and let's round the figure up to 50 percent for convenience's sake—you should really target a margin of 50 to 55 percent as your general goal. Anything less simply wouldn't do the job.

You've already set a price for your bud vase. Next let's figure out how to establish a retail price for a shipment of wind chimes that just came in. Wholesale, they cost you $18 apiece. The shipping cost, according to the invoice, was $24. There were a dozen wind chimes in the case, so the per piece shipping cost was $2. Add that to the cost of one of the wind chimes, and you arrive at an actual cost to you of $20 per wind chime set. These chimes are exclusive to your store, so you decide to go for a 60 percent margin instead of the guideline 50 to 55 percent.

Now how do you get from there to an actual number to put on the price tag? Here's how:

$$\text{Retail price} = \frac{(\text{Cost + Freight})}{100 \text{ Percent} - \text{Margin Percent}} \times 100$$

$$\text{Retail Price} = \frac{20}{100 - 60} \times 100$$

$$\text{Retail Price} = .5 \times 100$$

$$\text{Retail Price} = \$50 \text{ (or, of course, } \$49.99)$$

On to the giant soap bubble blowers that came in on the same truck with the wind chimes. They're more common than the chimes, so you'll need to keep the price down. They cost you $3 plus 40¢ for shipping apiece. If you marked them up only 40 percent and balanced that out with the 60 percent the wind chimes will bring in, you'd still be able to maintain an average 50 percent margin.

$$\text{Retail Price} = \frac{3.40}{100 - 40} \times 100$$

$$\text{Retail Price} = .057 \times 100$$

$$\text{Retail Price} = \$5.70$$

Here I'd be tempted to round the figure up to $5.95. Then again, if I were pushing the giant soap bubble blower as a by-the-register impulse item, I'd probably lower it to $5.69. You get the general idea, though. *You do basic pricing with a formula that assures you the minimum margin called for by your financial projections. You adjust your final, real price by a little twiddling and a feel for what the market will buy.*

Price isn't everything, but without the right price for the market you can't sell. Wal-Mart, Target, and other megadealers know this, and they push the consumer's value button hard by heavily promoting low-cost, high-visibility items that are often on people's minds—cameras, jewelry, bras, Nintendo games, sheet sets, paint, motor oil, exercise equipment. You'll find them also conspicuously touting easily identifiable brand-name products and seasonal merchandise such as lawn seed.

A Feel for Value

Keep an eye on your competitors' circulars. There will be fifty or so items that they advertise constantly. Make sure you don't advertise the same products listed at a much higher price. While you can't and don't want to compete on price, if you must stock the same products, keep the prices on those particular articles as low as you can, even if it means cutting your gross margin down to nearly nothing.

Then make up the remaining price difference in service. Maybe you charge a little bit more for that twenty-five-pound bag of grass seed, but you also load it into the customer's car. Remember that consumers don't always necessarily buy at the lowest price. They buy what they feel is the best value for their money, and they may well measure that value partly or even largely in terms of service.

An even better solution than trying to keep your prices in line with those of the sprawling competition is to stock items similar to theirs but carrying a different brand name, preferably a more prestigious one. Then you can boost both your margins and the perception of your store as a unique quality establishment at the same time.

Surprisingly, in some instances you may find that you're charging less than the competition. The fact is that not every item the megadiscounters carry is the cheapest of its kind. By perception, the megastores' prices may be the lowest, but in reality you may discover that certain items you stock are priced lower, perhaps because of the particular formula you used in pricing them.

Where that happens, don't hesitate to mark them up a bit more. Remember that the image you're trying to project is that of a store competitive with the category killers because, while your prices might be a little higher than theirs, yours is the more pleasant place to shop. Your staff is friendly, eager to help, and really knowledgeable. Besides, you carry a lot of specialty items not found elsewhere. Given that perception, the fact that you might be selling some little thing for less than the discounters are charging won't even register with the customer, unless perhaps as an anomaly. So you might as well up the price to that of the competition.

What your customers believe about your store is as important as the reality of what it in fact is. Value perception goes far beyond any pricing structure or strategy. *You're in show biz, remember. You're Peter Pan challenging your audience to believe in you. If it doesn't, well, then your business simply isn't going to fly.*

There's a fine line to be trod between inviting belief and overstepping its bounds, inducing incredulity instead. Just as insincerity in service is instantly recognized, so is insincerity in pricing.

If, in your efforts to remove yourself from the bargain-basement outlets and create a caring, helpful image, you price yourself out of the market, obviously you've lost the customer. Overpricing is an affront to the shopper's intellect. Concern for your gross margins may be critical from the mercantile standpoint, but never forget that the customer ultimately determines the price he or she is willing to pay.

When You're the Shopper

Another way to raise your margins, besides raising prices, is by better buying. *You make your money when you buy.* Everything you do after that is simply collecting. If you haven't bought right in the first place, even the most astute of pricing strategies won't help you.

From your very first encounters with the distributors and manufacturers with whom you'll do business, check for quantity specials and other wholesale discounts. Build working relationships with reps. However, don't get stuck in a rut, especially a comfortable one. Always be on the lookout for new sources, not only because you're constantly shopping for price, but because you also need to vary your stock.

Complacency has always spelled slow death for a business. This is even more true in today's mercurial retail environment. Unless you're innovative in your product mix and your supply sources, you'll be left behind.

Empty Railcars Full of Opportunity

Innovative buying opportunities are all over the place. Finding them is largely a matter of perception. In the 1870s, before the railroads became regulated, the Lake Shore & Michigan Southern charged more for westbound than for eastbound freight. Going west, the charge was 2.02¢ per ton-mile, going east it was 1.56¢ per ton-mile. Most of the haulage was eastbound, and so the westbound traffic was charged enough to cover pulling the empties back. That seemed perfectly sensible. After all, running westward, the loaded cars had to produce enough revenues to cover their own haulage as well as that of the empties. If the Lake Shore & Michigan Southern didn't collect this extra charge, it would go broke.

Some years later, as the story is related by John H. White, Jr., in his history *The American Railroad Freight Car* (Baltimore: The Johns Hopkins University Press, 1995, p. 37), the railroad concluded that "the tide of traffic with the most empty cars would benefit most from lower rather than higher rates." The reasoning was quite as sensible as that supporting the company's former conclusion. By reducing the rates for westbound freight, the railroad found it could increase the traffic of loaded freight cars westward bound and thus increase earnings. Where they had been a burden, the empty cars became an opportunity, all because of a change in perception.

An excellent example of building on buying perception is the Christmas Tree Shop, a chain of gift stores in the Northeast. The owners, like most retailers, attended merchandise and trade shows to see what was new. One thing they noticed at these shows was the number of exhibitors grumbling about packing up their displays after each exhibition.

The booths themselves were one thing. Designed to be packed and unpacked and repacked over and over again, they were usually a cinch to break down. The wares stocking the booths were another matter entirely. As I'm sure you well know, once you've unpacked a stereo or some small household appliance, putting it back in the box—getting the baffles, bulges, support frame, and other accoutrements of modern packing to fit inside the carton again and maneuvering the article into place among them all—is close to impossible.

Enter the Christmas Tree Shop entrepreneurs. They made a deal with all the exhibitors to buy the entire show merchandise at a huge discount. "Leave the merchandise and the packing to us, and you can go home early, hassle-free. We'll clean up." Now there was a well-nigh irresistible offer leading to some deep discounted buys for the Christmas Tree Shop.

The buying strategy was innovative and resourceful. The name of the establishment wasn't. In fact, it squarely symbolizes much of what is wrong with retailing today. Christmas year-round isn't Christmas anymore. Even where it's Christmas in name only, literally a mere designation for a store, the everyday reference dilutes the significance of the expression and the selling power the image once had.

When a Sale Isn't

Likewise, the very word *sale* has become meaningless in most people's eyes. Shoppers have been inundated with the word—in print, on the radio, on television. Pitchmen prod consumers, for all the world as if they were lemmings, "Come on down, we're selling our entire inventory at 30 to 50 percent off, and on Sunday you can take another 50 percent off the sale price."

Make us an offer, special purchase, closeout, cash-raising—there's a sale for every day of the year and then some. The winter sale now starts in fall. The summer clearance ends on the Fourth of July. The shopper more or less laughs at the whole ludicrous spectacle.

All the same, there are still some sound reasons for throwing a sale, and the event can still be a good promotional tool. The trick is to be timely. Don't put winter merchandise on sale in the summertime. Make sure there's high demand for what you're

Basic Rules for a Sale

1. Whatever you're putting on sale should be something you normally carry. You should have it in stock both before and after the sale. Otherwise, people won't be able to sense that you've really reduced the price.

2. Be sure you have enough stock on hand to meet anticipated demand. A rain check is a poor substitute for the real thing.

3. Don't be timid when it comes to price reductions. The savings must be at least 20 percent, and 30 percent is better.

4. Always try to tie a sale item in with an item priced at the regular markup. If you put school notebooks on sale, make sure you have plenty of pens carrying their normal price tags displayed next to them.

5. Persuade your vendors, whether manufacturers or distributors, to contribute to the sale by giving you a discount on top of the discount, ad support, or co-op money. Better yet, procure all three.

6. Make sure there are plenty of in-store signs covering the sale.

7. Ask your staff to mention the upcoming sale to customers whenever possible.

featuring. Putting your leftover stock of Pet Rocks on sale in 1997 is meaningless.

Whatever the reason for your sale, it won't have an impact, obviously, unless shoppers are alerted to it. The usual means of getting the word out is general advertising. However, if you keep an up-to-date list of active customers—something you should contrive to do if at all possible—you could have an invitational sale, say an after-hours shopping gala exclusively for your regular clientele. Customers are flattered by such personal attention. Another way of having a sale without the customary burst of advertising is by means of a club card.

Building Customer Loyalty

Club cards and similar frequency marketing devices give loyal customers a special discount, free item, or other bonus as a token of their steady patronage. "Buy ten and the next one's on us!" reads the slogan emblazoned on the free coffee club card recently distributed to shoppers by Borders & More. The card was designed to serve a dual purpose, selling more coffee at the coffee bar and encouraging those lured into the store to buy books.

Similarly, for $10, shoppers can become card-carrying members of Waldenbooks' Preferred Reader club. Membership entitles them to a 10 percent discount on all the books they buy plus an additional $5 gift certificate mailed to them whenever they've purchased $100 worth of merchandise. Here again, the club approach encourages repeat business. In this case, it also gives the store $10 right up front every time someone joins the club. This is money collected for selling air, and you get to keep it all.

When a card club works, it's great. When it doesn't, all you've lost is what you spent having the cards printed up. It's a good, safe way to encourage buying. There's really no way you can insult any customers with this kind of promotion.

Actually, let me take that back. There is one way of doing just that, although I've only seen it in operation once. Posted by the cash register of a local food co-op is an obtrusive sign reading, "Nonmembers pay 10 percent above the sticker price." Anyone walking into that store for the first time is greeted with the choice of laying out an unexpected $25, the annual membership fee, or paying 10 percent more for his or her purchase than the register shows. Talk about making the customer feel unhappy!

The approach is all wrong. The underlying idea isn't a bad one, though. Had the sign read "All members get 10 percent off the sticker price," then when, say, a $14.98 sale was rung up for a member, the person could be told that he or she had just saved $1.49. The member would feel good, and a first-time shopper would be encouraged to join. The whole perception would be positive.

Mistakes in approach happen more often than you might realize. Often they're not recognized until they've been discarded for a new and better approach. A local community college had very few takers for a course called "Home Economics for Men." If students noticed the listing at all, they perceived the class as one that would be really dull. When the same course was renamed "Bachelor Living in Comfort," the college had to turn students away.

Coupons, either in print media such as local shopper's guides or in booklets distributed directly to consumers by mail, can be very effective sales tools. Even coupon pads posted on supermarket community bulletin boards pull well. As long as your shop is a small neighborhood one, the store won't usually mind your taking advantage of this distribution point. The cost involved in printing and distributing the coupons is relatively low, even for a mailing, which typically runs between $300 and $500 per 10,000, and you usually get a lot for your money in terms of response.

Shoppers today are quite coupon-oriented. They're used to clipping along the dotted lines, and they're good-natured about the chore. Then, too, the physical presence of a coupon anchored to the refrigerator with a magnet or tucked into a wallet acts as a reminder. In effect, you're giving them a shopping list as well as a discount.

The Six Ps of Retail

The right *product* at the right *price* in the right *place* with the right *promotion* and the right sales*people* = *profits.*

If you do use this sales technique, though, make sure there's a logic behind the coupon and that the product so promoted has broad appeal. A florist's coupon good for 25 percent off the price of any wedding package ordered in May is timely, an attractive offer made at a logical moment. However, only a small percentage of the population within driving distance of that store could probably be expected to get married in May of any given year. A coupon for a dozen roses at half the regular price has much wider appeal.

Beyond these conventional promotional devices lies a whole realm of innovative strategies, some of them still waiting for you to discover them. Cable television can be a cost-effective advertising source for stores carrying high-ticket items such as durable goods. Who knows the future of the Net and how it might impact even local retailers? There's a world of promotional possibilities out there. They just haven't been endowed with the right perception yet.

In researching innovative ways to publicize your enterprise, there are two things to keep in mind. The first of these is that some of the promotional ideas promulgated by the numerous books on marketing available today—many of which are worth reading, if for no other reason than that they provide mental stimulation—aren't half as clever as they initially appear.

When Marketing Goes Wrong

There's an oft-told story about a pizza chain that was entering a competitive new market area. Looking for publicity gimmicks, the company hit upon the notion of offering two pizzas for the price of one if the customer brought in the competition's Yellow Pages advertising. The idea was, of course, that anyone looking up pizza parlors in the Yellow Pages of that particular phone book in the future wouldn't see the rival ads. Clever, eh?

Now think about it for a minute. What's missing here? Well, for one thing, people don't tear out an ad from a telephone book. They tear out the whole page. This is not a coupon, and they're not clipping. So chances are that by this clever-sounding ruse, the pizza chain effectively ensured that its ad would disappear along with the competition's.

Now maybe the pizza chain's ad happened to be on a facing page. Maybe whoever thought up the gimmick checked that out first. In any case, the other thing wrong with the scenario that is far more telling than the missing ad is the missing page. A stunt like this is simply unethical.

To suggest that people tear up telephone books is to foster destructive behavior. Some of those telephone books with the pages torn out are going to be ones in telephone booths, where they are intended to serve as a public information source.

Besides making sure that the sales you hold have a purpose and the promotional strategies you use make a real point, you need to make sure as well that neither could negatively affect your image. Otherwise they will turn the consumer from your door, not only defeating their aim but dealing your whole image a ruinous blow.

The original purpose of a sale was to dispose of leftovers or slow-moving stock. While today you may have other, promotional reasons for throwing a sale as we've noted, the original one highlights an important aspect of running a store, namely, monitoring your inventory. *Track your inventory correctly, and you should never need to have an overstock sale.* That, however, is easier said than done, especially when you're first starting out in retail.

Timing Turnover

Inventory is evaluated in terms of turns, or turnover. Any item that moves at half the average rate of your stock turnover is a candidate for elimination—but only a candidate. There are many reasons for keeping a particular item in stock. It may contribute an unusually high margin, for example, or you may carry it as a customer service, something whose value to the store is not measurable in dollars and cents.

The need to be able to assess value of this kind is the reason why it's so important for you and your staff to be attentive to your customers' wants. It's easy enough to design a computer program that will automatically drop from future inventory all merchandise that is moving at half your average rate of turnover. It's impossible to design a computer program that will take into account the fact that

The Turn-Earn Ratio

Most retailers focus their buying efforts on getting the best price, really stocking up in order to do so. Certainly, the buying price, particularly of one-shot specials, is crucial, but when it comes to the staples of your inventory, you should also gauge their rate of sale as it affects earnings. You do this by using the turn-earn ratio.

The turn-earn ratio measures how many dollars you take to the bank for every dollar you invest in inventory. If a particular item turns over four times a year and has a margin of 60 percent, then for every $1 you spend stocking it, you'll deposit $2.40 in sales. The item's turn-earn ratio is 2.4.

Now let's say you reduce the margin on the item to 50 percent and that, as a result of the reduction in price, it turns over six times a year. Your turn-earn ratio becomes 3.0 and you take $3 to the bank for every $1 you spent. You've actually improved your take considerably by reducing the margin.

Mr. Smith visits your store once a month to get a special filter cartridge and that, while he's one of the few customers who buys that aquarium accessory, he also picks up a gratifying number of other articles. For the small, service-oriented store, buying right is rarely just a matter of going by the numbers.

Even when you've done everything possible to buy right for your store and your clientele, there will still be occasions when you have remainders. When that happens, it's time for an overstock sale. *Your inventory should be working for you, you shouldn't be working for the inventory.* It's very expensive to keep inventory that's not selling. Reduce its price by at least 25 percent. If it hasn't sold the first week, reduce the price by another 25 percent. The sale shouldn't drag on.

Don't fret, though, when you see otherwise unsalable merchandise going out the door at 50 percent off what you'd expected to get for it. You're no longer losing money. You lost the money back when the merchandise didn't sell. Now you're acquiring cash to buy different merchandise to sell at full price. Take the cash and get back on the profit track.

9 Never Say "May I Help You?"

In contemporary corporate circles, employees are referred to as human resources. As Orwellian as this allusion might appear in the gobbledygook of personnel managers, it does in fact sum up the real nature of such individuals. They are, first and foremost, human beings. By treating them as such, you'll enjoy a far more successful business, not to mention an easier life. Then, too, these people are indeed resources—second in mercantile importance only to the actual merchandise you sell.

Considering that retail positions are several steps below the average manufacturing job on the pay scale and equivalent to yesterday's door-to-door peddler in the social pecking order, a shortage of ideal personnel beating down your newly opened doors should come as no surprise to you. However, while there's no earthly reason for the low regard in which retail selling is held in today's service economy, the preconception—and prejudice—works to your advantage. Sales employees expect the worst. Offer them the best, and you can build unparalleled team loyalty and a quality staff.

The best doesn't necessarily mean the highest salaries, although the wages offered must be competitive. The best I'm talking about here is the most satisfying work environment, where the store attitude is buoyant and congenial, and where, above all, the staff is addressed humanly.

Trite though the reminder may sound, niceness works at every level of retailing, from transactions with your best customer to interaction with the employee at the bottommost rung of the totem pole. The old saying that bosses who coat themselves with honey are eaten by the flies is still true, of course, but my own feeling is that a genuinely nice boss is almost always a good boss. A sympathetic employer, friendly fellow employees, and a pleasant workplace are as crucial in retailing today as extending the same ambience to the customer. These qualities will only increase in importance as our society becomes more and more depersonalized.

Being nice starts with the very first job description you draw up. Yes, I know, here we're not talking about a megacorporate human resources department on a major hiring spree replete with all the promotional bells and whistles. We're talking about your first retail operation, starting out with maybe half a dozen employees. Surely, you think in disbelief, I'm not asking you to compose a radiant description of your personal virtues and your store's merits to peddle to headhunters. Well, actually, I'm doing something of the sort, and for the following reason, which I introduce with a question.

Did your eyes linger momentarily on the words *half a dozen employees*? Six employees isn't an unusually large staff for a store's first year of operations. Even if your venture is a small record or stationery shop, if it keeps mall hours, it will require more than one shift, although some of its employees may be part-time. Furthermore, the entire personality of your establishment will be represented by these few sales associates on the shop floor. So you'd better focus on the employee question right up front. It should be accorded the same attentive, thoughtful consideration that you devote to the merchandise you expect to sell.

Any job description you write up should be honest, accurate, and detailed. Fair play is part of being nice, and it's only decent to let people know the various tasks involved in the position for which they're applying. Being hired to sell cameras when photography is your favorite avocation can make you feel great. Being told two weeks into the job that you're also responsible for cleaning the employees' bathroom and taking out the garbage every night can add a veneer of disappointment, at the very least, to the whole affair. "Hey, I wasn't hired to clean toilets" is the protest. And, indeed, the person wasn't, unless that chore was expressly written into the job description.

In putting together the summary that is to portray a given position, you need to consider each and every obligation you're going to require of the person who fills that position. Mention the unpacking, shelving, pricing—and vacuuming. Remember that you're not hiring someone simply to ring up sales. You're hiring a staff member who will have a broad range of responsibilities in helping your store to become successful.

An incomparable aid in writing up a job description is a store manual, or employee handbook. Many of the tasks needing mention in your appraisal of what a particular position involves will be suggested by a quick review of the categories outlined in this reference, and it's something you'll need to have on hand in any case, before you hire your first employee.

Employee Lawsuits Are a Growth Industry

A store manual is not a reference work found in some trade library. It's a very focused document you create to describe your shop's concept and style and to delineate its policies and procedures, large and small. In the old days, if you liked the job an employee did, you gave the person two weeks' paid vacation. If you didn't like the individual or the individual's attitude, you doled out twenty hours of time off. Today such favoritism, once considered a natural reward, or the withholding thereof, comes back to haunt you. *You can still reward an employee, but when it comes to things like vacation time, everybody must be treated equally, and the only way not to be accused of discrimination is to detail your policies in your employee manual.*

You live by that manual. If you don't, you'll probably be sued. The fastest-growing legal specialty in the retail trade today is employer/employee relations. An entire industry has sprung up expressly to deal with the individual's legal rights as they pertain to employment. The rights so addressed are those of employees. As an employer, you won't have many. Make sure your attorney looks over your handbook.

It cost me $500 to have my first store manual reviewed from a legal point of view. Was it worth the tab? Let me tell you a story.

An ex-employee sued my store for three weeks' vacation pay. The handbook clearly stated that full-time employees were entitled to one week's paid vacation after twelve months of work and that the vacation time was to be earned from January through December. The vacation so earned was to be taken between May 1 and September 10 of the following year.

The state of Connecticut, where the business in question was located, does not require the granting of paid vacations. This particular employee, however, was of the opinion that everybody should be entitled to three weeks' vacation, and after working for a year, one fine February day she quit her job. Then she sued for the three weeks' pay she felt was owed her.

Leaving when she did, before the scheduled vacation period, she wasn't entitled to any vacation time at all, as the store's employee handbook clearly informed her. Without the manual and her signed acknowledgment that she had read it, I could have had a protracted lawsuit on my hands.

You'll find that *there will be countless occasions when a simple "Let's see what the manual says" will cleanly and clearly resolve a dispute.* At the same time, your employee handbook is far more than an arbitrator. It will set the substance and tone of your operation. It needn't be slick and fancy, but it does need to be detailed. So let's take a closer look at what it should include. (See Appendix D for a sample store manual. Yours will probably be quite different in its particulars, but the bases covered will be the same.)

The initial section of a shop's policy manual is where the business is introduced to the employee. This short preface is devoted to a brief history of the enterprise and a clear statement of its underlying philosophy. If you're just starting out in retail, obviously you don't have a history. You do have a philosophy, though. It's probably all that differentiates your establishment from the competition, and it lays the groundwork for how your store will be run.

It may seem hokey or pretentious for a small venture consisting of a single store to expound on its ideology. Nevertheless, defining your goals and modus operandi, very much as you did in your business plan, will give you targets to shoot for and a style to cultivate in your daily transactions.

Your First Job Is to Make the Staff Believers

Unlike the business plan, a tool primarily benefiting yourself and your financiers, your mission statement in the store manual directly affects everyone who works for you. Besides sharing your vision of the business, it sells the store to your sales team. Your employees are your inside customers, so to speak. Before they can knowledgeably, enthusiastically, and effectively peddle your wares to the external customers, they need to buy into the store concept.

If the introductory remarks in your manual are there to set the mood and pace of your establishment, the operational section is where you set forth the actual working principles by which your staff should be guided. Spell them out. "Our Company's Most Important Principles" was the heading I chose for this section in my pet store manual. With a clue like that, no employee could miss the point I was making.

The operational section tells your staff, right up front, how you expect your customers to be treated. Yes, I know, the customer is almost always right. We've all heard that. The directives you provide need to be more specific. In the shop manual for my pet stores, for example, I stress fun. Animals are fun, after all. They should be seen in that light in my shops. Pearl necklaces and ebony bracelets, on the other hand, are fashionable. The principles involved in merchandising them are more flash than simple fun. So the jewelry store's approach needs to be different.

Besides setting the tone for your customer relations, the operational section of the manual deals with the whole practical substructure supporting those relations—quite literally from the floor up. In short, the floor does need to be swept or vacuumed or mopped, because keeping the shop clean is part of keeping it attractive to customers. Such matter-of-fact maintenance rules, easily overlooked, are emphasized by being put in writing. Employees know what's expected of them, and why, more clearly than when they're just asked to please sweep the aisles.

How the internal affairs of the shop are conducted needs to be covered in your manual item by item. All the practices and procedures to be followed on the premises must be addressed. Label this section clearly. My heading reads "Company Policies and Procedures."

Under that category are subsumed such precise and prosaic specifics as on which ring to pick up the phone, steps one through four in handling customer complaints, and the dress code, including uniform and badge. Payday is defined. Overtime is defined. Vacation pay is defined. So is the use of the telephone for personal calls. The manual sets forth the store's discipline policy, pilferage policy, and safety rules. Even such relatively rare occurrences as jury duty and bereavement leave are detailed. In the event of a death in an employee's immediate family, two days' paid leave are permitted. The immediate family is then explicitly defined—spouse, parents, children, siblings, mother-in-law, father-in-law. You may be close to your uncle, but he's not included, at least not in my manual.

How your employee handbook handles such eventualities is up to you—and any state laws that apply. Read up on them. The objective is to cover as many conceivable contingencies as you possibly can. Then, when a personnel question comes up, you can say, "Let's see what the manual says about that," and expect to find a legitimate, indisputable answer written there.

Once you have both a store manual and the job descriptions drafted, written up, and reviewed, you're ready to start looking for prospective employees. This search won't be easy. One or two discerning and sagacious individuals might have noticed the new shop opening up and thought to inquire whether employment might be found within its doors. Don't hold your breath waiting for them. Such resourcefulness is rare.

Never Hire Anyone You Couldn't Fire

That leaves you with the more usual sources, which range from employment agencies—usually the least promising of the lot—to family and friends—the most problematic. My personal rule is never to hire anyone I might have trouble firing. First and foremost, that precept encompasses relatives and friends. Obviously, you don't hire with the intent to fire. Nevertheless, the option to do so must be free and unencumbered, and it rarely is in the case of people close to you in your private life.

Another group of people I refrain on principle from employing is my staff's circle of family and friends. As I've learned to my sorrow, it's difficult, if and when the necessity arises, to fire an employee who's referred a friend to me without losing the friend as well, and vice versa. I once hired the sister of a really good assistant manager on my payroll. After I caught the sister stealing, I lost them both. On a subsequent occasion, I hired the daughter of one of my employees, which turned out very well, but then I hired her son, who proceeded to give merchandise away to his friends to demonstrate what a great guy he was. I lost the mother as well as the son, although, interestingly enough, not the daughter. That was when I learned at last not to hire relatives and friends of my employees.

If family and staff are, to all intents and purposes, off limits to you in your search for qualified job applicants, and if employment agencies rank at the bottom of the efficiency scale in screening likely candidates, the want ads in your local newspaper—the ones placed by people looking for work or the ones placed by you looking for people looking for work—lie somewhere in the middle range of the effectiveness scale as a means of ferreting out possible employees.

Frankly, *the two very best ways I've found to staff my stores are to hire customers and to recruit employees from other stores.* The latter is particularly useful in yielding good managers. It doesn't make me overly popular with the competition, but then I'm not too happy with them when they do the same to me. They know and I know that we're operating in a free-market economy, after all.

The plain marketplace fact is that when you're impressed by a clerk in somebody else's store, you've found someone who would be ideal for yours. Offer that person improved working conditions and a higher salary than the other establishment has provided, and hiring him or her becomes a benefit to both of you. The salesperson gets a better job, and you get a better salesperson.

As to garnering staff from among your clientele, regular customers are excellent source material. You'll be talking to regular patrons of your store often. Should you happen to learn that one of them is in the market for a job, part-time or full, by all means follow up on the lead. Here's someone who knows the store, knows the merchandise, and, assuming he or she has the temperament and personality for it, might prove to be a super sales associate.

If your own personal scouting fails to unearth good staffing prospects and you end up having to advertise for employees, go beyond the classified pages of your local newspaper in placing your ads. Should the nature of your store be such that student help on weekends might fill a need, contact the local high school guidance counselor. This works particularly well in schools with a business department or a Junior Achievement program. Community bulletin boards in supermarkets, churches, and other gathering places often draw well, too.

Making use of community displays requires follow-through. Remove or replace your ads after they've been up for a week or two. Leaving dog-eared file cards exhibiting your shop's logo tacked up on the boards does nothing for your store image.

Classified newspaper ads are not cheap. They should be worded as succinctly and directly as possible. Start off with a one- or two-word head identifying the position—Sales Associate, Cashier, or whatever counterpart is appropriate in your case. Follow the head immediately with a description of the type of environment involved—Shoe Store or Record Shop, for instance. Then say whether the job is full-time or part-time, and provide some indication of the hours involved.

Most employment specialists suggest that you add the line "Experience preferred" to your ad. In the case of entry-level positions, though, the phrase really doesn't accomplish much, and *there's often a lot to be said for hiring someone with no retail experience but with a personality that happens to be just right for the job.* It gives you a chance to train the individual by the standards you've set for your store personnel without first having to break bad habits acquired elsewhere.

How to Hire

When someone responds to your ad, have an employment application ready to be filled out. Pads of standard applications are available at any well-stocked stationery store. You can also draft your own simple form, leaving blanks for personal data to be filled in. There should be lines for name, address, social security number, and telephone number. In addition, inquire about education and job experience, and ask for the names and addresses of former employers and at least three references. In choosing a suitable model for your questionnaire, your safest bet is to ask for a sample form from the local office of your state department of labor. It should be politically correct, although there's no guarantee of this.

Employment applications serve a number of functions in even the smallest business. First of all, they put a job category on a professional footing. Second, if you go on to hire someone who's filled out an application form, the relevant data pertaining to that employee will already be all together in one spot. Third, there's the assistance the form contributes to the hiring process itself. The questionnaire will tell you certain things about an applicant, and not all of these things will be specific answers to specific questions.

The way in which an application is filled out may be a good indicator of how a prospective employee would work out. Someone who completes the form neatly and in detail will normally prove a more dependable employee than someone whose application is sloppy and full of mistakes or missed items. Omissions may be simple oversights or more serious evasions. Carelessness may indicate a basic inattentiveness or even indifference that could reflect poorly indeed on your store's image.

Review the form you've drawn up and make a mental note of the spots where telltale warning flags might go up. Then, ads in place and application forms and manual in hand, you're ready for the telephone to start ringing.

Some of the inquiries you receive in answer to your ads may be odd enough to warrant your dismissing the caller out of hand. "I was just curious" almost always indicates a dead end as well. With the exception of such responses, however, anyone who calls deserves a crack at an interview. Some people who come across poorly on the telephone turn out to be highly personable in the face-to-face world of the sales floor.

Six Hiring Disqualifiers

1. The applicant comes in with his or her mother or a group of friends. Who are we supposed to be hiring here?

2. The parent comes in alone to pick up an application form for the prospective employee. Yes, this happens often.

3. The individual comes in, is given an application, and then asks if you have a pen. Such unpreparedness, while not fatal, is usually a sign of trouble ahead.

4. "I'll take the application home and fill it out." No, you won't. If the application is completed on the premises, you'll know that the person possesses at least the rudimentary skills required to perform that task.

5. The applicant is dressed either for the beach or for the prom. An inability to grasp the concept of appropriateness is detrimental to retail sales.

6. The interviewee would just love to work in your store but mentions, in the course of the conversation, certain prior commitments—four weddings, three funerals, night school, marching band practice—and constraints—doesn't work weekends, the month of August, and nights with a full moon. Hire this person, and you can count on an employee who will work straight through an eclipse, the appearance of Halley's comet, and February 29th—unless, of course, there's a wedding.

In setting up each interview, after agreeing on a date and time, advise the caller to arrive about ten minutes beforehand to fill out an application. Specifying that advance arrival time is an excellent test of the individual's ability to understand instructions and follow through. It's also not a bad test of your own ability to state plainly what you want or expect. Be sure you make quite clear the fact that the person should come early enough to complete the paperwork.

The interview itself is very much an individual matter, influenced considerably by your own comfort level and that of the interviewee. *The one cardinal rule is never to let the interview become too personal.* There are laws severely restricting the questions you can ask a prospective employee. To be on the safe side, you should check the current rulings with both your attorney and your state's equal opportunity office or civil rights commission.

What You Can't Talk About When Hiring

In brief, the laws prohibit discussing an applicant's race, sex, religion, place of birth, marital status, or age. You can ask someone if he or she is over the minimum age for full-time employment in your state, but you can't ask how old the person is. If you do, and if the applicant later decides to take you to court, claiming that your hiring policy isn't based purely on merit, then you're liable to incur hefty court costs and penalties.

That warning on record, start the interview by going over your job description. Hand a copy to the would-be employee and review it point by point. You want to be sure you're both on the same wavelength. Then let the interviewee talk.

You'll have to develop a feel for what information is relevant here. While friends are sometimes reluctant to share their innermost thoughts, strangers will often share everything. As a result, interviews can take some strange turns.

What you're listening for is the tenor of the applicant's personality. Does he or she seem people-oriented? As a rule, although there are exceptions to it, extroverts make the best salespeople. Does the individual appear dependable, punctual, self-motivated, a team player? In a brief interview, discerning the presence or absence of such attributes is largely a matter of going by your gut feelings. If these feelings aren't accurate at the beginning of your hiring endeavors, they will be by the time you've engaged half a dozen staff members. By then, too, you'll have gotten over that strange new feeling of being perceived as the boss, and you'll have learned to look beyond the bias that this image interjects into conversations.

Beyond heeding your gut feelings, you'll need to ask two specific questions. The first of these is: how much notice would the person have to give his or her present employer if hired? Should the applicant indicate a willingness to start right away, without serving notice, don't offer that individual the job. You're almost certain to get the same treatment. Besides, the telltale inconsiderateness revealed in that casual approach bodes no good for business. The exception to this particular rule, of course, is the situation where the person is unemployed. In that instance, obviously, the question isn't even applicable.

The second question to ask is: how much does the person need to live on? If the position you have open won't pay enough to cover the rent and buy the groceries and meet other expenses, you won't be hiring an employee, you'll be borrowing one, and probably an already disgruntled one at that.

Bring the interview to a close by thanking the applicant for his or her time. Mention that there are others who have applied for the job, and say that you'll call with your decision by a specific date. Be sure you call every interviewee by that date, even if only to let the person know that he or she wasn't hired. Be courteous. You may end up hiring one of them in the future.

There's been a tendency lately in most businesses not to check employment references. Along with strictly censoring what you ask a job applicant in order to protect yourself from being sued, you'll find that the present-day sociopolitical environment severely circumscribes what an employer listed as a reference will tell you about someone formerly on the payroll. Here, too, the threat of lawsuits is ever present.

Still, *I always check references*. Because retail hiring usually draws on a local employee pool, I find I can often drive to a previous employer's establishment and speak with him or her privately. People will tell you a lot in person that they would never put in writing.

Provided no salient doubts about a prospective employee have been raised in the course of talking with an applicant's past employers, you've probably reached the point where a decision is in order. When all the various applicants' good and bad points have been judiciously considered, check back with your gut feelings once more. It's your store and your concept. Which of the applicants who've applied for a given job best fits into the picture? Will he or she be able to convey that concept to the customer?

Once you've decided to hire someone, have your reasons for the verdict ready, jotted down and in front of you, before you call. That way you can put a positive spin on the event by telling the applicant why you'd like him or her to join your team. Give a specific starting date and the beginning salary that goes with the position. Mention how long the training period is and when new employees are eligible for a raise. These details add some continuity and future to the job.

If the applicant wants time to think things over, agree on a definite date for a yes or a no. Where an applicant says no right off the bat, try to determine why he or she came to that decision. A really good candidate should be given the benefit of your flexibility. Wherever possible in such a circumstance, adjust your offer.

When Prospective Employees Tell You You Are Wrong

Should your top three employee choices all say no, you need to sit down and do some serious thinking about what you and your venture have to offer. Three refusals from people looking for work and going to the trouble of completing an application and coming in for an interview bespeak something seriously wrong with your operation—in the eyes of conceivable employees but also, in all probability, in the eyes of those already on your payroll.

On a happier note, let's assume that the prospective staff member accepts your offer. There you are, it's Monday morning, and the new employee is coming in. Now what do you do?

Putting Them to Work—Right

Far too many employers acquaint staff with their operation by giving them a quick tour of the premises, pointing out the goods in the major sales areas, showing them the storeroom, and waving a hand in the general direction of the bathroom. If the boss happens to be in a particularly expansive "Let's make the hireling feel good" mood, the coffeemaker may be presented. Then it's off to work we go. This is a bad beginning.

The first thing to do after welcoming a fledgling employee is to present the newcomer with his or her own copy of the store manual. With the manual, provide an acknowledgment form indicating understanding and acceptance of its terms, to be signed that evening after the handbook has been read at home.

SELL FAB

No, we're not talking about the Beatles here, or laundry detergent. SELL and FAB are two acronyms for a basic sales training program. SELL covers the presentation—Show the features, Explain the advantages, Lead into the benefits, Listen to the customer talk.

The first three sales points come naturally to most enthusiasts. If your product is computers and you've hired people who like computers to sell them, your staff will have no difficulty mastering the SEL. Their natural ardor will take care of that. It's the last L, for Listening to the customer, that you'll need to emphasize in your training.

In order to SELL, your staff will need to know the merchandise—its Features, Advantages, and Benefits—in short, its FAB. Don't introduce a new line of merchandise, put it on display, and expect it to move by itself. Whenever you add significantly to your product mix, call a brief staff meeting to tell your sales associates about the product. Go over its FAB thoroughly, so all your salespeople know exactly what they're selling. Even if you have only one employee and you feel that the idea of holding a staff meeting just for the two of you is ludicrous, take a coffee break with that employee sometime when you're both shelving the new stock and point out the FAB highlights. If you don't know what you're selling, the selling is twice as hard. Clue in your staff.

Apart from this inaugural protocol, a new employee's first day on the job should be spent as a trailer hitched to another salesperson, observing, assisting, learning the ropes. If this is your first employee, you're the one to be trailed. The buddy system is an invaluable training tool. It's particularly effective in teaching the sales approach used in a given store.

If the staff person to whom the trainee is assigned has himself or herself been well trained in turn, one thing the new employee will not observe, hopefully, is that long since outdated traditional salesclerk/customer ritual. It runs, "May I help you?"/"No thanks, just looking."

"May I help you?" is a tired and—pardon the pun—shopworn expression, a leftover from the white-glove heyday of Wanamaker's, that today tends to elicit a negative response. Train your employees never to use this phrase or any greeting that can be answered with just yes or no.

A simple friendly hello is always appropriate when greeting a customer. A comment about the weather might be an opener. Where the customer seems bewildered or baffled, "What can I help you find?" is the modern-day replacement for the "May I . . ." response. The more open-ended the approach, the more conducive it will be to conversation, which makes the customer feel at home. "Are you looking for a current release or an oldie?" expresses interest and invites the shopper to talk.

An encouraging "Try it on, it should look good on you" offered a customer looking at a sweater is complimentary, cheering, and conducive to a sale. "Let me get that down for you" and "Here, take it out of the box" are other ways to get the merchandise into customers' hands, and once in their hands, the goods are much more likely to be bought.

Along the same lines, *train your sales staff to respond positively and actively when a customer asks for something specific.* Pointing or saying vaguely "Over there in the third aisle" isn't very helpful. Instead, the salesperson should escort the customer to the goods. I call this the walk that sells. It's the perfect opportunity to interject a cordial, personal comment as the merchandise is handed to the customer.

Not every customer is going to buy something every time he or she visits your store. A salesperson new to your staff needs to know this. Otherwise, discouragement over a failure to make a sale may set in. It's the concern for the customer—the interest expressed in a search the person is conducting for some particular item, the sympathy voiced over a particular problem or dilemma—that brings the customer back another day. A contented customer who doesn't buy is simply a deferred customer, that's all.

The Sincerest Form of Flattery

A point you need to stress to your sales personnel is that customer involvement must be sincere. One chain's checkout clerks look at a credit card, find the customer's first name, and recite it as they hand over the merchandise. This is personal marketing carried to a rote, sometimes off-putting extreme.

Contrast this approach with one I encountered in a shoe store not long ago. I was looking over the latest in running shoes displayed out front. One particular pair looked great. It also happened to be the most expensive shoe in the shop.

Three Sure Ways to Lose a Customer

1. You're busy stocking shelves or talking with other sales personnel, and you keep the customer waiting. Show customers that you don't have time for them, and they'll certainly take the hint and go elsewhere.

2. You don't take returns. The customer made a mistake? That's the customer's problem. Why should you pay for it? If you want to be a real sport about it, you take returns, but you make the process as difficult as possible. Have dissatisfied customers fill out forms, swear that they never actually used the merchandise, and wait an interminable time before they get their credit slip. Everybody loves a hassle. Don't you?

3. Run out of stock on sales items. There's nothing quite like being told there's none left for you. It makes you feel gypped, and your feelings about the store are suddenly not very kindly.

The clerk, who was a runner, must have caught my ambivalent expression. "Those are great, aren't they," he agreed, "but for your type of foot, I'd suggest these," and he pulled down an attractive pair 30 percent lower in price. "They'll give you better support." The shoes felt great, and you know I'll be going back there. A separate episode illustrates perfectly another instance of good salesmanship. I wandered into a bookstore at nine o'clock one evening looking for a gift. Not being sure how much time I had to shop, I asked, "How late are you open?"

"We're open as long as you're here," was the simple, sunny reply. Talk about being made to feel at home!

Your staff's response to customers is what produces—or fails to produce—the return customer. A purchase is a vote cast for your store. Stress to your personnel the need to validate the customer's vote, not only by a thank-you conveyed with a genuine smile, but by an affirming comment on the purchase as well. "I bought that for a friend" or "I've got a popcorn popper just like that, it's great" supports the shopper's choice and makes him or her feel good.

Turning Returns into Sales Instead of Failures

No matter how pleased your customers normally are, there will still be the occasional return. This is another aspect of customer relations calling for good salesmanship, and it takes training. Resolving problems for existing customers is far easier in the long run than acquiring new customers. Returns are one of these problems.

Like most store owners, I no longer give cash refunds. They're an open invitation to the drug trade's petty thieves trying to unload stolen goods. The sign by the cash register in my shop reads "No Fault Credit Policy" and goes on to explain that the store offers replacement or return for credit and extends all manufacturers' warranties for thirty days beyond their normal warranty period. Outside of the no-cash policy, I impose no restrictions on returns. I don't care whether the customer has a receipt or not, I don't care whether or not the merchandise is in its original box, and I don't even care whether it was purchased yesterday or seven months ago.

If I can establish that the article is an item we carry or have carried in the not-too-distant past, I give the customer a new one or, if preferred, store credit. I simply send the returned merchandise to the distributor to be credited to my account in turn.

The incidence of abuse of a generous return privilege pales in significance when compared with the goodwill such a policy generates. The real abuse in retailing is that misery called shoplifting. If this is your first foray into retailing, be aware that 2 to 3 percent of a store's average sales volume is sacrificed to theft, theft that knows no economic borders.

Dealing with the Inevitable— Shoplifting

My first job in the retail industry was with a large chain discount store situated in an impoverished ethnic neighborhood. We caught five to twenty shoplifters on a weekly basis on or about the premises of the store. Because of the sheer numbers involved, a special court day was set aside once a month to accommodate our security chief, who would spend that entire day prosecuting these shoplifting cases for the company.

Four years later, I was assigned by the same discounter to a new location, a store catering to an upscale white-collar clientele— engineers and middle-management groupies drawn primarily from a giant defense contractor's complex across the street. You guessed it. We caught five to twenty shoplifters on a weekly basis on or about the premises of the store. Because of the sheer numbers involved. . . .

In both of these stores, the predominant common factor was— as it is in many instances of shoplifting—teenagers stealing. They stole on a dare or for the thrill of it or because they wanted something they couldn't pay for but intended to have, by whatever means necessary. Your staff must be trained from day one to deal with the probability of theft.

That training begins with surveillance maneuvers. Sad to say, your staff must learn to monitor your customers, however unobtrusively, at all times. They should be especially observant of people with loose coats, large purses, totes, shopping bags, and umbrellas.

Professional shoplifters often work in teams. Make sure your employees realize that if there's a commotion in the store—say a display is knocked over or a jar is dropped—their job is not only to help set things right again, but to keep their eyes on persons removed from the scene as well. Bedlam is often a distraction, focusing attention on the immediate vicinity of the upheaval and averting it from something going on elsewhere in the store.

A security force, the police, or at the very least another employee should be called upon to help a staff member deal with a thief. Under no circumstances should a single staff person try to tackle the job alone. Above all, make very clear to your employees that a shoplifter is always to be apprehended outside the store.

In the retail industry, theft is euphemistically called *inventory shrinkage* or sometimes just *shrink*. Besides shoplifting, it includes in-house pilferage. *Professional shoplifters and surreptitious customers slipping past the checkout counter can cause considerable financial loss, but internal shoplifters doing business as employees can literally put you out of business.* The most diabolic external shoplifter is in your store for a few minutes at most. The pilferer within your ranks is there for some forty hours a week, during which he or she can steal volumes for self, friends, and family.

Is this common? No. Does it occur? You bet it does. Over the years I've caught dozens of employees giving so-called discounts to friends, stealing outright, or worse. And what might that be? Well, in an electronics store, part of a chain for which I was working at the time, I was asked to find the source of a considerable amount of shrinkage. What I found was that the receiving manager had made a deal with the regular delivery driver whereby the manager would sign off for a shipment and the truck driver, rather than unloading the cargo, would then drive off to a warehouse they'd rented and drop the goods off there. The shrinkage in this particular case came to $100,000 a year.

To minimize that kind of shrinkage, you need to make sure your staff is aware of and understands the internal security operative on your premises. There are certain rules and regulations to be followed, certain prohibitions. They're all right there in the employee

You Know You Have an Internal Shrinkage Problem When—

1. Your employees dress better than you do.

2. Staff purchases are down, an indication that they're not buying from you, yet they still wear the merchandise you sell or give great gifts that came from your store.

3. Your sales rep tells you how well you're doing on reorders in certain categories for reorders, but you can't remember those items coming through the register.

4. Customers routinely return the same high-priced items without any sales slips or other proof of purchase.

5. Your inventory is down, your sales are flat, your accounts payable are up, and your checkbook balance is hurting.

6. You feel it in your gut, you notice that there are holes in your inventory that weren't there when you left for your night off, and on checking the register you find that you didn't have a sale on those items of merchandise.

manual. They have nothing to do with the individual, with trust, or with distrust. They are part and parcel of good business practices. And they are enforced. Your personnel will get the point. Most employees, like most people, are good, honest individuals.

Running the Cash Register Right

Central to store security are the rules applying to cash registers. Only one employee on a shift should be authorized to work the register, unless, of course, there's more than one register, in which case one person is assigned to each register. The registers must be cashed out at each change of shifts. Cashing out requires, besides a physical count of the take, a register total printed out on the tape. This total enables you to match the register record with the actual money.

Use the *x* key, not the *z* key, to total the take. The *z* key blatantly invites theft. It sets the register to zero, allowing a salesclerk to *z* out, pocket everything that comes into the till after that, and *z* out again, leaving no evidence of the deceit. Never *z* out a register.

Void slips must be filled out in full, listing the customer's name, address, and phone number and the reason for the canceled sale. Each slip should be signed by the employee handling the void. From your point of view as an employer, such a tight rein on voids, besides being a security measure, shows up any difficulty a member of your staff might be experiencing in dealing with the cash register. Not all theft is intentional.

In addition to knowing and respecting the rules of the register, your personnel should be trained to use the shop's security mirrors effectively. These funny-looking image-distorting reflectors aren't there to glamorize the store like disco spheres. Neither are they or their office-mounted, one-way counterparts there to discourage professional shoplifters, who aren't fazed by them. They're there to intimidate the ordinary, everyday shoplifter and to help the staff catch the spur-of-the-moment petty thief. The mirrors won't help, however, if they're not used. They should be glanced at often.

The same holds true for closed-circuit television. I have a small video camera set up by the front register in my pet stores. The camera's monitor is in the office, allowing me to peruse the environs of the register occasionally from my desk while I'm paying bills and shuffling paperwork.

I point out the camera to new employees their first day on the job, explaining that it's there so I can monitor customers and come to their aid if too long a line forms at the checkout counter or some other customer problem develops. Obviously, it occurs to the employee that, with the aid of the camera, I can clearly see the register itself from my office, but the focus on the customer emphasizes the "We'll solve the problems together" team approach.

One last internal security check I have in my stores is the employee discount book. As a benefit, all *my employees may purchase anything in one of my stores at a discount equivalent to their normal working hours.* If they work twenty hours a week, they get 20 percent off. If they work thirty hours a week, they get 30 percent off. The rule is that while they may buy whatever they want whenever they want it, to simplify the paperwork, it's all to be paid for on payday.

Firing Employees

If hiring the right employee for your operation is difficult, firing one that turns out to be wrong for that operation is doubly trying. An employee may have to be fired for a number of reasons. Dishonesty, violent behavior, substance abuse, and sexual misconduct are all just causes for dismissal. So is simply not working out.

Alfred Sloan, the formative power behind General Motors, is quoted as saying, "I think we have lacked and perhaps still lack courage in dealing with weaknesses in personnel. We know weaknesses exist, we tolerate them and finally after tolerating them an abnormal length of time, we make the change and then regret that we have not acted before" (James R. Cook, *The Start-Up Entrepreneur*, New York: Harper & Row, 1987, p. 197). Fire only as a last resort, but forestall the regret that comes from putting off the onerous task long after the need for it has become obvious.

When you do have to fire someone, be ready. Have the employee's final paycheck, which should include any back pay or other monies due the individual, in hand. Stay calm, show no anger, but be prepared for tears, verbal abuse, or worse. Do the firing in private, and always do it yourself.

Whenever an employee buys something, the transaction is written up in the employee sales book, and a copy of the sales slip signed by the purchaser is attached to the page. I check this book every week or so to see who's buying what.

Know Your Employees

While I'm no employee's buddy—a fatal stance for an employer to take in personnel relations, I know my staff well. I know their hobbies, their pets, their likes and dislikes. If they're not buying the obvious things they need from me, at a very respectable discount, I have to wonder why. Is it because they're buying elsewhere or because they're shopping at my store without paying?

If they're doing their shopping at my place, for free, then I have a problem on my hands. If they're buying elsewhere, then I'd better find out why, because I might have an even bigger problem on my hands. If I can't sell my wares to my own employees, at a really good discount, how can I sell anything to the general public?

Besides what they let you know inadvertently, your employees can tell you a lot about what you're doing right, as well as what you're not, directly. They're constantly in touch with your customers, your products, your services. Train your team from the start to listen to the customer, to pay attention to suggestions and ideas from the floor. Then, for your part in turn, listen to your team.

Not far from where I live, there's a small general store. For quite some time, it went through a new owner every six months—when it wasn't closed for business. A little over a decade ago, I dropped in, looking for some shoelaces, only to be told by the clerk at the checkout counter that the store didn't carry laces. A couple of weeks later, I stopped by the store to pick up a newspaper. The owner came up to me and said, "By the way, we now have shoelaces. They're over there next to the laundry detergents. Thanks for the suggestion."

It's been ten years since that brief conversation took place, and the store has had a thriving business for all those years. It's bigger now, and the owner has since purchased a couple more stores to increase his buying power.

Yes, You Need Staff Meetings

The best way to find out what your employees are thinking and what they're hearing from your customers is to hold regular staff meetings. Be objective in these meetings, and accept both suggestions and criticism without going on the defensive. No one says you have to take any advice that's proffered, but since you've asked for it, have the good grace to listen to the answers you get courteously. *Employees' number one complaint about their jobs is that their bosses don't listen to them.*

Jot down all the suggestions made in your staff meeting. Then give yourself until the next meeting to think about them, unless they're ones that clearly should be implemented right away. At the next meeting, bring up those suggestions again, let your team know you've been thinking them over, and give the good ones your go-ahead. When you turn down a proposed idea, give a reason for your decision.

Small suggestions can effect big changes. As well as eliciting those, however, once in a while, throw out a really leading question for your team to brainstorm. The single best one I know of is: if this were your store and your money, would you be doing what we're doing now?

Then sit back and listen. You'll both be rewarded.

10 How Much Is That Window in the Store?

The fifties hit song "How Much Is That Doggie in the Window?" sums up the marketing strategy of that booming decade. Put something lively in the shop window and, the customers, they would buy.

Today's video-saturated consumers, bombarded with vibrant visual images and seductive sound, are not so easily wooed. Even so, the display window remains your least expensive and, at the same time, your most powerful marketing tool. Windows make your store, both defining it and inviting shoppers into it.

The incorporation of windows into shop architecture during the late 1700s, when declining prices made glass an increasingly affordable luxury, was a primary formative influence in the evolution of a consumer society. Mass production and disposable income were essential preconditions of consumerism as well. Machine manufacture had to take over what was once done laboriously and in small lots by hand, and large numbers of people had to have the means with which to buy the plentiful goods so made available. Without the wish-for factor, however, our consumer culture would never have blossomed. That factor is what today is fostered by the graphic media, the insistent merchandising of television and glossy magazines, and in earlier days by that doggie in the window.

People in our society are both lonely and bored to distraction. Given the chance and the wherewithal to alleviate this ennui and emptiness, they will do so. That's why an engaging manner on the part of your sales staff is so important. A good salesperson is selling the sizzle—the flash of excitement, the human contact, a momentary feeling of friendship—as much as the steak.

Your salespeople won't get their turn at bat, though, unless you first get the customer's attention. That's where the window comes in. Catching the shopper's eye is the job of your display.

Making the Window Work

Shop windows have come a long way since their inception. Increasingly, and especially in malls, the open storefront is replacing the early boxed-in display case. Retail behemoths such as warehouse discounters and price clubs have even eliminated the window altogether. For them, it has served its historical function and can safely be discarded. The wish-for factor is addressed by other means, and theirs is but to deliver the goods, at the best conceivable price.

Despite this trend, the more traditional display window still has its uses for the smaller, individually owned store. Like a movie poster, it sparks the interest of the passerby and telegraphs a story.

One corollary of this is that, *like the movie poster, the window display should be changed frequently.* Another is that it shouldn't convey mixed messages. Particularly if your display window is a see-through one rather than an enclosed case with a backdrop, look closely at what's behind your window display. If someone gazes at a gorgeous window, a window to end all windows, and sees in the shop beyond it stacks and stacks of sloppily arrayed, cheap merchandise bearing no resemblance to what's in the window, you've lost a customer. Your window display and your store must convey a unity of image.

Fashion stores and trendy boutiques take the best advantage of the focused window display, in which the sizzle takes the stage. While selection and pricing may have ceded the spotlight here, however, they should still be waiting in the wings. The ideal window leads the customer into the store, eager to buy. If the customer is captivated by the tantalizing diorama in the window and then finds the selection inside limited and the prices not competitive, that's one disappointed customer.

The same holds true, obviously, for window dressing that's nowhere to be found inside the shop at all, in any size, shape, or form. Yet it's not uncommon for a merchant who has contrived a particularly zingy window display to keep it long after the merchandise has been sold out. Why not? The window looks great.

The unity, or disunity, of a store's image is more highly visible to the shopper where the display is part and parcel of an open storefront. The shop wide open to the street or the mall floor hides no secrets.

Open Versus Closed Store Fronts

The open-front store traces its line of descent to the teeming bazaars of the Orient and medieval days. More recent in its lineage are the bargain stores that once made Delancey Street in New York City an immigrant's ladder to financial success and a shopper's paradise. Like the pickle barrels and fruit crates lining the grocery stalls of yore, and like those racks of clothing pushed out onto the sidewalks by the Delancey Street merchants, the wares of the open-front store are in clear view and within tangible reach.

This has its advantages and disadvantages. The customer can see more or less at a glance what's in the store, so false hopes aren't as likely to be raised by a come-on display. On the other hand, the area on view is bigger than that of a window, so it's harder for the shopkeeper to make everything work together.

The open storefront is as different from the window display in psychological effect as it is in physical appearance. The entire storefront wall, usually in the form of sliding glass panels or collapsible partitions, actually moves out of the way when the store is open for business, leaving no barrier between the street or the mall floor and that of the shop. Passing by, you practically enter the store, whether you planned to or not.

For this reason, the open-front store is most effective in a high-traffic location such as a busy Main Street or mall, where people going past on their way to somewhere else are likely to stop and buy something on impulse. The driving force behind impulse buying is usually money—the perceived bargain, which is why the apple barrel always had a placard proudly proclaiming its "2 for 5¢" twofers and the Delancey Street merchants had price banners fluttering above their coatracks.

The savings pennant or a striking display or the strategic placement of merchandise may be what guides passersby into a store, but the fact that they're in the mall or on Main Street in the first place is no accident. One didn't pass Delancey Street on the way to anywhere. One went to Delancey Street to buy clothes. One ended up buying them at a particular place because that's where the best

The Four Most Common Window Display Errors

1. Misdirected lighting. To be effective, a display needs drama. The merchandise must stand out from the backdrop and props.

2. Busyness. A customer visually bombarded with too many items, a clutter of things, won't really see any of them.

3. A failure to keep stock on the floor to match the window display. If a customer comes in to buy that doggie in the window and finds out that it's already been sold and you kept it in the window just because it was such a cute draw, you've lost a customer, maybe permanently.

4. A window that lacks unity and clarity, in turn leaving the customer unfocused on what to buy.

bargain was. In due course, provided its prices stayed competitive, that place became a destination store.

In keeping prices competitive, the open-front store has an advantage over the enclosed one in that its display entails no real window costs, either those of construction or those generated by the need for constant display changes. At the same time, having no windows or facade allows the shopkeeper to merchandise all the way to the front of the store. The dumps and displays right at the entrance or even projecting a bit into the common space beyond the actual lease line all represent merchandising space gotten for free. The extra expanse of high-visibility selling space again helps in keeping prices down and margins up.

The content of a display, whether it's windowed or open, isn't limited to wares. There are myriad ways to get a sales message across, and the nonmerchandise part of your display is truly limited only by your imagination.

Crate & Barrel features the containers from which it took its name both on its catalog covers and in its store displays. What could be more practical and down-to-earth than the boxes and barrels the merchandise comes in? What could better send a message of practicality and economy, even if one ends up building some crates specially for the display because what the merchandise actually arrived in was battered corrugated cartons? The point is that the name, the catalog, the window display, the store itself, and all the merchandise fit into one focused picture announcing that here is something new, inexpensive, and sturdy. Now there's a tremendous display vision.

Contrast that with a fashion display in the window of a boutique I passed recently. The vibrant, well-lit presentation featured the latest hot trend—paraded by aged mannequins looking as if they'd been on the low end of a bid from a men's hair club. The picture wasn't whole, and the discord surely turned potential customers off.

While you don't want to use mature mannequins to flaunt miniskirts, you also don't want to use a display vehicle from the twenty-first century to reach a mature market. *When doing your windows, remember the maxim that everything should coordinate.*

At the same time, the startle factor can sometimes be utilized quite effectively in attracting consumer attention. Witness a really clever sales ruse recently employed in a fashion promotion. Antique mannequins without wigs or any of the other usual accoutrements began appearing in windows. Ancient display dolls suddenly took on the air of futuristic skinheads, appealing to a youthful sci-fi crowd on the cutting edge of designer fashion.

Even for nonfashion displays, think in terms of wardrobe and accessories. Match the look and the message. Christmas decorations don't go with bathing suits, and toothpaste doesn't belong with shoe polish. The customer doesn't put gleaming teeth in the same category with gleaming shoes. The flashing smile doesn't go with the sparkling footwear.

As always, there are exceptions. One of the most remarkable instances of successful marketing in the restaurant field is New York's Russian Tea Room, which has survived a declining menu quality over the decades by the simple expedient of maintaining its trademark Christmaslike ambience year-round. Talk about chutzpah!

Your window should have a reason for its existence. In other words, besides telling a single story, it should have a theme. Christmas, that nirvana season in retailing, is one obvious focus. But unless you're the Russian Tea Room, you can't sell Christmas all year long. Other seasonal displays probably come to mind—spring ones set off by flowers to dispel the gloom of a dull, dark winter, or a Halloween one ringed with pumpkins. These have their place. Tradition sells.

However, there are other excellent reasons for a particular display. Celebrating hot, new, trendy stock is one of them. Waving the banner for the local high school football team's undefeated season is another. If the Dow Jones just went through the roof, take advantage of the news and build a display around bulls and jagged charts reaching for the sky.

Announcing that there's just been a new addition to your family might seem to stretch the point a bit, but remember that customers long for the personal touch. Including them in a birth announcement is a little like making them part of the family.

In working out a theme for your window display, don't forget that there's a balance to be struck between the goal of creating an unusual, arresting window and representing your store and your merchandise. You want your store to be noticed, but you need to make sure the window doesn't reflect something you're not.

A Retailer's Display Calendar

February 1.   The Valentine's Day displays should be up. Valentine's Day has a much shorter sales span than Christmas does. Don't miss it by waiting any longer to turn the spots on it.

February 15.   The day after Valentine's. Easter starts no later than this. The immediate contrast between all that traditional red and Easter pastels is always a startling draw.

May 1.   If you're in a college area and your sales environment encompasses a school focus, graduation begins now. June 1 is fine for high schools.

August 1.   The back-to-school impetus supplants the graduation flurry of activity. The lengthening school year in many areas may soon drive this date back to mid-July. Incidentally, nothing says your stock has to be school related in order to qualify for a back-to-school sale. One very successful late-summer special featured early winter coats for women along with a message to mom that she deserved to look good and be warm while standing out there with the kids waiting for the school bus.

October 15.   Thereabouts, the Christmas push begins in earnest. It used to start on the Friday after Thanksgiving, but that was a long Dickensian time ago.

Since you bought this book, obviously you're fairly serious about opening your own store. Chances are you've already strolled up and down Main Street and through nearby malls casting a critical eye over the shops. Now do it again—with a particular assignment in mind. Roam the malls and Main Street concentrating on the shop windows. What are the stories they're trying to tell? Have they succeeded or failed? Are they selling price or fashion or volume, or is the message such a mishmash that you can't even tell which of these it is? How does one store's display set it off from the competition?

Look for displays indicating that the shopkeeper has grasped the value of promoting uniqueness. Recently, I came across a sewing machine in the window of a fashion shop. It might have sent a very confusing message indeed were it not for the fact that an attractive sign disclosed the store's readiness to monogram any purchase for free. This was a service duplicated nowhere else in the mall, and it certainly drew customers.

That very thing—providing what the picture in the window implies is going to be available inside—is the next thing you want to look for. Do the premises support the promise made out front? Do the salespeople champion it, leading the customer from display to actual purchase?

I recently scouted out a men's store specializing in clothing for hard-to-fit extra-large individuals, not only portly ones, as the overweight were once tactfully called, but men well over six feet tall who could never find pants long enough to fit. All the salespeople were in their late teens or early twenties, and nary a one of them wore anything but 30 × 30 pants and size 38 jackets—not a comfortable environment for individuals of uncommon height or girth.

Turning a Fringe Benefit into a Sales Tool

That particular store furnishes a conspicuous example of the blatant failure to carry a focus through from the outside to the in. Its opposite is a jewelry store in the same mall where the salesclerks wear the jewelry the store carries. One of their fringe benefits is that they buy the merchandise at cost plus 10 percent. Everyone wins. The salespeople get a real bargain, and the shopkeeper gets a living display with the merchandise always modeled right before the customer's eyes.

Not only the image projected by your sales associates, but that suggested by the layout and the fixtures of your store as well, should harmonize with the message conveyed by your display. Fixtures in particular lend a certain definite aura to a store. The style, colors, materials, and finishes should all blend into a coherent whole complementing the picture you're trying to present.

Victoria's Secret and Gloria Jean's are two excellent examples of shops featuring a warm, woodsy, continental environment. Gleaming modern chrome racks, no matter how fine in quality, would simply be out of place in either store.

Servicing Your Silent Salesmen

End caps, the displays at the ends of the aisles, dominate the customer's view, set apart as they are from the length of the aisles. Known in the trade as silent salesmen, these displays need to be changed as often as every two weeks if they are to be effectual.

My Aunt Martha had a piano in her living room. Every couple of months she would move the piano from one corner of the room to another. Once she even moved it into the middle of the room. She was very proud of that piano, though no one played it, and she was afraid that someone coming by to visit might overlook it. Now you might think a piano pretty hard to overlook, but people do become used to familiar surroundings and fail to really notice them anymore. Unless things are changed and moved around sometimes, they get lost in the background of our lives.

Simply changing the end caps frequently isn't enough, however. They need to tell a story, and the story needs to be a one-liner—short, simple, and to the point. A really focused, direct winter end cap in a clothing store might be a cornucopia of assorted gloves for the whole family. An auto supply might feature a dozen different basic winter driving aids such as dry gas, starter fluid, ice scrapers, and windshield washer fluid. In a gourmet shop, an appropriate end cap might consist of an array of low-fat products. Even a collection of items all under $3 in price could be an effectively unified end cap in an establishment where the bargain is the selling point.

Whatever you do, make your end caps inviting to touch. Don't build pyramids that are going to fall down whenever a customer picks something up. An item in hand is almost a sale.

On the whole, you'll probably be wise not to use the displays provided by manufacturers. The one place where you might consider taking advantage of them is next to the register, although you do have to be very careful not to make this area too much of a jumble.

Why You Don't Want Promotional Displays

A major shortcoming of most manufacturers' displays is that they tend to be simply too large. They block aisles. They disrupt the flow of traffic and attention. They break up the uniformity and continuity of the shop. Except in bookstores, usually designed from the outset to accommodate dumps parading twenty, thirty, or even fifty copies of the same title, such displays rarely either fit or fit in. Where they do, everybody has them, and when everybody has them, they lose their individuality. Dumps are almost impossible to personalize. They're making a strong statement of their own, and all too often it's not the one you're trying to make.

Another problem with most promotional displays is that they're designed to hold far more units than you would normally stock. You might have considered carrying four electric styling combs in your store, for instance, but on finding that a special boxed display of two dozen such combs is available, you go for the deal. A week later you find that you've sold fourteen of the combs. Now the display looks empty, disorganized, and unappealing.

What do you do? Well, you could order another dozen units to fill out the display, but would they sell within a reasonable amount of time or have you made all the easy sales within your clientele? Alternatively, you could take the display down and put the extra combs in with your regular stock, but since you normally wouldn't carry that many of this particular item, such a move would entail shuffling all your other stock around. All in all, the manufacturer's display probably wasn't worth the trouble it caused.

That said, I'll be the first to admit that I do take advantage of manufacturers' display promotions on occasion. Provided the special discount or other added value thrown in by the supplier makes the promotion worthwhile from a dollars-and-cents point of view, I'll take it. Then, if the display itself doesn't suit my purposes, I'll simply throw it out and assemble my own spotlighting for the merchandise.

In this case, I'm referring to spotlighting in the literal sense of the word, and that brings us to an important consideration in merchandising. *Lighting is one of the most crucial components of retail marketing.* If the customer doesn't see the goods, your chances of a sale are slim. Beyond that more or less self-evident point, however, lighting can greatly enhance a product, turning it from something ordinary and easily overlooked into something notable and desired.

One of the most common applications of light enhancement in retailing is found at your local supermarket. Special bulbs are used over the vegetables to intensify their greenness and hence their presumed freshness. Next time you're in a supermarket, pick up some leaf lettuce or a bunch of carrots with the tops left on and take it from the vegetable section toward the windows—usually far away. It will seem to wilt before your very eyes as you get closer to the outdoors. Yet nothing will have changed, really, besides the lighting. The same holds true for the meat section, except that there, as you might surmise, the illumination emphasizes red.

Technologically speaking, you have the same basic choice in light sources for your store that you have for your home. You can opt for either fluorescent or incandescent lighting. Now fluorescent lamps have improved a lot since the fifties, when every kitchen in America installed this economical form of illumination, and every American family gathered around the kitchen table took on the aspect of Mme. Tussaud's wax figures. Never depend on fluorescents as your sole source of store lighting.

The economics of fluorescent lighting are such that it will probably be your major source of illumination, just the same. The fact of the matter is that incandescent light is really inefficient by comparison. The bulbs have a shorter life and generate a lot of heat besides.

A blend of warm and cool fluorescent bulbs should give you good, reliable, economical—and rather uninteresting—general illumination for your store. Never mind, what you're doing here is setting the preliminary stage only. The spotlights go on later. If you plan to use display cases in your store, though, one thing to watch out for when you're installing these overheads is the angle between them and the cases. Unless you're careful, the overhead lights will be reflected in the glass tops of the cases so customers don't get a clear view of the merchandise. Also watch that the overheads don't cast shadows about the store. You want pleasant, even, bright but

Design Tips to Minimize Shoplifting

1. Except along walls, display fixtures should reach no higher than eye level.

2. Fitting rooms, if needed, should be situated where they will be in full sight of your sales staff, not secluded at the back of the store.

3. The manager's office ought to be in a conspicuous spot and feature, as well, an obvious one-way mirror. One-way mirrors are immediately noticed by shoplifters, rarely remarked by honest shoppers.

4. Easily palmed expensive items are best exhibited in showcases, designed to safeguard such merchandise. If they are to be on open display, at least put them on—or, better yet, above and behind—a counter that's continuously and uninterruptedly staffed.

5. Checkouts, besides being close to exits, should be so manned that the customer is never delayed in paying for merchandise. In today's make-your-morals-as-you-go society, even normally honest people will sometimes walk out with a few small unpaid-for items if they're compelled to wait too long to make their purchases. "If they don't want to take my money," goes the reasoning, "it serves them right."

unobtrusive illumination throughout the shop—except where you're highlighting the merchandise. Shadows and dark corners not only reduce the visibility of your merchandise, but increase the opportunities for shoplifting as well. In mapping out your lighting system, as with all other design considerations, keep the effect on shoplifting in mind.

Spotlights, either the standard incandescent variety typified by the familiar track light spots or the brighter tungsten-halogen ones, are excellent to heighten the consumer's awareness of certain articles in your store. To be effective visually, however, a spotlighted display on the shop floor needs to be about two to two and one-half times as bright as its surroundings. That's an average easy enough to specify and a bit more difficult to implement.

Both lighting and its measurement can be very tricky. That's why there's so much lighting apparatus being manipulated by so many people in every movie shoot.

As a shopkeeper, you too can hire professional lighting consultants. If you can afford it, this might not be a bad idea. However, most start-up operations are better off putting that cash into goods and simply spending a little extra time really focusing on the question of lighting in first setting up shop. Visit a couple of attractive, well-lit stores, check out the number and power of their lights, study how the spots are placed, observe the distance between the spots and the merchandise they highlight, and so on. Then copy the results you like.

Remember, whatever you decide on, that it's important to move the spots around inside the store. Change the highlighting at least once a month. Twice a month is better. These variations in display are what put the action into your show, and action, particularly in this age of thirty-second commercials, is what people crave.

If spots are crucial to a floor display, they're even more pivotal in a window. A store window is, after all, 100 percent display. This is a riddle little concerning the owner of an open-front mall store. There, no particularly brilliant lighting statement is needed. The illumination at the door need only be bright enough to pull customers in from the mall's common space, normally kept subdued lightwise in any event, to make the stores themselves seem visually brighter. Even if your shop has an open front, though, you might well want to have a spotlight or two shining on any displays that extend that little bit past the lease line, say a foot or two, onto the mall floor itself. Customers will tend to step over the lease line and into the shop for a closer look. At that point, once more a sale is halfway made.

The problem faced by the shopkeeper whose establishment features a traditional store window is more or less the same whether the space is an enclosed display or one opening onto the store floor so that the shopper looks through and beyond it. A window demands innovation and continuous care, and both of those involve critical issues of illumination. Should one give the whole window a high degree of illumination? Should the focus be put on the merchandise with strategically placed spots? Should one use high-contrast lights, spotlights, color filters?

If yours is a store with a display window, don't be afraid to experiment. Try them all—the spotlights, contrast, color. Small programmable switchboxes permitting alternating cycles of bright and muted lighting or a sequence of various colors are well worth having on hand. You wouldn't run such an animated light show in your window all the time, but doing so three or four times a year to interrupt longer interludes of bright but quiet illumination could really help to set your store apart from others that never vary their lighting.

Between worrying about the spotlights here and the overheads there, a shopkeeper is all too apt to overlook the bottom of the picture. Understandable though this may be, the bottom of a window display is as important as the rest of it. Yet it easily and often ends up being a mass of overlapping shadows. Erase these by the judicious use of footlights. Lamps at the bottom of the window illuminating the display frontally will counterbalance the light beamed onto it from above, eliminating the disquieting dark circles lurking beneath.

Whatever your display, and whatever lighting you use, remember to go out and look at it from the customer's vantage point every day. Merchandise shifts in a display. Bulbs burn out. Things you'd never expect to go wrong go wrong. When they do, you need to make sure they're corrected right away. If your end caps are your silent salesmen, then the window display is your ace sales associate and greeter.

11   A Day at the Store

Whatever time of day your store opens, someone should be there half an hour earlier to do what *shouldn't* have been done the day before. Most retail operations, be they large chains or single-store outlets, have a policy of cleaning the premises daily, usually beginning about half an hour before closing. The idea is to ensure a spick-and-span store all ready for a hassle-free start the next day. It sounds logical, but it's absolutely wrong.

Think about your own reaction when, toward the end of the day, you walk into a store where a clerk is busy vacuuming the aisles. Do you feel a bit intimidated or in the way? Most people sense that they're imposing. Far too many, confronted with this driven machine, the cord perhaps snaking across the entrance, won't even enter the store in the first place. They'll simply walk away.

Malls in particular induce such near-closing-time feelings of rejection. So if your store is situated in a mall, take advantage of the other shops' mismanagement. Don't allow any cleaning before the doors of the shop are shut for the day. Resist that urge to get the job done early, even in the hectic, messy pre-Christmas shopping season when the store, after a few hours of being rummaged through by customers, looks as if it had been hit by a tornado. Train your personnel to be at their liveliest and best just before closing. Shoppers drifting out of the large anchor stores already humming with vacuums will quite often drop by. They're in the mall. They're in a buying mood. One more stop in an inviting emporium is a natural impulse.

Schedule the half hour of cleaning not done before closing time for the beginning of the next day. If your store opens for business at 10:00 A.M., whoever is to tidy up the place should be there by 9:30. For a dry cleaning establishment with only fifty square feet of customer space in front of a counter, ten minutes is probably plenty. A pet store, on the other hand, needs someone two to three hours before opening to clean up after all the animals. A puppy eating may be cute, but cleaning up the mess afterward doesn't sell the merchandise. Whatever the time needed, *when you're open for business, you're not cleaning. If you're cleaning, you're not really open for business.*

The same principle holds true for counting your money. Don't cash out, as the procedure is known in the trade, at closing time. Do it an hour or so beforehand. Then customers won't feel rushed. They'll know the store is going to be open for some time yet, whatever you're doing with the cash register. In a successful retail operation, the last hour's sales belong to tomorrow.

Where Did the Money Come From?

Cashing out isn't just a matter of counting the day's take, and there's more to the cash register than the money drawer. The retail business is dynamic, and the daily cash out sheet is your trend indicator and early warning system. It's the thermometer of the register, so to speak, the way you take your business's temperature. It's backed up by the cash register tape itself.

Every morning, before the shop opens, you should go over the previous day's cash out figures. (See Appendix E for an example of a cash out sheet and matching register tape. You'll note that the cash out sheet shown is divided into first and second cash outs. You might have three, four, or even more separate cash outs, depending on how your operation is set up.) If you have more than one shift, there should be a cash out each time a manager goes off. Let's say you open the store yourself and run it till 4:00, and then someone else takes over. You should cash out before you leave, and your second manager should cash out for that shift. The same holds even truer if someone other than yourself is in charge at all times, since in that case neither shift will be under your direct supervision. Multiple cash outs give you more control over potential cash shrinkage problems.

Another function of multiple cash outs is periodically to reduce the amount of cash accumulating in the register. Less cash, less temptation, less likelihood of theft.

The Cash Out Sheet Is Your Business Day Snapshot

The first item on a cash out sheet, the date, is self-explanatory. Note, however, that in retailing the date, besides simply establishing chronological order, also fixes the day's sales for comparison purposes. Sales depend a lot on the weather, the second item, and other irregular factors.

Here an old-fashioned device called the Beat Yesterday Book (a sample page follows) is something well worth putting together. Nothing else will give you quite the same feel for the pulse and trends of a business. This said, I'll be the first to admit that I no longer bother to keep one. The operative phrase, however, is *no longer*.

A Beat Yesterday Book is like a diary. At one time or another in our lives, most of us have resolved to keep a diary. Many of us have even started one, though few people manage to keep one for very long. Do try, however, to keep a Beat Yesterday Book for the first couple of years you're in business. It could prove invaluable.

Beat Yesterday
Your Store, Inc.

Jan 96

Date	Notable	Weather	Total Sales	Total Customers
1 Mon	New Year's Day	Clear	$1,668	103
2 Tues		Clear	980	61
3 Wed	Coupon	Snow	1,112	69
4 Thurs		Snow	730	46
5 Fri		Lots of snow	530	33
6 Sat		More snow	829	52
7 Sun		Cold	1,232	77
8 Mon		Pleasant	1,453	91
9 Tues		Pleasant	1,926	120
10 Wed		Snow	631	39
11 Thurs	Senior citizen sale	Cloudy	1,503	94
12 Fri		Pleasant	1,864	116
13 Sat	Mall winter carnival	Clear	2,193	137
14 Sun		January thaw	856	54
15 Mon	Martin Luther King Day	Warm	1,031	65

Simply comparing sales, say for the second week in January of this year with the second week in January of last year, can be misleading. Taken alone, the figures might indicate that sales improved vastly. Unfortunately, your Beat Yesterday Book might show that a major snowstorm really snarled traffic and kept shoppers at home during much of that particular week last January, so the increase in sales was largely illusory. Or perhaps no snow fell at all that week, but the coupon promotion you did this year during the second week in January was really effective, temporarily inflating sales. Don't count on your memory. You need the Beat Yesterday Book records for a reliable comparison of the years day by day and week by week. Plain and simple, calendar days are just numbers.

The third item on your cash out sheet is the customer count. The term *customer count* may conjure up visions of someone standing by the door, clicker in hand, pressing the button when anyone enters the store. That's not what I have in mind. What you want is a tally of the number of people actually making a purchase on a given day. If a customer buys something, leaves the store, remembers another needed item, and comes back for it, that's two separate purchases on the customer tally.

Every item of a sale is recorded on the detail tape of the cash register, and each total sale is assigned a transaction number. Take the transaction number of the previous day's last sale, subtract it from the final transaction number of the current day's sales, and you have the actual customer count for the day.

This tally can give you, in turn, the average ticket value of the day's sales.

$$\frac{\text{Total dollar sales}}{\text{Customer count}} = \text{Average ticket value}$$

Any change in the average ticket value is worth noting and trying to analyze in terms of its business value. For instance, an increase in the average ticket value indicates that customers are buying pricier merchandise. This could mean that your shop is becoming a destination store, one that people set out to visit with a specific purpose in mind, rather than a nondescript emporium that just happens to be there as they are passing by. It could also mean a trend toward quality purchasing instead of value seeking, or buying on price.

Then again, an increase in average ticket value might be due to a change in attitude on the part of your staff. Maybe your sales personnel are pushing higher-priced items because you recently implemented a bonus system. Maybe they've given up on the less expensive sale.

Your job is to analyze the trend, applying all the knowledge of local circumstances and events you have at your disposal, and determine how you can turn a profit from it. *From an operational point of view, the big difference between a large- and small-scale retailer is that the small store can react much more quickly—and profitably—to trends.*

If an increase in sales of big-ticket items makes it appear that your shop is becoming established as a destination store, experiment with new, higher-priced lines. If low-ticket but high-markup merchandise isn't moving, see what you can do to improve its location and display. These small high-markup items can figure significantly in your overall profits.

The preliminary figures of your cash out sheet provide a quick reference to the day-to-day health of your business as a whole. However, in addition to this overview, you want a breakdown of where in the store the profits and potential problems actually lie. For this you need some means by which to analyze and assess what's happening in the different departments. Thus, the bulk of your cash out sheet is devoted to the separate categories of merchandise sold in the various departments. Pet store sales, for instance, might be broken down into dogs (department I on the cash register tape shown here), dog supplies (department II), fish (department III), and so on.

Another focus of sales to be separated out from the cash out sheet for analysis is specials such as coupon offers and other promotional highlights you may be featuring. The total here is an effective measure of whether or not a particular promotion is paying its way.

The tax line on your cash out sheet is self-explanatory. It is also, alas, unavoidable, a necessary part of the earnings picture.

The Crucial Below-the-Line Items

Add all the lines together, and you have your gross sales, the total dollar volume for the cash out period. This isn't the amount actually in the drawer, however, because you'll also have paid outs and voids offsetting the day's receipts. Monitoring these below-the-line items, as they're called, is crucial to your survival and success as a retailer in any situation where you are not the sole person running the register.

I know one very successful small-scale retailer who had a quaint brass mechanical register with a bell that gonged loudly as each sale was rung up and the drawer sprang open to receive its money. Although he had half a dozen employees to assist him with customers, not one of them was ever within six feet of the register. You won't see that sort of operation often in this country, but working out of a cigar box is still common in many less developed nations, where a simple cash box is often quite adequate to the task.

Where a business is a little more complex, however, and especially where hands other than yours have access to the till, a close watch over revenues and expenses is essential. So back to reality.

The first below-the-line item, paid outs, includes the outlay for duct tape to hold up a fixture, a postage-due disbursement, the purchase of paper towels for the bathroom—in short, all the small costs that crop up unexpectedly in day-to-day operations. All paid outs should be authorized and initialed either by you as owner of the shop or by your store manager if you have one. No exceptions.

The second below-the-line item is voided sales. Even an obvious void such as a sale rung up as $980 instead of 98¢ should have a void slip filled out by the staffer who made the mistake and be signed by the manager.

Such attention to detail might seem petty to someone unused to the vagaries—and value—of a recording cash register, but *enforcing a strict accounting policy from the outset of operations could save you an immense amount of grief later.* Not only does the careful documentation of payouts and voids ensure honesty, but it reduces the incidence of cash register errors as well, because they're such a nuisance to rectify. Efficiency, both apparent and real, is improved in turn.

Subtracting the paid outs and voids from your gross sales gives you your actual take, your net sales, for the cash out period. This is the money that should be in the till, either as cash or in the form of credit card charge slips.

In the real world, of course, the amount actually in the till never matches the net sales line. That's why there's an over/short line on your cash out sheet.

Too Much Money Is a Problem

Overages and shortages are both problems. Yes, having more money in the register than you were supposed to have is indeed a problem. In my book, in fact, overages are the more serious of the two discrepancies.

Most of the time, you'll be $4 to $5 to either side of your mark, and the error or errors will be traceable to something like giving the wrong change. If you're over by a large amount, say $120, the problem will be relatively easy to locate. Usually, it's a large sale the sales associate failed to ring up while talking to a customer. When the overage is $10 to $30, though, you have a potentially serious problem on your hands.

A peculiar-looking overage may turn out to have a simple, innocent explanation. Someone doesn't understand the use of the register, say. Then again, someone may have decided to become your unannounced partner. This self-appointed cohort may be not ringing up sales, intending to pull the cash out later. Possibly the opportunity to do so fails to arise. Possibly he or she loses track of how much hasn't been rung up. Whatever the case, your job is to identify the suspect.

After you've checked over your shop's cash out sheet, the next stop on your morning inspection tour is the stockroom. There, you want to make sure all new orders received have been moved out. A delay here can be very costly from a cash flow perspective. If incoming merchandise sits in the stockroom for a week—which isn't unusual, sadly enough, particularly once one box has been stacked on top of another "just for a minute"— that's a week during which it can't be sold, a week during which you own and pay for that merchandise. Owning merchandise isn't what retailing is all about. Turnover is.

If you find you have a lot of stock in the back room because you already have plenty of the same items out on the shelves in the shop, chances are you're ordering too much of that particular line. As a rule of thumb, 80 percent of your merchandise should be on the floor and no more than 20 percent in the stockroom.

Of course, an unexpected run on an item may create blank shelf space no one could have anticipated. If there's no replacement stock in the back room, fill in the space anyway, even if it means moving merchandise around. The shelves in the store should always be full.

Once you're through surveying the back room, make a quick sweep of the store itself. In doing so, try never to walk through the aisles without moving something. Straighten out a display here, pull some stock forward on a shelf there, check a price tag, or rotate some items. Stay in touch with your merchandise.

Look for other things to be done, and try to give everyone on the staff at least one specific task to accomplish that day. The message you're sending is that you're involved and interested in the day-to-day details of the operation. Then, later, mention to each person how the job was or wasn't done. Comments, however brief, are an effective way to let staffers know you're on top of the situation.

Focus on the Cash Register Area for Profit

As you approach the front of the store on your inspection tour, focus your attention on the cash register area. The four feet to either side of the register and the space directly below it constitute a separate business domain. Major brands have evolved by concentrating their marketing efforts on this impulse zone alone.

Consider Edward John Noble, an enterprising salesman of advertising space. In 1914 Noble bought the rights to an obscure and unsuccessful brand of mints called Life Savers. Part of the reason sales of these 5¢ mints were lagging was that, encased in flimsy cardboard tubes, the mints became stale and lost their flavor within a couple of weeks on candy store shelves. Noble came up with a foil wrapper to solve that problem.

Still sales went nowhere. To broaden the market, Noble decided, he needed to expand sales beyond the realm of the traditional candy store. Pondering the matter, he came up with a brilliant idea. Where there's a cash register, there's change, and where there's change, there are nickels. Now a nickel is only a nickel. People aren't hesitant to spend it. So why not put the Life Savers where the nickels were?

With that in mind, Noble approached a host of proprietors of barbershops, drugstores, restaurants, smoke shops, and a whole gamut of other small businesses. "Put the mints next to your register with a big 5¢ card, be sure all your customers get a nickel in their change, and see what happens," he suggested.

What happened was that Life Savers became a huge success and the concept of cash register impulse buying was launched.

Within a short time, free enterprise being what it is, the area around the cash register had become a jumble of competing candy displays. Noble remained undeterred. Turning the chaos to his advantage, he designed a large sectional candy tray to help store-keepers organize the displays. Of course, the tray had *Life Savers* boldly emblazoned on it, and the top row, the choice location, was specifically fashioned to hold—you guessed it—Life Savers. You'll see these racks by many a cash register to this very day.

Noble's original goal and yours are a bit different. Noble wanted to make sure that Life Savers were always near that crucial location for spur-of-the-moment buying, the cash register. Your goal is to make sure that *different* impulse items are always clustered around the cash register. Refresh and change the display at least once a month. Focus on high-markup items.

Here, incidentally, is one place where a half-empty display case is acceptable and sometimes even advantageous. Modern consumers have acquired a certain affinity for the odd lot and the closeout, and while ordinarily you don't want to broach these merchandising are-nas, the contents of an occasional bin of marked-down "last ones" tucked in by the register often fly out the door. Experiment.

The register display is just about the last stop on your morning inspection tour. Put the day's operating cash into the register drawer, and you're ready to open for business. As you unlock the front door, move out any sidewalk displays you have planned for the day.

Sidewalk displays are both a boon and a burden. In some loca-tions they aren't even allowed, which takes the decision of whether or not to use them out of your hands. Mall managers tend to be stricter on this score than the overseers of freestanding locations and urban stores are. Even in cities, however, outside displays may be restricted because crowds milling around sidewalk exhibits or shopping racks can block traffic.

Where displays are allowed, the burden of deciding whether or how best to use them falls on the storekeeper's shoulders. Here shoplifting becomes a primary consideration. Sticky fingers cling most readily to merchandise arrayed outside the store itself.

Given that drawback, *sidewalk displays can nevertheless be some of your most profitable retail footage*, particularly since the space they occupy is effectively rent free. They're customer magnets, virtually extending your window dressing and at the same time proffering impulse merchandise.

While you're outside the shop, scrutinize your storefront with a critical eye. You're perusing it from the customer's first vantage point, outside looking in. Remember Hemingway's search for a "clean and well-lighted" place. Burned-out bulbs should be replaced and damaged signs repaired as soon as possible. It's all too easy for a sign to chip, fade, or acquire a coat of grime without your noticing the change because it's been so gradual. Make sure that all your lights are on, giving the store a welcoming, open look.

The rest of the day is for selling. Nurture friendliness and enthusiasm among your staff—by example. Attitude, knowledge, and quality stock are your most effective tools in competing with the big chains and discounters. You'll never be able to match their prices or sheer volume of inventory. What you can do is offer better stock and service—at the right time.

Timing is a sales factor not easily embraced by the big retail outlets. Caldor's, an anchor store at one of the malls where I have a shop, is a case in point. Invariably, come the last week in August, Caldor's bedding section is completely empty. Not a sheet or a towel is in sight.

Now it so happens that there are two colleges nearby. Yet no one on the Caldor staff, even after twenty years of doing business in the area, has connected the yearly influx of students with the missing sheets, arrived at the conclusion that students buy a lot of white goods during their annual move into the dorms, and concluded that the store should stock more sheets and towels. The reason no one has worked out this simple formula is that this store, like every other Caldor's, is stocked by central purchasing, which is unaware of the local situation.

Know your neighborhood. It's an invaluable key to good marketing.

Listen to the Customer

One of the best ways to get to know your neighborhood is to keep a customer request pad by the register. Customers ask the darnedest questions, to paraphrase an old book title, and just as the book itself made a mint for its authors, your customers' queries can be a great source of revenue. Both you and your personnel should jot down any requests shoppers make, even the ones that seem a little silly. Future review may prove them far from pointless.

There you are, running a lingerie shop, for instance. Your request pad shows that over the space of the last couple of months six different customers have asked whether you carry jumpsuits. Now that's puzzling, to say the least. Are jumpsuits sexy, luxurious, frivolous? What does an upscale rendering of workmen's overalls have to do with lingerie?

Plenty, apparently. *Yours is not to reason why. Yours is to offer the right thing to buy.* Originally, Victoria's Secret was a modestly successful purveyor of underwear. Those garments may still be the draw, but today they're a minor part of the shop's overall inventory. The store's line has grown and expanded to keep up with what the customer wanted.

So a day of selling is a day of listening as well. The cutting edge of a new consumer trend may be reflected in that request pad by the register. If you experiment, stocking the occasional item that seems to be coming into demand, you may soon find your hunch confirmed by your cash out breakdown.

The mechanics of closing, tallying the day's register receipts and completing the cash out sheet, are simple. Well before lockup time, the hour when you actually shut the doors behind the last customer, hit the *x* key on the register for the day's total take. However many separate cash outs you have in order to accommodate different shifts or managerial changeovers, this is your final sales score for the day. Remember, never *z* out a register for your total.

Transfer the data from your register tape to your cash out sheet, entering the day's receipts and expenses on their respective lines. Now you're ready to turn your attention to deposits.

First, stamp all the checks *For Deposit Only*. Add them up, add up the cash, and fill out the deposit slip. Make sure you save a copy to match against the bank's records when they come in. Then put the checks and cash in a night deposit bag. You should keep three or four of these on hand so there's always an extra in case you need to make another deposit before picking up the empties at the bank the following day.

Next, add up the credit card receipts, comparing them with the charges recorded on the register tape. If the figures don't agree, you have some detective work on your hands. Otherwise, you can go ahead and type in an OK on the credit card machine so the money will actually be transferred to your account.

Keep a copy of each and every charge slip. Clip all the day's slips right to the cash out sheet along with the detail tape from the register and any other pertinent record-keeping items such as void slips, store credits issued, coupons turned in, delivery payouts, or other expenses. This is your paper trail substantiating all your business transactions.

Once a week, tuck all this paperwork into an envelope and give it to the bookkeeper. If you use a computerized accounting program, the data needs to be entered weekly at minimum. When you or the bookkeeper is finished with the paperwork, put the envelope in a box. At the end of the year, put the box in a safe place. Seven years later, if you happen to think of it, you can throw the box out, since that's the end of the required IRS record-keeping period.

So you've cashed out, with an hour to go before you actually close the doors. This could be your most profitable hour. Evenings and weekends are usually the busiest times for retailers. The exception is a brief interval after Christmas, when stores are often crowded during the weekdays and quiet at night as well as on the weekend.

The fact that business happens to be slow is never an excuse for closing early, though. Close half an hour before the scheduled time, and you can safely bet that a good customer will come by fifteen minutes later, sure that you'll be open. That's one customer who won't be back, or at least not for a year.

One of the most valuable times for the owner of a store to be there is at the very end of the day. One Christmas Eve, when Puppy Love Pet Center was supposed to close at 5:00 P.M., there was a knock on the glass as I was turning out the lights. It was 5:15, and every store in the mall was shut. I let the customer in and, soon after, a second one desperately needing a lovebird for his wife and, of course, a cage to go with it. . . . The first customer bought a dog. Between the two of them, the register rang up an extra $1,500 in sales that day. Plus, I was the retailer who saved Christmas for at least two families.

Appendix A

Payroll Service Bill

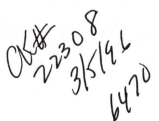

ADP

100 CORPORATE DRIVE
WINDSOR CT 06095

Invoice # 965929
February 2, 1996   *Page   1*

Accounts receivable number:
00012-701695

**Any questions? Call your ADP
service representative,**
Mary Jambard (203)688-8900

C005

lll....ll....ll.l.lll.....ll.ll.l...ll.l
RUTH BROWN
PUPPY LOVE PET CENTERS
XX Xxxxxx Xx-Xxxxxxx Xxxxx
Xxxxxxxxxxx, XX XXXXX-XXXX

Current Charges	Autopay Plus	Company code 4QC	
	Processing charges for period ending 01/27/96		
	28 Pays		35.79
	Direct Deposit		6.00
	Check Stuffing		8.00
	28 Bank Check Charge	$.05 each	1.40
	Official Bank Charge		6.00
	Total Tax		13.76
	PR Delivery(Supply Delivery N/C)		4.00
Total			74.95
Special Adjustment			-13.91
		Sub-total current charges	61.04
		Tax	3.66
		Total due this invoice	**$64.70**

Ck# 22308
3/5/96
6470

Please return the portion below with your payment in the enclosed return envelope. Include
your accounts receivable number on your check made out to Automatic Data Processing, Inc.

Appendix B

Sample Letter of Intent

February 25, 1993

Mr. Tom Xxxxxx
XX Xxxxxx Road
Xxxxxx, XX XXXXX

RE: Xxxxxx Corner
Xxxxxx, XX

Dear Tom:

I am pleased to submit the following proposed lease terms for your review:

1) Shopping Center:	Xxxxxx Corner XXX Xxxxxx Avenue Xxxxxx, XX
2) Tenant:	Xxxxxx, Inc. d/b/a/ Lox & Bagels
3) Guarantor:	Tom Xxxxxx XX Xxxxxx Road Xxxxxx, XX XXXXX SS#_____
4) Permitted Use:	Operation of a restaurant selling bagels, sandwiches, salads, soup and related accompaniments for on- and off-premises consumption. Maximum seating: 16 seats.
5) Leased Premises:	Approximately 809 s.f.
6) Condition Upon Delivery:	As-is
7) Construction:	Tenant shall obtain all permits and approvals and shall perform all construction at Tenant's sole cost and expense, with prior written approval of Landlord
8) Term:	Five (5) years
9) Commencement:	30 days from delivery or when open for business, whichever is first to occur

February 25, 1993
Mr. Tom Xxxxxx
Page Two of Three

	Year	Annual	P.S.F.
10) Base Rent:	1	$21,843.00	$27.00
	2	$22,652.00	$28.00
	3	$23,663.00	$29.25
	4	$24,674.50	$30.50
	5	$25,685.75	$31.75

11) Percentage Rent:

7% of gross sales in excess of:
$312,043   year 1
$323,600   year 2
$338,046   year 3
$352,493   year 4
$366,939   year 5

12) Common Area
Maintenance/Fire
& Liability
Insurance:

Pro Rata - initial annual escrow ★
$2.16/s.f. (Escrowed monthly,
adjusted yearly)

13) Taxes:

Pro Rata - initial annual escrow ★
$1.77/s.f. (Escrowed monthly,
adjusted yearly)

14) Utilities:

Separately metered or submetered;
Tenant's responsibility

15) Security Deposit:

$2,500.00

16) M.A./Promo. Fund:

Tenant shall participate in the
Merchants' Association. Initial
dues are $0.50 psf, subject to
increase by Merchants' Association
member vote.

17) Leasing Agent:

Xxxxxx Management Corporation, paid
by Landlord

February 25, 1993
Mr. Tom Xxxxxx
Page Three of Three

I believe these terms will be acceptable to the ownership of
Xxxxxx Corner; however, the submission of these proposed
lease terms for your consideration does not constitute an
offer to lease the above-referenced premises to you or a
reservation of or an option for said premises. Any lease will
become effective only upon execution and delivery thereof by
both the Landlord and Tenant.

If these terms meet with your approval, please sign below
indicating your intention to lease and return to me, together
with your most recent financial statement and restaurant
menu. Thereafter, I will submit the information to Landlord
for its review and acceptance.

If you have any questions, please contact me.

Very truly yours,

                                        ACCEPTED AND AGREED:

Leasing Representative   _____

                                _____

                                                Date

Appendix C

A Typical Store Lease

INDENTURE OF LEASE

THIS INDENTURE made this 26th day of March, 1986 by and between WILLIMANTIC ASSOCIATES, a Connecticut Limited Partnership, acting herein by RICHARD D. BRONSON, with offices c/o Bronson Hutensky Companies, CityPlace, 185 Asylum Street, Hartford, Connecticut, hereinafter referred to as "Landlord", and MORTON BROWN, Colonial Drive, Columbia, Connecticut, hereinafter referred to as "Tenant".

W I T N E S S E T H :

1. PREMISES

(a) Landlord leases to Tenant and Tenant rents from Landlord those certain premises, as part of now or hereafter to be erected in the Shopping Center (hereinafter referred to as "Shopping Center"), located on the westerly side of Connecticut Route 195, in the Town of Mansfield, County of Tolland and State of Connecticut, which premises are more particularly described as follows:

> A kiosk has a gross leasable area of approximately 200 square feet designated as K-3 on Exhibit A attached.

(b) Wherever in this lease reference is---------------------- made to the "Shopping Center" it is understood to mean that portion of the property owned by the Landlord or controlled by the Landlord under a leasehold interest. (c) The boundaries and location of the Demised Premises are outlined in red on a diagram of the Shopping Center, which is attached hereto and made a part hereof and marked Exhibit A. Said Exhibit A sets forth the general lay-

Sam: pg. 21 section 28 § Merchants Assoc.
pg. 21 section 27 license to common area

out of the Shopping Center and shall not be deemed to be a warranty, representation or agreement on the part of Landlord that
said Shopping Center will be exactly as indicated on said diagram
Landlord may relocate the Demised Premises and may increase,
reduce or change the number, dimensions or locations of the walks
buildings and parking areas (in any manner whatsoever) as Landlord shall deem proper, and reserves the right to make alterations or additions to, and to build additional stories on the
building in which the Demised Premises are contained and to add
buildings adjoining the same or elsewhere in the Shopping Center.
(d) Use and occupancy by Tenant of the Demised Premises shall
include the use in common with others of the common areas and
facilities, as hereinafter more fully provided. (e) Nothing
herein contained shall be construed as a grant or rental by Landlord to Tenant of the roof and exterior walls of the building or
buildings of which the Demised Premises form a part, or of the
walks and other common areas beyond the Demised Premises.

     2.   TERM

          The term of this Lease shall be for ten (10) years
commencing as provided in Paragraph 3 below, unless sooner
terminated or extended as hereinafter provided

     2A. RENEWAL OPTION

     Landlord herein grants Tenant the right and option to
extend this Lease for one (1) period of five (5) years from
the termination date hereof, providing written notice is given
to the Landlord at least six (6) months prior to the termination of the original term, and providing that the Tenant is not
then in default. If Tenant shall have exercised the option
as aforementioned, the term of this Lease shall be extended for

-2-

said additional period upon all of the same terms, provisions
and conditions, except as hereinafter provided. The mean level
of the Bureau of Labor Statistics Cost of Living Index (National)
during the year XXXX 1996 shall be the base for the adjustment upward
of minimum rent during the said option period. If upon the
commencement of the option period, the Level of said Cost of
Living Index shall be in excess of the aforesaid base, the minimum annual rental payable during such option period shall be
increased by the same percentage as the percentage change in
said base level; but in no event shall the minimum annual
rental be less than the minimum annual rental during the last Lease Year of the
original term. As an illustration only: If the Cost of
Living Index as of the first day of the option period has
gone up to 10% over the base, then the minimum annual rental
payable during such option period shall be increased by 10%.

As soon as all facts are known, the parties agree to
execute an instrument modifying the minimum rental figure, if
the same needs to be modified with respect to the option
period.

In the event that the aforesaid option to extend is duly
exercised, all references contained in this Lease to the term
hereof, whether by number of years or number of months, shall
be construed to refer to the original term hereof, as extended
as aforesaid, whether or not specific reference thereto is
made in this Lease.

-2A-

3. COMMENCEMENT DATE

                                           (the "Commencement Date")

        The term of this Lease shall commence/upon the earlier

of the following dates: (a) * ~~Novixlxdxxx1986xx~~ or (b) the date

on which Tenant shall open the Demised Premises for business.

In the event Tenant shall, or be required to, open for business

on a---

day other than the first day of the month, then the rent shall

be immediately paid for such partial month prorated on the

basis of a thirty (30) day month and the term of this Lease shall

be extended for the number of days from the commencement date to

the first day of the month next succeeding. Tenant shall, upon

request by Landlord, execute and deliver to Landlord a written

declaration in recordable form: (1) ratifying this lease; (2)

expressing the commencement and termination dates thereof; (3)

certifying that this lease is in full force and effect and has not

been assigned, modified, supplemented or amended (except by such

writings as shall be stated); (4) that all conditions under this

lease to be performed by Landlord have been satisfied; (5) that

there are no defenses or offsets against the enforcement of this

lease by the Landlord, or stating those claimed by Tenant; (6)

the amount of advance rental, if any, (or none if such is the

case) paid by Tenant; (7) the date to which rental has been paid;

and (8) the amount of security deposited with Landlord. Such

declaration shall be executed and delivered by Tenant from time

to time as may be requested by Landlord. Landlord's mortgage

lenders and/or purchasers shall be entitled to rely upon same.

  * Thirty (30) days subsequent to Tenant's Possession date.

-3-

4.   <u>USE</u>

Tenant shall use the Demised Premises solely for the purpose
of conducting the retail business of sale of boxed and loose
candy, caramel corn and small novelties. Tenant shall not use
or permit or suffer the use of the Demised Premises for any other
business or purpose without the prior written consent of Landlord,
which consent shall not be unreasonably withheld.

5.   <u>MINIMUM RENT</u>

(a) Commencing with the Commencement Date, the minimum rent
shall be as hereinafter provided, which rent shall be payable in
equal monthly installments, in advance, on the first day of each

month during the Lease term. The minimum rent shall be ~~EIGHT~~ TEN
THOUSAND DOLLARS ($10,000.00) ~~X$8,000X~~ per annum, for the ~~XXXBXXt wXXXX2XXXX6%X~~
term of this Lease.
~~XXXXXXXXXXXXXXXXXXXXXXXXXXXXXXXXXXXXXXXXXXXXXXXXXXXXXXXXXXXX~~
~~XXXXXXXXXXXXXXXXXXXXXXXXXXXXXXXXXXXXXXXXXXXXXXXXXXXXXXXXXXXXXXXX~~
~~XXXXXXXXXXXXXXXXXXXXXXXXXXXXXXXXXXXXXXXXXXXXXXXXXXXXXXXXXXXXXXXXXX~~
~~XXXXXXXX~~ However, the mean level of the Bureau of Labor Statistics
Cost of Living Index (National) during the year 1986 shall be the
base for the adjustment upward of annual minimum rent during the
sixth through tenth Lease Years. If upon the commencement of each
Lease Year commencing with the sixth Lease Year, the Level of said
Cost of Living Index shall be in excess of the aforesaid base,
the minimum annual rental payable during such Lease Year shall be
increased by the same percentage as the percentage change in said
base level; but in no event shall the minimum annual rental be less
than the minimum annual rental during the immediately preceding
Lease Year. As an illustration only: If the Cost of Living Index
as of the first day of the sixth Lease Year has gone up to 10% over
the base, then the minimum annual rental payable during the sixth
Lease Year shall be increased by 10% of $12,000, i.e. $13,200.

As soon as all facts are known, the parties agree to execute
an instrument modifying the minimum rental figure, if the same
needs to be modified with respect to the sixth Lease Year and
each Lease Year thereafter.

-4-

HYMAN, HARDING, SBARGE & DRONEY, P.C. • CORPORATE CENTER WEST • 433 SOUTH MAIN STREET • WEST HARTFORD, CONNECTICUT 06110 • (203) 561-3250

(b) The phrase "minimum rent" shall mean the fixed minimum rent above specified without any set-offs or deductions whatosever and without any prior demand being required therefor. Further, the fixed minimum rent shall be increased by any sales or rent tax which is or may be chargeable against the Demised Premises, the minimum rent, the additional rent and/or the percentage rent as herein defined. Simultaneously with the execution of this Lease, Tenant has paid to Landlord the first month's rent, receipt whereof, if by check subject to collection, is hereby acknowledged.

(c) It is the intention of the parties that the rent payable hereunder shall be net to Landlord, so that this Lease shall yield to Landlord the net annual basic minimum rent specified herein during the term of this Lease, and that all costs, expenses and obligations of every kind and nature whatsoever relating to the Demised Premises shall be paid by Tenant, except as specifically set forth in this Lease, and shall be deemed to be and shall become additional rent hereunder whether or not the same be designated as such and Landlord shall have the same remedies for failure to pay same as for a nonpayment of rent.

(d) Lease Year shall mean each twelve (12) consecutive month period from the first of the month immediately following the Commencement Date plus, for the first Lease Year, the number of days from the Commencement Date, if other than on the first day of a month, to the first day of the following month. For example, if this Lease commences March 10, 1986, the first Lease Year is March 10, 1986 through March 31, 1987 and the second Lease Year is April 1, 1987 through March 31, 1988.

HYMAN, HARDING, SBARGE & DRONEY, P.C. • CORPORATE CENTER WEST • 433 SOUTH MAIN STREET • WEST HARTFORD, CONNECTICUT 06110 • (203) 561-3250

PARAGRAPHS 6, 7 and 8 INTENTIONALLY OMITTED.

9. <u>ADDITIONAL RENT</u>

In addition to the foregoing minimum rent,----------
all other payments to be made by Tenant, either to Landlord or to
Merchants' Association, if any, shall be deemed to be and shall
become additional rent hereunder whether or not the same be designated as such; and shall be due and payable on demand or together
with the next succeeding installment of rent, whichever shall
first occur together with interest thereon at the then prevailing
legal rate; and Landlord shall have the same remedies for failure
to pay the same as for a nonpayment of rent. Landlord, at its
election, shall have the right to pay or do any act which requires
the expenditure of any sums of money by reason of the failure or
neglect of Tenant to perform any of the provisions of this lease,
and in the event Landlord shall at its election pay such sums or
do such acts requiring the expenditure of monies, Tenant agrees
to pay Landlord, upon demand, all such sums, and the sum so paid
by Landlord, together with interest thereon, shall be deemed additional rent and be payable as such.

10. <u>NO PARTNERSHIP</u>

Landlord shall in no event be construed, held or become
in any way or for any purpose a partner, associate or joint

HYMAN, KEITH, HARDING & HUTENSKY   100 CONSTITUTION PLAZA, HARTFORD, CONNECTICUT 06103

venturer of Tenant or any party associated with Tenant in the
conduct of its business or otherwise.

    11.   PLACE OF PAYMENTS

    All payments required to be paid and all reports required
to be rendered by Tenant to Landlord shall be delivered to the
office of Landlord as above mentioned and, except as is provided
in Paragraph 9 above, without any prior demand for the same, and
without deduction or offset.

    PARAGRAPH 12 INTENTIONALLY OMITTED.

    13.   CONSTRUCTION

    Tenant shall accept the Demised Premises in their "as is"
condition on the express understanding that Landlord has made no
representations or warranties concerning the Demised Premises or
the equipment therein or thereon.

    Tenant shall have the right to remodel or renovate the
kiosk on the following terms and conditions:

    (a) the plans for the remodeling or renovation are
approved in writing by Landlord prior to any such work being com-
menced. Such approval not to be unreasonably withheld.

    XXXXXXXXXXXXXXXXXXXXXXXXXXXXXXXXXXXXXXXXXXXXXXXXXXXXXXXX
XXXXXXXXXXXXXXXXXXXXXXXXXXXXXXXXXXXXXXX

    14. · TENANT'S INSTALLATIONS AND ALTERATIONS

    Tenant shall not do any construction work or alterations,
nor shall Tenant install any equipment or trade fixtures
without first obtaining Landlord's written approval and consent.
Tenant shall present to Landlord plans and specifications for such
work at the time approval is sought. Tenant shall not commence
any such work without first delivering to the Landlord a policy
or policies of compensation, liability and property damage insurance, naming Landlord as additional insured, in limits and with

companies acceptable to the Landlord, as well as a completion
bond in a form and issued by a surety company acceptable to the
Landlord. Any alterations, additions, improvements and fixtures
installed or paid for by the Tenant upon the interior or exterior
of the Demised Premises, other than unattached moveable trade
fixtures and decorations, shall upon the expiration or earlier
termination of this Lease become the property of the Landlord.
Landlord shall have the right to order Tenant to terminate Tenant's
construction work at any time when such work interferes with
normal operation of the Shopping Center. Upon notification from
Landlord to Tenant to cease work, Tenant shall remove from the
premises all agents, employees and contractors of Tenant forthwith,
until such time as Landlord shall have given its consent in writing for resumption of work, which consent shall not be unreasonably
withheld, and Tenant shall in connection therewith have no claim
for damages of any nature whatsoever against Landlord. In the
event that Tenant engages in the preparation of food or baked goods
or engages in the use, sale or storing of inflammable or combus-
tible material, Tenant shall install chemical extinguishing devices
(such as ansul) approved by the fire insurance rating organization
and shall keep these devices under service as required by the
fire insurance rating organization; and shall also install a gas
cut-off, if gas is used in the Demised Premises. If Tenant fails
to install said installations and subscribe to the servicing of
such installations, Landlord shall have the right to enter the
Demised Premises to make necessary installations and charge the
cost of such installations to Tenant as additional rent. If
Landlord does not elect to make such installations, Tenant shall
pay as additional rent any increase in insurance premium attributable to the failure to make such installation.

-7-

15. OPERATION OF BUSINESS

Tenant shall (a) conduct its business in the entire
Demised Premises; (b) remain open for business during customary
business days and hours for such business in the city or trade
area where the Shopping Center is located and shall remain open
with respect to times of opening or closing for such days, nights
and hours as the department store(s) and/or the majority of the
tenants located within the Shopping Center are open for business
or for such further days or additional hours as required by Landlord; (c) ~~xxxxxxxxxxxxxxxxxxxxxxxxxxxxxxxxxxxxxxxxxxxxxxxxx~~
~~xxxxxxxxxxxxxxxxxxxxxxxxxxxxxxxxxxxxxx~~ (d) adequately staff its store
with sufficient employees to handle the maximum business and carry
sufficient stock of merchandise of such size, character and quality
to accomplish the same; (e) maintain displays of merchandise in
the display windows, if any; (f) keep the display windows, and
signs, if any, well lighted during the hours from sundown to 12
midnight; (g) keep the Demised Premises and exterior and interior
portions of windows, doors and all other glass or plate glass fixtures in a neat, clean, sanitary and safe condition; (h) warehouse
store or stock only such goods, wares and merchandise as Tenant
intends to offer for sale at retail; (i) if the Demised Premises
contain a mezzanine, restrict the use thereof for storage purposes
only; (j) neither solicit business nor distribute advertising
matter in the parking or other common areas; (k) not place any
weight upon the floors which shall exceed Seventy-Five (75)
pounds per square foot of floor space covered; ~~(xxxxxxxxxxxxxxxxx~~

xxxxxxxxxxxxxxxxxxxxxxxxxxxxxxxxxxxxxxxxxxxxxxxxxxxxxxxxxxxxxxxxxxxxxxxxxxxxxxxx
xxxxxxxxxxxxxxxxxxxxxxxxxxxxxxxxxxxxxxxxxxxxxxxxxxxxxxxxxxxxxxxxxx (m) Tenant
shall not have any displays on the sides of the kiosk; and (n)
use the insignia or other identifying mark of the Shopping Center
designated by Landlord in Tenant's advertising, whether printed
or visual, and make reference to the name of the Shopping Center
in each instance of audio advertising.

16. COMPLIANCE WITH LAWS

Tenant shall, at its own cost and expense: (a) comply
with all governmental laws, ordinances, orders and regulations
affecting the Demised Premises now in force or which hereafter
may be in force; (b) comply with and execute all rules, requirements and regulations of the Board of Fire Underwriters,
Landlord's insurance companies and other organizations establishing insurance rates; (c) not suffer, permit or commit any waste or
nuisance; (d) not conduct any auction, distress, fire or bankruptcy sale; and (e) install fire extinguishers in accordance
with insurance requirements.

PARAGRAPH 17 INTENTIONALLY OMITTED.

18. SIGNS, AWNINGS AND CANOPIES

If required by the Landlord, the Tenant shall purchase
identification signs, both for the interior of the mall (if a mall
exists) and for the exterior of the building, each of said signs
to be of a size and design to be approved in writing by Landlord,

-9-

and installed at a place designated by Landlord. Other than the
foregoing and except as provided in Exhibit B, Tenant shall not
place or suffer to be placed or maintain any sign, awning or canopy
in, upon or outside the Demised Premises or in the Shopping Center
or within a half mile of the Shopping Center; nor shall Tenant
place in the display windows, any sign, decoration, lettering or
advertising matter of any kind without first obtaining Landlord's
approval and consent in each instance. Tenant shall maintain any
such signs or other installation, as may be approved in good condition and repair.

19. ASSIGNMENT

Tenant shall not assign, mortgage or encumber this lease,
in whole or in part, or sublet all or any part of the Demised
Premises without the prior written consent of Landlord, which consent shall not be unreasonably withheld with respect to a subletting or assignment. The-------------------------------------
consent by Landlord to any assignment or subletting shall not
constitute a waiver of the necessity for such consent to any subsequent assignment or subletting. This prohibition against
assigning or subletting shall be construed to include a prohibition
against any assignment or subletting by operation of law. If this
lease be assigned or if the Demised Premises or any part thereof
be occupied by anybody other than Tenant, Landlord may collect
rent from the assignee, or occupant and apply the net amount
collected to the rent herein reserved, but no such assignment,
underletting, occupancy or collection shall be deemed a waiver of
this provision or the acceptance of the assignee, undertenant or
occupant as Tenant, or as a release of Tenant from the further performance by Tenant of the provisions on its part to be observed or
performed herein. Notwithstanding any assignment or sublease,
Tenant shall remain fully and primarily liable hereunder and shall
not be released from performing any of the terms of this Lease.

-10-

20. REPAIRS

Landlord shall not be required to make any repairs or
improvements of any kind upon the Demised Premises except for
necessary structural repairs. Tenant shall at its own cost and
expense, take good care of and make necessary repairs to the
interior of the Demised Premises, and the fixtures and equipment
therein and appurtenances thereto, including the exterior and
interior windows, window frames, doors, door frames and entrances,
store fronts, signs, showcases, floor coverings, non-structural
interior walls, columns and partitions; and lighting, heating,
air conditioning, plumbing and sewerage facilities and equipment.
All parts of the interior of the Demised Premises shall be painted
or otherwise decorated by Tenant periodically as determined by
Landlord. Tenant agrees to keep and maintain in good condition
the electrical equipment and heating equipment in the Demised
Premises and keep in force a standard maintenance agreement on all
heating and air conditioning equipment and provide a copy of said
maintenance agreement to Landlord.

21. TENANT'S FAILURE TO REPAIR

If Tenant (a) refuses or neglects to make repairs, or
(b) if Landlord is required to make exterior or structural repairs
by reason of Tenant's negligent acts or omissions, Landlord shall
have the right, but shall not be obligated, to make such repairs
on behalf of and for the account of Tenant. In such event, such

work shall be paid for in full by Tenant as additional rent
promptly upon receipt of a bill therefor.

      22. LIENS

        Should any mechanic's or other lien be filed against
the Demised Premises or any part thereof for any reason whatsoever by reason of Tenant's acts or omissions or because of a
claim against Tenant, Tenant shall cause the same to be cancelled
and discharged of record by bond or otherwise within Ten (10)
days after notice by Landlord.

      23. UTILITIES

        Landlord shall not be liable in the event of any interruption in the
supply of any utilities, except if caused by the negligence of Landlord, its
agents, servants or employees. Tenant agrees that------------------------

it will not install any equipment which will exceed or overload
the capacity of any utility facilities and that if any equipment
installed by Tenant shall require additional utility facilities,
the same shall be installed at Tenant's expense in accordance with
plans and specifications to be approved in writing by Landlord.
Tenant shall be solely responsible for and shall promptly pay
all charges for use or consumption for heat, sewer, water, gas,
electricity or any other utility services from the date it enters
the Demised Premises to commence fixturing and throughout the term
of this Lease. Should Landlord elect to supply any utility
services either individually or through a private contractor,
Tenant agrees to purchase and pay for the same as additional rent
at the applicable rates charged by the utility company furnishing
the same. Should Landlord elect not to install a water meter in
the Demised Premises, or be required by the local water authority
to channel Tenant's water through the Landlord's master meter,

the Tenant agrees to reimburse the Landlord each month as additional rent, an amount based upon the Tenant's estimate of the Tenant
average annual water supply, except that in the event the local
water authority, at any time during the term of this Lease, estim-
ates that Tenant's consumption of water exceeds Tenant's estimate,
then the monthly reimbursement shall thereafter be based upon
the local water authority's estimate. Should the Landlord elect to
install a central heating and/or air conditioning system and
offer to supply either chilled air or water, or warm air or water,
Tenant agrees to adapt Landlord's heating and cooling equipment
and at Tenant's expense to connect said equipment to facilities
provided by the Landlord, and to pay for such chilled air or
water and/or warm air or water, as metered through meters installed
by the Landlord at rates agreed upon, provided that Tenant shall
not be charged more than the rates it would be charged for the same
services if furnished direct to the premises by a public utility
company.

  In addition to the foregoing, Tenant shall pay its
pro rata share (using the same ratio as set forth in Paragraph 24)
of any flat charge for sprinkler heads imposed by the utility
supplying water.

  24. <u>TAXES</u>

  Landlord will pay in the first instance all real property
taxes, including extraordinary and/or special assessments, (and
all costs and fees incurred in contesting the same) hereinafter
collectively referred to as "Taxes", which may be levied or
assessed by the lawful taxing authorities against the land,
buildings and all other improvements in the Shopping Center.
For the purposes hereunder, the cost of sanitary sewers shall
be included as part of Tenant's obligation for real estate taxes
and assessments-in the event said sewers are installed during the
term hereof.

Tenant shall pay to Landlord as additional rent that portion of such Taxes equal to the product obtained by multiplying said taxes by Tenant's Proportionate Share. As used in this Lease, Tenant's Proportionate Share shall mean a fraction, the numerator of which shall be the gross leasable area of the Demised Premises and the denominator of which shall be (i) 253,866 for the first five Lease Years, and (ii) 101,835 commencing with the sixth Lease Year and thereafter during the term of this Lease and any renewal thereof.

Tenant agrees to pay said share of Taxes in advance in monthly installments as reasonably estimated by Landlord, along with Tenant's regular monthly rental payment. Should the actual taxes attributable to the Demised Premises be more than the amount estimated by Landlord and paid by Tenant as aforesaid, then Tenant's monthly payment as aforesaid shall be adjusted from time to time throughout the term of this Lease to more nearly reflect the actual Taxes.

Within thirty (30) days from the date upon which the first tax payment accruing during the terms of this Lease is due, Tenant shall pay to Landlord in a lump sum its proportionate share of said payment in accordance with the formula hereinbefore set forth. Thereafter, Tenant shall pay to Landlord its monthly tax payment as hereinbefore computed (and as adjusted from time to time) which payment shall be an advance against the next payment of Taxes due with respect to the Shopping Center.

HYMAN, HARDING, SBARGE & DRONEY, P.C. • CORPORATE CENTER WEST • 433 SOUTH MAIN STREET • WEST HARTFORD, CONNECTICUT 06110 • (203) 561-3250

Within thirty (30) days from the date Landlord presents each ensuing tax bill, Tenant will pay to Landlord in a lump sum that amount by which Tenant's actual Proportionate Share of the Taxes exceeds the amount of Tenant's estimated payments theretofore. Should the amount of Tenant's estimated payments exceed Tenant's Proportionate Share of the Taxes, then Landlord shall, within said thirty (30) day period refund such overpayment to Tenant. A tax bill (or copy thereof) submitted by Landlord to Tenant shall be sufficient evidence of the amount of Taxes assessed or levied against the parcel or real property to which the bill relates. Tenant's Proportionate Share of Taxes shall be adjusted in the first and last year of the Lease to take into consideration the fact that Tenant may only be in possession for a partial tax year.

The Tax year of any lawful authority commencing during any lease year shall be deemed to correspond to such lease year. Should the taxing authorities include in such Taxes the value of any improvements made by Tenant or include machinery, equipment, fixtures, inventory or other personal property or assets of Tenant, then Tenant shall also pay the entire personal and real estate taxes for such items.

Should any governmental taxing authority acting under any present or future law, ordinance or regulation, levy, assess or impose a tax, excise and/or assessment (other than an income or franchise tax) upon or against or in any way related to the land and buildings comprising the Shopping Center, either by

way of substitution for or in addition to any existing tax on
land and buildings or otherwise, Tenant shall be responsible for
and shall pay to Landlord, as additional rent, its proportionate
share as set forth above of such tax, excise and/or assessment.

25. COMMON MALL AND COMMON PARKING AREA MAINTENANCE.

All common areas, parking area and other facilities in
or about the Shopping Center provided by Landlord shall be subject
to the exclusive control and management of Landlord. Landlord
shall have the right to construct, maintain and operate lighting
and other facilities on all said areas and improvements; to police
the same; to change the area, level, location and arrangement of
parking areas and other facilities; to build multi-story parking
facilities; to restrict parking by Tenant, their officers, agents
and employees; to enforce parking charges (by operation of meters
or otherwise) and in such event the net proceeds from such
charges after deduction of the cost of the same shall be applied
toward the reduction of the cost of parking area maintenance; to
close all or any portion of said areas or facilities to such
extent as may be legally sufficient to prevent a dedication
thereof or the accrual of any right to any person or the public
therein; to close temporarily all or any portion of the parking
areas or facilities to discourage non-customer parking. Landlord
shall operate and maintain the common facilities in such manner
as Landlord in its reasonable discretion shall determine, and
Landlord shall have full right and authority to employ and discharge all personnel with respect thereto.

26. COST OF MAINTAINING THE COMMON PARKING AREAS AND COMMON MALL AREAS

A.   Common Area Maintenance

The Tenant agrees to pay to the Landlord, as additional rent, payable in advance as additional rent in monthly installments as reasonably estimated by Landlord, that proportion of the annual total cost incurred by the Landlord in operating and maintaining the common areas in the shopping center, equal to the sum of the total cost of said common area maintenance multiplied by a fraction the numerator of which is the gross leaseable area of the premises demised to the Tenant and the denominator of which is ~~XXXXXXXXXXXXXXX~~ ~~XXXXX~~ Landlord shall, prior to pro-rating the cost of such maintenance as set forth herein, deduct from the total annual cost incurred by Landlord in such Common Area Maintenance the total of the actual amounts of the contributions toward such cost received by Landlord from Caldor, Sage-Allen and A & P.   Landlord shall have the right to periodically, but not more frequently than monthly, compute the actual cost of common area maintenance and bill Tenant its proportionate share of said cost for said period. Said bill shall be paid by Tenant as additional rent within ten (10) days of the date rendered.   Should the amount of the common area maintenance paid by Tenant during any Lease Year exceed Tenant's actual Proportionate Share of the cost of common area maintenance for said Lease Year, Landlord shall within thirty (30) days from the end of such Lease Year, credit such excess payment against Tenant's common parking area charges in the next succeeding Lease Year.   Within sixty (60) days after the commencement of each Lease Year, the Landlord may, at its option, adjust the Tenant's monthly contribution towards common

* 253,866 square feet during years One (1) through Five (5) of the term of this Lease and 101,835 square feet during the years Six (6) through Ten (10) of this Lease and any renewals thereof.

-16A-

HYMAN, HARDING, SBARGE & DRONEY, P.C.   •   CORPORATE CENTER WEST   •   433 SOUTH MAIN STREET   •   WEST HARTFORD, CONNECTICUT 06110   •   (203) 561-3250

area maintenance to more nearly reflect the actual expenses incurred during the prior Lease Year.

The term "common parking area maintenance" shall mean:
all costs and expenses of every kind and nature paid or incurred
by Landlord during the Lease Year (including appropriate reserves)
in operating, managing, equipping, policing (as and to the
extent provided by Landlord), protecting, insuring (including
all insurance required under Paragraph 29 hereof), lighting,
correcting, repairing, replacing and maintaining the shopping center's
common areas and facilities therein (including all curbs and
sidewalks), all as they may from time to time exist. Such common areas and facilities shall not, however, include the Enclosed
Mall. For the purposes of this Paragraph 26A, such costs shall
include, but not be limited to, all costs and expenses of
security, fire protection and traffic direction and control;
cleaning and removal of rubbish, dirt, debris, snow and ice;
planting, replanting and replacing flowers and landscaping;
water and sewerage charges; premiums for liability, property
damage, fire, extended coverage, malicious mischief, vandalism,
workmen's compensation, employees' liability and other insurance;
wages and fringe benefits, unemployment taxes and social
security taxes and personal property taxes thereon; fees
for audits, licenses and permits; costs and expenses of supplies,
operation of sound speakers and other equipment supplying music;
all charges for utility services, together with all costs and
expenses in maintaining lighting fixtures (including the cost
of light bulbs and electricity); reasonable depreciation of,
and rental paid for the leasing of equipment used in such common
areas and facilities; and administrative costs and overhead
expenses equal to 15% of the total of the foregoing costs

-17-

(except appropriate reserves). There shall be excluded from
the foregoing costs, the cost of equipment properly chargeable to the capital account and depreciation of the original
cost of construction of such common areas and facilities. Cost
of common area maintenance shall not include expenses incurred
by the Landlord solely for the operating, maintaining, repairing
or servicing of the Enclosed Mall and included as "common
mall area maintenance".

    B.   <u>Enclosed Mall Maintenance</u>

       Landlord shall maintain, repair, heat and air-condition
the Enclosed Mall and common facilities located therein, in the
same manner as the Landlord shall in its discretion determine.
Tenant agrees to pay to Landlord as additional rent payable in
advance as additional rent in monthly installments as reasonably
estimated by Landlord
along with the regular rental payments or that proportion of the
annual total cost incurred by the Landlord in operating and maintaining the Enclosed Mall and the common areas and facilities
therein contained, equal to the sum of the total of said cost
multiplied by a fraction the numerator of which is the gross
leaseable area of the premises demised to Tenant and the denominator of which is XXXXXXXXXXXXXXXXXXXXX*. Landlord shall
have the right to periodically, but not more frequently than
monthly, compute the actual cost of Enclosed Mall maintenance
and bill Tenant its proportionate share of said costs for said

---

*253,866 square feet during years one (1) through five (5) of the term of
this Lease and 101,835 square feet during the years six (6) through ten (10)
of this Lease and any renewals thereof.

HYMAN, KEITH, HARDING & HUTENSKY   100 CONSTITUTION PLAZA, HARTFORD, CONNECTICUT 06103

period, reduced by Tenant's monthly payments as hereinbefore set forth. Said bill shall be paid by Tenant as additional rent within ten (10) days of the date rendered. Should the cost of Enclosed Mall maintenance paid by Tenant during any Lease Year exceed Tenant's actual proportionate share of cost of Enclosed Mall maintenance, Landlord shall, within thirty (30) days from the end of such Lease Year, credit such excess payment against Tenant's Enclosed Mall maintenance charges in the next succeeding Lease Year.

Within sixty (60) days after the commencement of each Lease Year, the Landlord, at its option, may adjust the Tenant's monthly contribution towards Enclosed Mall maintenance to more nearly reflect the actual expenses incurred during the prior Lease Year.

"Enclosed Mall maintenance" shall mean: all costs and expenses of every kind and nature paid or incurred by Landlord during the lease year (including appropriate reserves) in operating, managing, equipping, policing (as and to the extent provided by Landlord), protecting, insuring (including all insurance required under Paragraph 29 hereof) lighting, ventilating, heating, air-conditioning, correcting, repairing, replacing and maintaining the center's Enclosed Mall and facilities therein, all as they

may from time to time exist. Such Enclosed Mall and facilities
shall not, however, include the parking areas. For the purpose
of this Paragraph 26B, such costs shall include, but not be
limited to, all costs and expenses of security, fire protection, cleaning and removal of rubbish, dirt, debris, planting, replanting and replacing flowers and landscaping; water
and sewerage charges; preimums for liability, property damage,
fire, extended coverage, malicious mischief, vandalism, workmen's compensation, employees' liability and other insurance;
wages and fringe benefits, unemployment taxes and social
security taxes and personal property taxes thereon; fees
for audits, licenses and permits; costs and expenses of supplies
operation of sound speakers and other equipment supplying music;
all charges for utility services, together with all costs and
expenses in maintaining lighting fixtures (including the cost
of light bulbs and electricity); reasonable depreciation of,
and rental paid for the leasing of equipment used in such Enclosed
Mall and facilities; and administrative costs and overhead
expenses equal to 15% of the total of the foregoing costs
(except appropriate reserves). There shall be excluded from
the foregoing costs, the cost of equipment properly chargeable to the capital account and depreciation of the original
cost of construction of such common areas and facilities. Cost
of parking area maintenance shall not be included in Enclosed
Mall maintenance.

27. LICENSE TO COMMON AREAS

In order to establish that the Shopping Center, and any
portion thereof, is and will continue to remain private property,
the Landlord shall have unrestricted right in the Landlord's sole
discretion, with respect to the entire Shopping Center, and/or
any portion thereof owned or controlled by the Landlord, to close
the same to the general public for one (1) day in each calendar
year, and in connection therewith, to seal off all entrances to
the Shopping Center, or any portion thereof. All common areas
and facilities which Tenant may be permitted to use and occupy are
to be used and occupied under a revocable license, and if any such
license be revoked or if the amount of such areas be changed or
diminished, Landlord shall not be subject to any liability nor
shall Tenant be entitled to any compensation or diminution or
abatement of rent nor shall revocation or diminution of such areas
be deemed constructive or actual eviction.

28. MERCHANTS' ASSOCIATION

In the event a Merchants' Association is established
for the Shopping Center, the Tenant will promptly become a member
of, and during the term of this lease, participate fully, and
remain in good standing in said Merchants' Association (as soon
as the same has been formed). Members will abide by the regulations
of such Association. The Tenant agrees to pay minimum dues to the
Merchants' Association in the amount of Ten (10.00) Dollars

-21-

per month, to be used solely for advertising and promotional purposes, payable in advance on the first day of each month, subject
however, to annual adjustments approved by a majority vote of the
members of the Association increasing said dues to the extent required by increases in the costs of promotional, public relations
and advertising services. The continuing monthly contributions by
Tenant to the Association will be adjusted by a percentage equal to
the percentage increase or decrease from the base period of the
United States, Department of Labor, Bureau of Labor Statistics
Cost of Living Index, provided that said Index has increased or
decreased by at least Ten (10%) Percent or more from the base
period. The term "Base Period" shall refer to the date on which
said Index is published, which is closest to the date of the form-
ation of the Merchants' Association. The Tenant agrees to advertise in any and all special Merchants' Association newspaper
sections or advertisements
and agrees to cooperate in the Merchants' Association special sales
and promotions. Nothing in the by-laws or regulations of the
said Association, a copy of which is attached hereto as Exhibit
D, shall affect Tenant's obligations under this lease. The
failure of any other tenant or any adjoining department store to
contribute or be a member shall in no way release the Tenant

HYMAN, KEITH, HARDING & HUTENSKY   100 CONSTITUTION PLAZA, HARTFORD, CONNECTICUT 06103

from Tenant's obligations hereunder, membership and participation in the Association being a covenant of this Lease. The Landlord agrees to contribute no less than Twenty (20%) Percent of the total amount of dues assessed and paid by the Tenant members of the Association. At the option of the Landlord, the Landlord may elect to contribute part or all of the services of a promotion director and/or secretary, in lieu of a cash contribution. The promotion director shall be under the exclusive control and supervision of the Landlord who shall have the sole authority to employ and discharge the promotion director.

29. INSURANCE

Construction work, described in Exhibit "B" hereof, whether performed or paid for by Landlord or Tenant, shall, upon its completion be insured by Landlord against fire and such other risks as are from time to time included in standard extended coverage endorsements in an amount equal to at least eighty (80%) percent of full insurable value thereof. With respect to all other decorations and improvements, Tenant shall maintain at its own cost and expense (a) Fire and extended coverage, vandalism malicious mischief and special extended coverage insurance in an amount adequate to cover the cost of replacement of all decorations and improvements in the Demised Premises in the event of a loss; and with respect to the Demised Premises generally and to any act or omissions of Tenant, its agents, contractors, employees servants, or licensees within the Shopping Center; and (b) PUBLIC LIABILITY INSURANCE on all occurrence basis with minimum limits of liability in an amount of Five Hundred Thousand ($500,000) Dollars for bodily injury, personal injury or death with respect to any one person and One Million ($1,000,000) Dollars for bodily injury, personal injury or death with respect to any one accident and

One Hundred Thousand ($100,000) Dollars with respect to damage
to property by water or otherwise; and (c) FIRE INSURANCE in an
amount adequate to cover the cost of replacement of all fixtures
and contents in the Demised Premises in the event of fire, extended coverage, vandalism, malicious mischief and special extended coverage.

Tenant agrees to pay to Landlord its proportionate share
of the cost of all insurance premiums paid in any lease year
with respect to the Shopping Center, including all insurance
premiums paid for fire and liability insurance with all its
endorsements, in the same proportionate share and as part of the
cost of common parking maintenance under Paragraph 26 hereof.

Tenant's proportionate share of insurance premiums as
aforesaid has been estimated at ten ($.10) cents per square foot
of gross leaseable area per annum or EIGHTEEN ($18) DOLLARS,
per annum. Tenant agrees to pay said share of insurance in advance in monthly installments of ONE and 50/100 ($1.50) DOLLARS,
along with Tenant's regular monthly rental payment. Should the
actual insurance premiums attributable to the Demised Premises be
more than ($.10) cents per square foot as aforesaid, then Tenant's
monthly payment as aforesaid shall be adjusted from time to time
throughout the term of this Lease to more nearly reflect the
actual insurance premiums. At the end of each lease year, Landlord shall compute Tenant's actual pro-rata share of the cost of
such insurance, and shall present Tenant with a bill indicating
such computation and Tenant shall pay within fifteen (15) days
of receipt of such bill, as additional rent, the amount by which
Tenant's pro-rata share of the cost of such insurance exceeds
Tenant's payments under this Paragraph 29.

30. LIABILITY

Except for the negligence of Landlord, its agents, servants and employees, Tenant shall (a) indemnify Landlord and save
it harmless from suits, actions, damages, liability and expense
in connection

-24-

HYMAN, KEITH, HARDING & HUTENSKY   100 CONSTITUTION PLAZA, HARTFORD, CONNECTICUT 06103

with loss of life, bodily or personal injury or property damage
arising from or out of the use or occupancy of the Demised Premises or any part thereof, or occasioned wholly or in part by any
act or omission of Tenant, its agents, contractors, employees,
servants, invitees, licensees or concessionaires, including the
sidewalks and common areas and facilities within the Shopping
Center development; and (b) Tenant shall store its property in
and shall occupy the Demised Premises and all other portions of
the Shopping Center at its own risk, and releases Landlord, to the
full extent permitted by law, from all claims of every kind
resulting in loss of life, personal or bodily injury or property
damage; (c) Landlord shall not be responsible or liable at any
time for any loss or damage to Tenant's merchandise, equipment,
fixtures or other personal property of Tenant or to Tenant's
business; and (d) Landlord shall not be responsible or liable to
Tenant or to those claiming by, through or under Tenant for any
loss or damage to either the person or property of Tenant that
may be occasioned by or through the acts or omissions of persons
occupying adjacent, connecting or adjoining premises; and (e)
Landlord shall not be responsible or liable to Tenant for any
defect, latent or otherwise, in any building in the Shopping Center
or any of the equipment, machinery, utilities, appliances or
apparatus therein, nor shall it be responsible or liable for any
injury, loss or damage to any person or to any property of Tenant
or other person caused by or resulting from bursting, breakage,
or by or from leakage, steam or snow or ice, running, backing up,

-25-

seepage, or the overflow of water or sewerage in any part of
said premises or for any injury or damage caused by or resulting
from acts of God or the elements, or for any injury or damage
caused by or resulting from any defect or act or omission in the
occupancy, construction, operation or use of any of said premises, buildings, machinery, apparatus or equipment by any person
or by or from the acts of negligence of any occupant of the
premises; (f) Tenant shall give prompt notice to Landlord in case
of fire or accidents in the Demised Premises or in the building
of which the Demised Premises are a part or of defects therein or
in any fixtures or equipment; (g) Tenant shall also pay all costs
expenses and reasonable attorney's fees that may be incurred or
paid by Landlord in enforcing the terms of this lease.

31. ADDITIONAL INSURANCE

Tenant agrees to insure and keep insured in the name of
Tenant and for and in the name of Landlord at Tenant's expense
(a) all outside plate glass in the Demised Premises, and (b) if
there is a boiler or air conditioning equipment in, on, adjoining
or beneath the Demised Premises, Tenant will insure and keep
insured said boiler or air conditioning equipment with broad form
boiler or machinery insurance in the amount of One Hundred Thousand ($100,000) Dollars.

32. INSURED'S WAIVER NOTICE

Any insurance procured by Tenant as herein required shall
be issued in the name of Landlord and Tenant by a company licensed
to do business in the state where the Shopping Center is located
and shall contain endorsements that (a) such insurance may not be
cancelled or amended with respect to Landlord by the insurance
company; and (b) Tenant shall be solely responsible for payment
of premiums for such insurance; and (c) in the event of payment

-26-

of any loss covered by such policy, Landlord shall be paid first
by the insurance company for its loss; and (d) Tenant waives its
right of subrogation against Landlord for any reason whatsoever,
and any insurance policies herein required to be procured by
Tenant shall contain an express waiver of any right of subrogation
by the insurance company against the Landlord. The original
policy of all such insurance shall be delivered to Landlord by
Tenant within Ten (10) days of inception of such policy by the
insurance company. The minimum limits of any insurance coverage
required herein shall not limit Tenant's liability under Paragraph
30.

33. INCREASE IN INSURANCE PREMIUMS

Tenant shall not stock, use or sell any article or do
anything in or about the Demised Premises which may be prohibited
by Landlord's insurance policies or any endorsements or forms
attached thereto, or which will increase any insurance rates and
premiums on the Demised Premises, the building of which they are
a part and all other buildings in the Shopping Center. Tenant
shall pay on demand any increase in premiums for Landlord's
insurance that may be charged on such insurance carried by Landlord
resulting from Tenant's use and occupancy of the Demised Premises
or the Shopping Center whether or not Landlord has consented to
the same. In determining whether increased premiums are the
result of Tenant's use, occupancy or vacancy of the Demised Premises, a schedule issued by the organization making the fire
insurance, extended coverage, vandalism and malicious mischief,
special extended coverage or any all-risk insurance rates for said
premises or any rule books issued by the rating organization or
similar bodies or by rating procedures or rules of Landlord's
insurance companies shall be conclusive evidence of the several

items and charges which make up the insurance rates and premiums
on the Demised Premises and the Shopping Center. If due to the
(a) occupancy, or (b) abandonment or (c) Tenant's failure to
occupy the Demised Premises as herein provided, any insurance
shall be cancelled by the insurance carrier or if the premiums
for any such insurance shall be increased, then in any of such
events Tenant shall indemnify and hold Landlord harmless and shall
pay on demand the increased cost of such insurance. Tenant also
shall pay in any such events any increased premium on the rent
insurance that may be carried by Landlord for its protection
against loss through fire or casualty.

Should the Tenant do any work within the Demised Premises
or carry on any activity not specifically allowed under the provisions of Paragraph 4 hereof and should such work or activity
cause the insurance premiums on the Demised Premises or the buildings of which the Demised Premises form a part to be increased,
unless the Landlord enter upon the Demised Premises to do any work
which may be required by the insurance carrier in order to prevent
such increase in cost, then the Tenant hereby agrees to pay, as
additional rent, the cost for said work plus ten (10) percent
of said cost for Landlord's profit and overhead. Said sum shall
be payable along with the next installment of rent following the
presentment of a bill to the Tenant.

34. DESTRUCTION

If the Demised Premises shall be partially damaged by any

casualty insurable under the Landlord's insurance policy, Landlord shall, upon receipt of the insurance proceeds, repair the same, and the minimum rent shall be abated proportionately as to that portion of the Demised Premises rendered untenantable. If the Demised Premises (a) by reason of such occurrence is rendered wholly untenantable or (b) should be damaged as a result of a risk which is not covered by Landlord's insurance or (c) should be damaged in whole or in part during the last Three (3) years, of the term or any renewal term hereof, or (d) the building of which it is a part, (whether the Demised Premises is damaged or not) or all of the buildings which then comprise the Shopping Center should be damaged to the extent of Fifty (50) Percent or more of the then monetary value thereof, or if any or all of the buildings or common areas of the Shopping Center are damaged, whether or not the Demised Premises are damaged to such an extent that the Shopping Center cannot, in the sole judgment of Landlord, be operated as an integral unit, then or in any of such events, Landlord may

END OF PAGE

-29-

either elect to repair the damage or may cancel this lease by
notice of cancellation within one hundred twenty (120) days after
such event and thereupon this lease shall expire, and Tenant shall
vacate and surrender the Demised Premises to Landlord. Tenant's
liability for rent upon the termination of this lease shall cease
as of the day following the event or damage. In the event Landlord elects to repair the damage insurable under Landlord's
policies, any abatement of rent shall end Five (5) days after
notice by Landlord to Tenant that the Demised Premises have been
repaired. Nothing in this paragraph shall be construed to abate
percentage rent, but the computation of such rent shall be based
upon the revised minimum rent as the same may be abated. If the
damage is caused by the negligence of Tenant or its employees,
agents, invitees, concessionaires there shall be no abatement of
rent. Unless this lease is terminated by Landlord, Tenant shall
repair and refixture the interior of the Demised Premises in a
manner and to at least a condition equal to that existing prior
to its destruction or casualty and the proceeds of all insurance
carried by Tenant on its property and improvements shall be held
in trust by Tenant for the purpose of said repair or replacement.

    35. CONDEMNATION

    (a) Total: If the whole of the Demised Premises shall
be acquired or taken by eminent domain for any public or quasi-
public use or purpose then this lease and the term herein shall
cease and terminate as of the date of title vesting in such
proceeding. (b) Partial: If any part of the Demised Premises
shall be taken as aforesaid, and such partial taking shall render that portion not so taken unsuitable for the business of
Tenant (except for the amount of floor space), then this lease
and the term hereof shall cease and terminate as aforesaid. If

such partial taking is not extensive enough to render the premises unsuitable for the business of Tenant, then this lease shall
continue in effect except that the minimum rent shall be reduced
in the same proportion that the floor area of the Demised Premises
(including basement) taken bears to the original floor area
demised and Landlord shall, upon receipt of the award in condemnation, make all necessary repairs or alterations to the building
in which the Demised Premises are located so as to constitute the
portion of the building not taken a complete architectural unit,
but such work shall not exceed the scope of the work to be done
by Landlord in originally constructing said building, nor shall
Landlord in any event be required to spend for such work an amount
in excess of the net amount received by Landlord as damages for
the part of the Demised Premises so taken. "Net Amount received
by Landlord" shall mean that part of the award in condemnation
after deducting all expenses in connection with the condemnation
proceedings, which is free and clear to Landlord of any collection
by mortgagees for the value of the diminished fee. (c) If more
than ten (10) percent of the floor area of the building in
which the Demised Premises are located shall be taken as aforesaid,
Landlord or Tenant may, by written notice to the other, terminate this Lease,
such termination to be effective as aforesaid. (d) If this lease
is terminated as provided in this paragraph, the rent shall be
paid up to the day that possession is so taken by public authority
and Landlord shall make an equitable refund of any rent paid by
Tenant in advance. (e) Award: Tenant shall not be entitled to
and expressly waives all claim to any condemnation award for any
taking, whether whole or partial, and whether for diminution in
value of the leasehold or to the fee, although Tenant shall have
the right, to the extent that the same shall not reduce Landlord's

-31-

award, to claim from the condemnor, but not from Landlord, such compensation as may be recoverable by Tenant in its own right for damage to Tenant's business and fixtures, if such claim can be made separate and apart from any award to Landlord and without prejudice to Landlord's award.

36. DEFAULT

If the Tenant shall make default in payment of the rents reserved hereunder for a period of ten (10) days after any of the same shall become due and payable as aforesaid, or if default shall be made by Tenant in any of the other covenants and agreements herein contained to be kept and fulfilled on the part of the Tenant for a period of ten (10) days after written notice of such default is given by the Landlord to the Tenant without action by the Tenant to remedy such default and continuance of such action to remedy such default to conclusion with reasonable diligence or if the Tenant shall file a voluntary petition in bankruptcy or take the benefit of any insolvency act or be dissolved or adjudicated a bankrupt, or if a receiver shall be appointed for its business or its assets and the appointment of such receiver is not vacated within sixty (60) days after such appointment, or if it shall make an assignment for the benefit of its creditors, or if the Tenant's interest herein shall be sold under execution, then and forthwith thereafter the Landlord shall have the right, at his option and without prejudice to his rights hereunder, to terminate this lease and to re-enter and take possession of the Demised Premises, or the Landlord, without such re-entry may recover possession of the Demised Premises in the manner prescribed by the statute relating to summary process, and any demand for rent, re-entry for condition broken, and any and all notices to quit, or other formalities of any nature, to which the Tenant

may be entitled, in such event, are hereby specifically waived;
and that after default made in any of the covenants contained
herein, the acceptance of rent or failure to re-enter by the
Landlord shall not be held to be a waiver of its right to terminate this lease, and the Landlord may re-enter and take
possession thereof the same as if no rent had been accepted after
such default. In addition thereto, on the happening of any of
the events hereinabove referred to, the Landlord may, at its
option, declare immediately due and payable all the remaining
installments of rent herein provided for and such amount, less the
fair rental value of the premises, for the residue of said term
shall be construed as liquidated damages and shall constitute a
debt provable in bankruptcy or receivership. For purposes of
this paragraph, "fair rental value" of the premises shall be deemed
to be, at any time during the term of this lease, seventy-five
(75%) percent of the minimum rent provided in Paragraph 5 above.

37. ACCESS TO PREMISES

Landlord shall have the right to place, maintain and
repair all utility equipment of any kind in, upon or under the
Demised Premises as may be necessary for the servicing of the
Demised Premises and other portions of the Shopping Center.
Landlord shall also have the right to enter the Demised Premises
at all times to inspect or to exhibit the same to prospective
purchasers, mortgagees, and tenants and to make such repairs,
additions, alterations or improvements as Landlord may deem
desirable. Landlord shall be allowed to take all material in,
to and upon said premises that may be required therefore without
the same constituting an eviction of Tenant in whole or in part
and the rents reserved shall in no wise abate while said work is
in progress by reason of loss or interruption of Tenant's business

or otherwise and Tenant shall have no claim for damages. If
Tenant shall not be personally present to permit an entry into
said premises in the event of an emergency,

Landlord may enter the same by a master key or by
the use of force without incurring liability therefore and without
in any manner affecting the obligations of this lease. The provisions of this paragraph shall in no wise be construed to impose
upon Landlord any obligation whatsoever for the maintenance or
repair of the building or any part thereof except as otherwise
herein specifically provided. During the Six (6) months prior to
the expiration of this lease or any renewal term, Landlord may
place upon the said premises "To Let" or "For Sale" signs which
Tenant shall permit to remain thereon.

38. EXCAVATION

If an excavation shall be made upon land adjacent to the
Demised Premises, Tenant shall permit the person authorized to
cause such excavation to enter upon the Demised Premises for the
purpose of doing such work as such person deems necessary to pre-
serve the wall or the building of which said premises form a part
from damage and to support the same by proper foundations without
any claim for damages or indemnification against Landlord or
abatement of rent.

If as a result of an entry by Landlord, or its agents,
servants or employees, pursuant to Paragraphs 37 and 38 hereof,
Tenant is required to close its business and such closing continues
for ten (10) consecutive business days, then rent shall abate from
the date of such closing until Landlord's entry ceases.

-34-

39. <u>SUBORDINATION</u>

At the option of Landlord or any mortgagee, this lease and the Tenant's interest hereunder shall be subject and subordinate to any mortgage, deed of trust, ground or underlying leases or any method of financing or refinancing now or hereafter placed against the land, and/or the Demised Premises and/or any and all of the buildings now or hereafter built or to be built in the Shopping Center by Landlord; and to all renewals, modifications, replacements, consolidations and extensions thereof.

END OF PAGE -34A-

-34A-

40. ATTORNMENT

Tenant shall in the event of the sale or assignment of Landlord's interest in the Shopping Center or in the Demised Premises, or in the event of any proceedings brought for the foreclosure of, or in the event of exercise of the power of sale under any mortgage made by Landlord covering the Demised Premises, attorn to the purchaser or foreclosing mortgagee and recognize such purchaser or foreclosing mortgagee as Landlord under this lease.

41. ATTORNEY-IN-FACT

Tenant shall, within ten (10) days after written request from Landlord, execute and deliver to Landlord such instruments to evidence the intent of Paragraphs 39 and 40. Tenant hereby irrevocably appoints Landlord as attorney-in-fact for Tenant with full power and authority to execute and deliver such instruments for and in the name of Tenant. If Tenant shall not have executed and delivered such instruments as aforesaid, and Tenant's actual execution is required by the party requesting the instrument(s), Landlord may cancel this lease without incurring any liability on account thereof and the term hereby granted is expressly limited accordingly.

42. QUIET ENJOYMENT

Tenant, upon paying the rents and performing all of the terms on its part to be performed, shall peaceably and quietly enjoy the Demised Premises subject, nevertheless, to the terms of this Lease and to any mortgage, ground lease or agreements to which this lease is subordinated.

43. FORCE MAJEURE

Landlord shall be excused for the period of any delay in the performance of any obligations hereunder, when prevented

from so doing by cause or causes beyond Landlord's control which
shall include, without limitation, all labor disputes, civil
commotion, war, war-like operations, invasion, rebellion, hos-
tilities, military or usurped power, sabotage, governmental
regulations or controls, fire or other casualty, inability to obtain any material, services or financing or through acts of God.

44. END OF TERM

At the expiration of this lease, Tenant shall surrender
the Demised Premises in the same condition as it was in upon delivery of possession thereto under this lease, reasonable wear and
tear excepted, and shall deliver all keys and combinations to
locks, safes and vaults to Landlord. Before surrendering said
premises, Tenant shall remove all its personal property including
all trade fixtures, and shall repair any damage caused thereby.
Tenant's obligations to perform this provision shall survive the
end of the term of this lease. If Tenant fails to remove its
property upon the expiration of this lease, the said property
shall be deemed abandoned and shall become the property of Landlord.

45. HOLDING OVER

Any holding over after the expiration of this term or
any renewal term shall be construed to be a tenancy at will at
the rents herein specified (pro rated on a daily basis) and shall
otherwise be on the terms herein specified so far as applicable.

46. NO WAIVER

Failure of Landlord to insist upon the strict performance
of any provision of this lease or to exercise any option or any
rules and regulations herein contained shall not be construed
as a waiver for the future of any such provision, rule or option.
The receipt by Landlord of rent with knowledge of the breach of

any provision of this lease shall not be deemed a waiver of such breach. No provision of this lease shall be deemed to have been waived unless such waiver be in writing signed by Landlord. No payment by Tenant or receipt by Landlord of a lesser amount than the monthly rent shall be deemed to be other than on account of the earliest rent then unpaid nor shall any endorsement or statement on any check or any letter accompanying any check or payment as rent be deemed an accord and satisfaction and Landlord may accept such check or payment without prejudice to Landlord's right to recover the balance of such rent or pursue any other remedy in this lease provided, and no waiver by Landlord in respect to one Tenant shall constitute a waiver in favor of any other tenant in the Shopping Center.

47. NOTICES

Any notice, demand, request or other instrument which may be or are required to be given under this lease shall be delivered in person or sent by United States Certified or Registered Mail, postage prepaid, and shall be addressed (a) if to Landlord, at the address as hereinabove given; and (b) if to Tenant, at the Demised Premises. Either party may designate such other address as shall be given by written notice.

48. RECORDING

Tenant shall not record this lease but will, at the request of Landlord, execute a memorandum or notice thereof in recordable form satisfactory to both the Landlord and Tenant specifying the date of commencement and expiration of the term of this Lease and other information required by statute. Either Landlord or Tenant may then record said memorandum or notice of lease.

49. PARTIAL INVALIDITY

If any provision of this Lease or application thereof to any person or circumstance shall to any extent be invalid, the remainder of this lease or the application of such provision to persons or circumstances other than those as to which it is held invalid shall not be affected thereby and each provision of this lease shall be valid and enforced to the fullest extent permitted by law.

50. BROKER'S COMMISSION

Tenant represents and warrants that there are no claims for brokerage commissions or finder's fees in connection with the execution of this lease and agrees to indemnify Landlord against and hold it harmless from all liabilities arising from any such claim, including cost of counsel fees.

51. SUCCESSORS AND ASSIGNS

Except as otherwise expressly provided, all provisions herein shall be binding upon and shall inure to the benefit of the parties, their legal representatives, successors and assigns. Each provision to be performed by Tenant shall be construed to be both a covenant and a condition, and if there shall be more than one tenant, they shall all be bound jointly and severally, by these provisions. In the event of any sale of the Shopping Center, or of a lease of Landlord's interest in the Shopping Center, or of a sale or lease of Landlord's interest in this lease, Landlord shall be entirely relieved of all obligations hereunder. "Landlord" shall be deemed to be the Landlord in possession of the Demised Premises from time to time as fee owner or as ground lessee under a ground lease.

52. ENTIRE AGREEMENT, ETC.

This lease and the Exhibits, Riders and/or Addenda if
any attached, set forth the entire agreement between the parties.
Any prior conversations or writings are merged herein and extin-
guished. No subsequent amendment to this lease shall be binding
upon Landlord or Tenant unless reduced to writing and signed.
Submission of this lease for examination does not constitute an
option for the Demised Premises and becomes effective as a lease
only upon execution and delivery thereof by Landlord to Tenant.
If any provision contained in a rider or addenda is inconsistent
with any other provision of this lease, the provision contained in
said rider or addenda shall supercede said other provision. It
is herewith agreed that this lease contains no restrictive covenant
or exclusives in favor of Tenant. Should the Tenant at any time
during the term of this Lease claim rights under a restrictive
covenant, exclusive, failure of continued occupancy or inducement,
whether implied or otherwise, the Tenant herewith specifically
waives any such claim with respect to department stores, regional
or national chains and kiosks within the mall, in addition to other
merchants with whom leases had been signed prior to the date of
the signing of this lease by both Tenant and Landlord.

53. CAPTIONS

The captions, numbers and index appearing herein are
inserted only as a matter of convenience and are not intended to
define, limit, construe or describe the scope or intent of any
paragraph, nor in any way affect this lease.

54. RULES AND REGULATIONS

Tenant agrees as follows: (a) All deliveries or ship-
ments of any kind to and from the Demised Premises including
loading and unloading of goods, shall be made only by way of the
rear of the Demised Premises or at any other location designated
by Landlord, and only at such time designated for such purpose by

Landlord; (b) garbage and refuse shall be kept in the kind of
container specified by Landlord and shall be placed at the location within the Demised Premises designated by Landlord, for
collection at the times specified by Landlord; Tenant to pay the
cost of removal of garbage and refuse; Tenant shall store soiled
or dirty linen in approved fire rating organization containers;
(c) no radio, television, phonograph or other similar devices, or
aerial attached thereto (inside or outside) shall be installed
without first obtaining in each instance the Landlord's consent
in writing; and if such consent be given, no such device shall be
used in a manner so as to be heard or seen outside of the Demised
Premises; (d) Tenant shall keep the Demised Premises at a temperature sufficiently high to prevent freezing of water in pipes
and fixtures; (e) the outside areas immediately adjoining the
Demised Premises shall be kept clean and free from snow, ice, dirt
and rubbish by Tenant, and Tenant shall not place, suffer or permit any obstructions or merchandise in such areas; (f) Tenant shall
not use the public or common areas in the Shopping Center for
business purposes; (g) Tenant and its employees shall park their
cars only in those portions of the parking area, if any, designated for that purpose by Landlord; Tenant to furnish Landlord
with its and its employees' automobile license numbers within Five
(5) days after taking possession of the Demised Premises and
Tenant to thereafter notify Landlord of any changes within five (5)
days after such changes occur; if Tenant or its employees fail to
park their cars in designated parking areas, then Landlord may
charge Tenant Ten ($10.00) Dollars per day for each day or partial
day per car parked in any areas other than those designated, as
and for liquidated damages; Tenant hereby authorizes Landlord

-40-

to tow away from the Shopping Center any of Tenant's cars or
cars belonging to Tenant's employees, and/or to attach violation
stickers or notices to such cars; (h) plumbing facilities shall
not be used for any other purpose than that for which they are
constructed, and no foreign substance of any kind shall be thrown
therein; (i) Tenant shall use, at Tenant's cost, a pest extermina-
tion contractor at such intervals as Landlord may require; Tenant
shall not burn trash or garbage in or about the Demised Premises,
the Shopping Center, or within one mile of the outside radius of
the Shopping Center; (k) Tenant shall not place, suffer or permit
displays, decorations or shopping carts on the sidewalk in front
of the Demised Premises or on or upon any of the common areas of
the Shopping Center; (l) Tenant agrees at all times to maintain
the heating and air conditioning equipment in the Demised Premises
and at all times to maintain temperatures in the Demised Premises
consistent with the temperatures in the enclosed mall and in a
manner which will not cause any decrease in the mall temperature
while the mall is being heated or any increase in the mall temperature while the mall is being cooled; (m) Landlord may amend or
add new rules and regulations for the use and care of the Demised
Premises, the buildings of which the premises are a part, and
the common areas and facilities.

    55. <u>LIMITATION OF LIABILITY</u>

        Anything in this lease to the contrary notwithstanding,
Tenant agrees that it shall look solely to the estate and property
of the Landlord in the land and buildings comprising the Shopping
Center of which the Demised Premises are a part, and subject to
the prior rights of any mortgagee of the premises and subject to
Landlord's rights under a leasehold interest of the Shopping
Center or part thereof, if any, for the collection of any judg-

ment (or other judicial process) requiring the payment of money by Landlord in the event of any default or breach by Landlord with respect to any of the terms, covenants and conditions of this lease to be observed and/or performed by Landlord, and no other assets of the Landlord shall be subject to levy, execution or other procedures for the satisfaction of Tenant's remedies.

56. DEFINITION OF LANDLORD OBLIGATIONS

If there should be more than one Landlord or Tenant, the covenants of the Landlord or of the Tenant shall be the joint and several obligations of each of them, and if the Landlord or Tenant are partners, the covenants of the Landlord or the Tenant shall be the joint and several obligations of each of the partners and the obligation of the partnership. In construing this Indenture, feminine or neuter pronouns shall be substituted for those of masculine form and vice versa, and the plural for singular, and the singular for plural in any place in which the context may require.

57. RIGHT TO RELOCATE

Landlord shall have the right to relocate various facilities and premises within the Shopping Center if Landlord shall determine said relocation to be in the best interest of the development of the Shopping Center. Landlord shall not have the right to relocate the Demised Premises subsequent to the commencement date of the term of this lease without Tenant's consent.

PARAGRAPHS 58, 59 and 60 INTENTIONALLY OMITTED.

HYMAN, KEITH, HARDING & HUTENSKY   100 CONSTITUTION PLAZA, HARTFORD, CONNECTICUT 06103

61. PREJUDGMENT REMEDY, REDEMPTION, COUNTERCLAIM AND JURY TRIAL

The Tenant, for itself and for all persons claiming through or under it, hereby acknowledges that this lease constitutes a commercial transaction as such term is used and defined in Public Act No. 431 of the Connecticut General Statutes, Revision of 1973, and hereby expressly waives any and all rights which are or may be conferred upon the Tenant by said Act to any notice or hearing prior to a prejudgment remedy. Tenant further waives any and all rights which are or may be conferred by any present or future law to redeem the said premises, or to any new trial in any action of ejectment under any provision of law, after reentry thereupon, or upon any part thereof, by the Landlord, or after any warrant to dispossess or judgment in ejectment. If the Landlord shall acquire possession of the said premises by summary proceedings, or in any other lawful manner without judicial proceedings, it shall be deemed a reentry within the meaning of that word as used in this Lease. In the event that the Landlord commences any summary proceedings or action for nonpayment of rent or other charges provided for in this lease, the Tenant shall not interpose any counterclaim of any nature or description in any such proceeding or action. The Tenant and the Landlord both waive a trial by jury of any or all issues arising in any action or proceeding between the parties hereto or their successors, under or connected with this Lease, or any of its provisions.

HYMAN, KEITH, HARDING & HUTENSKY   100 CONSTITUTION PLAZA, HARTFORD, CONNECTICUT 06103

62. PAST-DUE RENT

If Landlord shall fail to receive, when the same is due
and payable, any minimum rent or any percentage rent or other
amounts or charges to be paid to Landlord by Tenant, as provided
in this Lease, Tenant shall pay as additional rent a late charge
equal to twelve (12%)   percent of each installment past due to cover
the administrative costs and expenses involved in administering
delinquent accounts.

63. GOVERNING LAW

This Lease shall be construed, and the rights and obligations of Landlord and Tenant shall be determined, according to
the laws of the state in which the Demised Premises is located.

IN WITNESS WHEREOF, the parties hereto have hereunto set
their hands and seals the day and year first above written.

Signed, Sealed and Delivered
  in the Presence of:

Patricia Bjornberg	As to Land-lord	WILLIMANTIC ASSOCIATES By _[signature]_ RICHARD D. BRONSON General Partner
Susan K. Roth		
[signature] PAUL B BAMM	As to Tenant	_[signature]_ (L.S.) MORTON BROWN

HYMAN, KEITH, HARDING & HUTENSKY   100 CONSTITUTION PLAZA. HARTFORD. CONNECTICUT 06103

EXHIBIT A

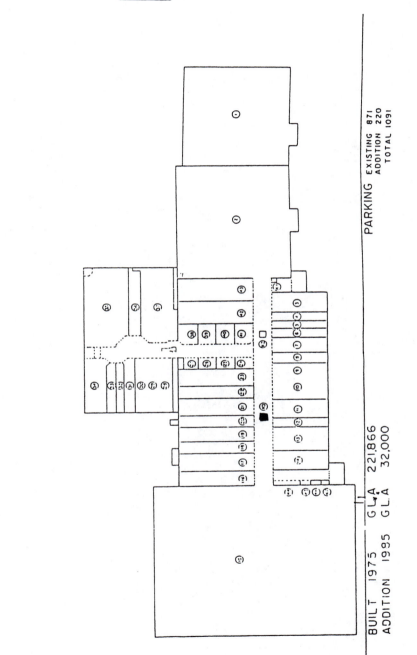

EAST BROOK MALL
MANSFIELD, CONN.

PARKING EXISTING 871 ADDITION 220 TOTAL 1091

BUILT 1975 G.L.A 221,866
ADDITION 1995 G.L.A 32,000

Appendix D

Puppy Love Store Manual
Revised July 1992

The following updated procedural manual will set up store criteria for the Associates to follow. The new hires will be able to get a jump start on the Puppy Love philosophy of doing business. It clearly sets up what the Company's priorities are and as a corollary what we feel our responsibility is to our customers, employees and the Companion Animals in our control.

Over the past 17 years the climate re: economy, customer, associate and the environment has undergone dramatic changes. The last update to our manual was done in 1984; since that time the profile of our customer has changed. A better educated consumer expects more for the retail $. The store that understands that value added grows the business has an advantage over the competition.

It is critical to the success of our operation that the better educated and informed our Associates are the more productive and adjusted they become to the store. To that end the manual will spell out in broad terms what we—as management—expect of them and what criteria for a successful performance are used.

Management is a team effort and if we are not all informed of what the objectives and goals are then the team concept will not work. Experience has taught me that the biggest challenge with new personnel is that they do not know what is expected of them; this manual should address that issue.

PUPPY LOVE PET AND AQUARIUM CENTERS
PERSONNEL GUIDELINES

Revised July 1, 1992

Welcome to the Puppy Love family. A brief history of our business may help expedite the process by which you become part of the Puppy Love heritage.

Ruth and Mort Brown founded the Company in 1975; the goals then and the goals today have not changed: to provide owners of Companion Animals a professionally trained team that care as much for our customers' pets as we would for ours.

The premise that we operate under is that our biggest asset is our personnel. We take great pride in the hundreds of people who have shared their time with us as Associates of Puppy Love. Our business is unique. We deal with the most wonderful of all things that people own, their Companion Animals. We do not take that responsibility lightly.

Naturally, we want you to be successful and enjoy yourselves while you are a member of the Puppy Love team. To that end we have found that education is the key. We will afford you every opportunity to learn, to make decisions, to grow as individuals and to be part of the best trained and educated group of professionals in our industry.

Has That Philosophy Been Successful?

We have been selected as one of the 10 best Pet Specialty Stores in the U.S.

In 1990, we received a State award from PETS of CT. for contributions to the pet industry in CT.

Since the inception of the Norwich Bulletin's "Best" in Eastern CT's readers' poll, each year we have been voted the "Best" Pet Store in Eastern CT.

Mort serves on the Dept. of Agriculture's Pet Shop Advisory Committee, representing the retail pet trade in CT.

Mort also serves on the board of the Pet Industry Joint Advisory Council, a nationally known and respected voice for the pet industry.

This manual is the Store Bible, but like all the other Bibles it won't answer all your questions; it will provide just an overview of the Company policies and procedures. Your Managers are your immediate contacts to help address any issues you may have concerning your stay with us at Puppy Love. Please read this manual a few times as soon as possible; it will help you adjust to our philosophy of doing business and make the transition as painless as possible. You will have questions so please ask, and again welcome to our family. After you've become familiar with the manual, please sign the last page (Acknowledgments) and return it to your Manager.

These personnel guidelines are intended to answer questions that you may have about your job and the employment procedures, practices and policies of Puppy Love.

All policies and practices contained in this handbook are subject to change at the discretion of Puppy Love. You will be notified of any and all changes through memos or other written notification. These guidelines do not and are not intended to create either an express or implied contract of employment or a warranty of benefits. Your employment with Puppy Love is on an at-will basis, which means that you have the right to terminate your employment at any time and Puppy Love has the right to terminate your employment at any time with or without cause and with or without notice. Any and all previous verbal and/or written policy or practice that is contrary to what is presented here is null and void. If at any time you are unclear about any of the personnel guidelines or work rules, please talk with your Store Manager.

- We want to be open to your suggestions and ideas.

- We want to provide a working atmosphere where we all grow and excel by providing exceptional support toward each other's needs.

Most importantly, WE WANT PUPPY LOVE TO BE A GREAT PLACE TO WORK!

Our Company's Most Important Principles:

These are the most important objectives and goals of our business. We will be successful only to the degree each of us recognizes and achieves these principles.

- OUR CUSTOMERS ARE CRITICAL TO OUR SUCCESS; without their loyal support we clearly have no business. Once we realize that, then as individuals and as a business our goal is clear. "EXCEEDING THE CUSTOMER'S EXPECTATION" is our challenge and to the degree that we have prospered over the past 17 years then Ruth and I feel that we have achieved some success in this endeavor. The only "problem" is that the goal becomes brand new with each customer so that we can never feel that our job is truly done. We do everything possible to make sure they are treated in the same manner that we would like to be treated under the same circumstances. We truly want Puppy Love to be a fun place to shop. If it's fun to be here, our customers will come back. To make our customers feel welcome, we must greet them when they enter our store and let them know we're here to help. We must provide accurate and helpful advice to customers who need information on pet care.

- OUR ANIMALS MUST BE GIVEN THE BEST CARE. We have consulting Veterinarians who are in the store on a weekly basis. If there are questions that can wait for their scheduled visit please funnel them through your management team; if there is a need for immediate attention for an animal then your Manager will contact the veterinarians' office where the problem will be taken care of. We at Puppy Love do not take shortcuts when we deal with our customers, and we do not take shortcuts when dealing with these wonderful Companion Animals that give us so much pleasure. Our veterinarians are experts in their fields. We even have consulting vets for reptiles, birds, ferrets or other specialties that may come up. At Puppy Love we take great pride in the care and health of everything that is in our care. Remember, we believe that GOOD ETHICS IS GOOD BUSINESS.

- Remember that each pet must be dealt with in a gentle calming manner, that in cases where a medication (i.e., worming or other preventative type of protocol) is being followed, all such implementation is done away from public view, and all conversations regarding veterinary care are done in private away from the public. It has been our experience that the public may misconstrue routine care as a negative, so rather than having to explain every procedure it is easier and more professional to deal with it out of view of the public sector. This also has a quieting effect on the animal you are treating.

- Our store must be kept clean and uncluttered at all times. Our customers measure us on the cleanliness of every aspect of our store.

- Our merchandise must be clean and well arranged so customers are motivated to buy the products.

- We must attempt to solve all customers' problems so that we retain their goodwill and repeat business.

- We must not argue or even debate with our customers. We will never win. We will only lose their support.

- We must not speak poorly about our competition but instead speak positively about our qualities.

- The only person that can really say no to a customer is a member of the Management team, so if you are in a position that you feel the answer is no to the customer's request, please check with the Manager in charge at the time.

- There is always something to do in our store so keep busy. Above all, however, be alert to the needs of our customers.

COMPANY POLICIES AND PROCEDURES

Store Opening and Closing:

Store Managers have responsibility for the opening and closing of the store each day. In the event a Store Manager is unable to open or close, a key person will be designated by the Manager to take responsibility for opening or closing. Only key people can open or close a store in the Manager's absence. If a key person knows that he/she will not be available to open or close, it is that person's responsibility to notify the Store Manager or the Asst. Manager to ensure that appropriate arrangements can be made.

Under no circumstances is someone who is not a key person to open or close a store. When the store is closed to the public for the day then NO ONE OTHER THAN SCHEDULED PERSONNEL SHOULD BE IN THE STORE. THIS MEANS FRIENDS, CUSTOMERS, UNSCHEDULED PERSONNEL, OR FORMER EMPLOYEES.

Store Coverage:

Store Managers have responsibility for appropriate coverage for all shifts on all days. It is critical that you give in writing as much notice as possible if you are not going to be at work.

Telephone Procedure:

A telephone call is an opportunity to create a customer. Since good customers are so difficult to find, it's essential that we recognize how important their call is to us.

Our objective is to answer the phone by at least the third ring. If you're with a customer and there's no one else to answer the call, excuse yourself by saying, "Would you please excuse me while I get the phone? I'll be right back." Customers do understand.

When you answer the phone, put enthusiasm in your voice. It's amazing how people can be positively influenced by your attitude when they hear a pleasant voice. Try this: "Good morning, this is Puppy Love. Bill speaking—how can I help you?" Be sure to use the complete store name and your name. Then, let the customer ask her/his question.

You'll find that questions will be as easy as, "What time do you close?" to questions that only a veterinarian should answer. Above all, be courteous.

Your real objective is to encourage customers to come into the store. You can answer their inquiry, but unless they come in, it's impossible to sell them the products they need. Even if they only want information, you want to extend an invitation to visit the store. "Have you ever been in our store? . . . Well, you should come down and see us. I'll be delighted to show you a couple of books which will explain your situation in detail." Also when you are on the phone you should be facing the store not the wall; also be aware of customers entering and exiting your store. It's good security and good manners.

If the store is busy or your customer is becoming impatient, you may have to ask the caller if you can get back to him/her. It is IMPORTANT TO REMEMBER THAT THE CUSTOMER STANDING IN FRONT OF YOU TAKES PRIORITY; he/she is in our store to purchase merchandise and must receive the best possible service. If you are with a customer when the phone rings, you can say "Thank you for calling Puppy Love. I'm with a customer right now. Can you hold for a moment?" It's also important to do one thing at a time. Don't talk to one customer on the phone when you are working with another customer. If you are on the phone when a customer approaches, simply tell the customer you will be right with him/her. If the phone call requires a lot of your time, ask the phone caller if you can get back to him/her. Then make sure you do call back or have someone else call. Remember, phone calls are not inconveniences but new customers looking for a store that will treat them nicely.

Handling Complaints:

Occasionally, you'll be faced with upset customers. It could be a product they purchased or perhaps even the service they received. Your role is to provide as much help as possible. If we can solve a customer's problem quickly and to his/her satisfaction, we'll usually retain their business. If they go away angry, they'll probably never come back and most of the time they'll tell others about how they were mistreated. We certainly don't want that to happen.

THE FOUR CRITICAL STEPS TO HANDLING CUSTOMER COMPLAINTS

1. Immediately show you'll listen to their issue. Don't argue, or get defensive, or make excuses. That just pours fuel on the fire. Instead, absorb their anger by saying things like, "I see what you mean," or "I can understand why you're upset." Keep your body language open—maintain eye contact and don't cross your arms.

2. Be sure you clearly understand the issue. Repeat back to customers the points they have made. "Let me see if I understand the situation. You purchased a hamster here a week ago, and it died." Avoid trying to shift the blame to customers even though you might believe it was partly their fault.

3. After you calm the customers down, ask them what they want. "What would you like me to do?" That usually takes them off the offensive. Most people want to vent their frustration.

4. IF THEIR REQUEST IS REASONABLE, DO IT IMMEDIATELY. Remember, if we resolve customers' complaints to their satisfaction on the spot, eight out of ten will continue to be repeat customers. If you have any question about how to resolve the complaint, ask your supervisor for help. We want customers to go away satisfied that we were concerned and addressed their problems.

A CUSTOMER COMPLAINT PROPERLY HANDLED IS AN OPPORTUNITY TO MAKE A LOYAL CUSTOMER.

Return and Exchange Policy:

It's important. Our priority above everything else is that we make our customers happy—even when we don't exactly feel they are right. There is an important business principle at work here: "Our customers are always right." We believe in that principle.

Very few customers will take unfair advantage of our policies, that's why we follow some of the most successful retailers by having a liberal refund and exchange policy. It's quite simple.

1. Any merchandise, other than livestock, can be returned for a full store credit.

2. If an item is used, new, partially abused or even if the customer thinks it should have performed better, it has always been our policy to give a full store credit with or without receipt; we are not the big chains with nine miles of rules. If a customer got in his/her car and brought back an item that was ours, then he/she deserves a full store credit. If they have their sales receipt that is fine, if they don't that is OK also. If you have any question about a return, ask your Store Manager. Our first priority is to satisfy the customer.

3. We do not give cash refunds. Please see our full return policy over the checkout at the front of the store.

4. Fish have a five-day health guarantee. Please review that policy with the Store Manager.

5. Any return or exchange involving livestock should be handled by the Store Manager or individual in charge at the time.

To ensure that we are providing the best possible service, it is essential that every customer be provided with a receipt for each transaction. If the customer is not given a receipt, the Store Manager will give the customer a $5.00 gift certificate. The $5.00 will be deducted from the cashier's wages that week.

Personal Grooming Standards:

We must always be conscious of our personal appearance. Frequently, customers make a judgment on our store by the way we dress or our personal grooming. Here are our guidelines:

1. Keep hair clean, well-groomed and in an appropriate style. Men may wear beards or mustaches but they should be neatly trimmed. Men's hair should be cut to shirt collar length, or to the same length that Mort is currently wearing his.

2. Fingernails should be cleaned and trimmed. For women, excessively long fingernails or bright polish is not appropriate.

3. For women, excessive makeup, cologne or heavy jewelry is also not appropriate.

4. Personal cleanliness is very important. Regular bathing and clean teeth will help present a positive personal image. (If you smoke, be sure to use breath fresheners regularly.)

5. Your clothing must be clean. Jeans are allowed, but they must be in good repair (no holes or patches).

6. Shoes must be appropriate—no sandals or thongs (socks must be worn).

7. Sunglasses are not appropriate; nor is gum or toothpicks.

8. Smoking or eating is not permitted on the sales floor.

Thanks very much for being cooperative and understanding about these personal grooming standards.

Pay Periods and Pay Days:

Pay periods start Sunday morning and end on Saturday evening. Because we must prepare payroll checks and do other paperwork, payday will be on the Friday of the following week.

Overtime:

All personnel will receive overtime for any hours exceeding 40 in a given week. Prior written approval must be given by the Store Manager.

Time Clock:

All employees must clock in and out in accordance with their work schedule as established by the Store Manager. Employees will record the time they work on a daily basis by:

1. Clocking in at the beginning of their scheduled hours.

2. Clocking out and in for meal periods.

3. Clocking out at the end of their scheduled hours.

Under no circumstances will an employee punch another employee's time card. Punching another employee's time card is grounds for immediate termination.

Only the Store Manager may sign an employee's time card to verify time worked.

Attendance:

If an employee is going to be absent from work, he/she must notify the Store Manager before the start of the workday. Excessive absenteeism is cause for termination.

Tardiness:

Tardiness is reporting to work after your scheduled starting time, leaving work before completing your scheduled hours or using more than your allotted time for meal or rest breaks. If you are going to be more than 10 minutes late for work or if you need to leave work early for any reason, you must notify the Store Manager. Excessive tardiness is grounds for termination.

Work Schedule:

Because Puppy Love is open seven days a week, you are required to work on all days for which you are scheduled including Sundays and holidays. If time off is needed, request it in writing from your Store Manager at least one week in advance.

Performance Reviews:

To be able to do your best work, it's important that you know what is expected of you and how well you are performing your assigned tasks. For this reason, your supervisor will discuss and evaluate your performance with you within your first six months of employment and at least once a year thereafter. These performance reviews will be formal and in writing. Shortly after you come to work for us your supervisor will work with you to develop your objectives for the year. These are the tasks and behaviors on which your performance review will be based.

Performance Reviews Serve Several Purposes:

1. They give a consistent, convenient format for you and your supervisor to review your progress and determine any areas for improvement.

2. They provide a fair basis for the application of our salary review policy as increases in salary are based on performance and are at the discretion of Puppy Love.

3. They provide a method for setting realistic performance goals for the next year.

The form used to record your review will be discussed with you, shown to you and signed by you before it becomes part of your personnel file. You have the opportunity and are encouraged to submit any written comment in response to the review which will also become part of your personnel file.

Meals and Rest Periods:

You are entitled time to eat your lunch or dinner if you work an eight hour day. No pay is deducted for time used for a break or a meal but because of scheduling problems it should be done in a timely manner and for evening personnel before 7:00 p.m. Any alteration to this schedule must be approved by the Store Manager. You are not permitted to eat on the public floor area. Notify your supervisor before leaving the floor.

You are also allowed to take a rest break if you work more than four hours. Please leave the sales floor during your break and don't invite customers or friends into the break room. As with meals, notify your supervisor before leaving the floor.

When taking lunch breaks and rest periods, keep your co-workers in mind. Let them know that you're on break and then return on time. Avoid taking breaks or rest periods while other employees are off the sales floor. Refrain from taking breaks or lunch periods with other employees since it creates a problem for floor coverage.

If you are on a break and a customer approaches you, find someone to help the customer. It's unacceptable to tell a customer that you're on a break and just walk away. This also applies if you're in the store on your day off. It only takes a minute to find someone to help the customer and it's one more reason our customers shop at Puppy Love—they know they can count on exceptional service. Just treat every customer the way you want to be treated when you are a customer.

Telephone Use:

Personal phone calls are to be brief and made only when absolutely necessary. Employees are to discourage personal calls made to them during working hours except in case of emergency.

VACATIONS AND OTHER FRINGE BENEFITS

Benefit and Description

Vacation with Pay:

Full-time employees are those that work an average week of 35 hours or more. Full-time employees are entitled to 1 week of vacation time after 12 months of continuous employment. Pay is based on average—over three months—scheduled work week. Two weeks of vacation pay is earned after three years of continuous service. Store managers receive three weeks vacation time after five years of continuous service. All benefits are terminated and all personnel are treated as new hires after a lapse of 30 days in Puppy Love's employ. VACATION TIME IS EARNED FROM JANUARY THROUGH DECEMBER OF EACH CALENDAR YEAR. The vacation must be taken between May 1 and September 10 of each year. Vacations may not be accumulated and if an Associate leaves before the vacation period it is lost. All vacation time must be approved by management. Because everyone needs time off, all vacation time should be taken each year or it will be lost. If two or more employees request the same dates for vacation, seniority will be the sole factor in determining who will get the vacation preference. Vacation pay can be issued in advance if the Associate gives us sufficient notice. Store Managers will receive four paid Holidays, New Year's, Thanksgiving, Christmas, and the Manager's birthday. Assistant Managers will receive two paid holidays, Christmas and Thanksgiving. All those entitled to paid holidays must work the scheduled day before and the scheduled day after the holiday to qualify for holiday pay. If an employee is ill before or after a holiday, a doctor's certificate will be required to qualify for holiday pay. If a paid holiday falls in a week in which an eligible employee has scheduled a vacation, the employee will be entitled to an additional day of vacation. The additional day is to be scheduled at a time convenient to both the employee and the company.

Days off scheduled in conjunction with a holiday can create coverage problems. Store managers are responsible for adequate coverage during holiday periods. Managers must approve any days off tied to a holiday for all full- and part-time employees. Puppy Love will approve any Manager's request for days off in conjunction with a holiday. For example: the Saturday before Memorial Day must be approved before it can be taken.

Profit Sharing:

Puppy Love is pleased to offer a profit sharing plan to its full-time employees after two years of continuous service as a way of saying Thank You. An employee will be eligible for a percentage of his/her pay based on the Company's performance. You must be 21 years of age or older, work 1,000 hours in each fiscal year and be in our employ on the 31st of July in the plan year in order to be eligible for that fiscal year. A full disclosure is available from our plan administrator at Tucker Anthony, One Corporate Center, Hartford, CT, 06103. Attention David Goldman, V.P. The plan is registered as the Puppy Love Pet Centers Profit Sharing Plan.

Each employee has an individual account with Tucker Anthony into which the sharing payment is deposited. Withdrawals before age 59.5 carry substantial penalties.

Medical Insurance:

Store Managers and Assistant Store Managers are entitled to a co-funded premium health insurance program currently with

Aetna Insurance through CBIA. This is available after 60 days in our employ. Please see Ruth Brown to see the benefits and the Managers' contribution to this plan. The health care plans are constantly changing so to be current with our information it is imperative that you receive full information from the Plan's coordinator Ruth Brown. The benefits included in these insurance programs are in keeping with present-day costs and will cover a portion of most normal medical bills.

Workers' Compensation:

As an employee of Puppy Love you are protected by Workers' Compensation Insurance, which covers injuries and occupational diseases that occur during the course of your employment. If you are injured during the course of your employment, please notify your supervisor within 24 hours because no benefits can be paid until a written report is filed with the insurance carrier and a doctor.

Uniforms:

As an Associate of Puppy Love you are required to wear a Puppy Love shirt, apron smock, and name badge when you are working. Puppy Love will contribute 50% of the cost of the shirts, and your contribution will be returned to you if you terminate employment with us and return your uniform.

Name Tags:

You must wear a visible name tag when you are at work. Puppy Love will provide each employee with two name tags. Any employee not wearing a name tag or requiring an additional name tag will be fined $1.00.

Employee Discount Plan:

One of the benefits of working at Puppy Love is our generous employee discount plan. Discounts are offered on most store merchandise. Because profit margins differ on our items, check with your Manager on the discount for a particular item. All employee purchases must be witnessed by the Store Manager. Shopping is to be done during meal or rest periods, on days off or before or after an employee's scheduled work hours. Discounts are for employees only.

Employee Discounts:

As a general rule of thumb: all part-time personnel under 30 hours are entitled to 20%. Full time—35 hours 40%. Store Managers at wholesale or distributors list without PL discounts.

Dog/Cat food 10%—Livestock at an individual specific basis.

Education:

Education seminars and workshops offered to employees are attended on a voluntary basis. Puppy Love will pay any fees for attendance and mileage. Education is an ongoing process in any business and adds to your ability to serve our customers. It is in your best interest to take advantage of any educational offerings. Full-time personnel are entitled to a co-sponsoring of any college courses that may have some value to your current job assignments. Managers and Assistants may have one-half to full compensation for any course taken, excluding the books. A "B" average in the course is mandatory. All courses must be reviewed by Mort to qualify for reimbursement.

Jury Duty:

Puppy Love wishes to cooperate with its employees who are summoned for jury duty. If you receive a summons, inform your Store Manager so your absence can be accommodated. You are expected to report to work whenever you are free of jury work during your regular working hours.

Bereavement:

Full-time employees are entitled to up to two days paid leave in the event of death in the immediate family. Immediate family includes spouse, parents, children, sibling, mother-in-law and father-in-law. One day paid leave for other deaths in the family may be given at the discretion of the owner.

Discipline Policy:

The following procedures are generally utilized with respect to disciplinary action. The management, however, will determine the course of action best suited to the circumstances and may skip one or more of these steps. The company expressly reserves the right to terminate an employee at will. Management may either orally warn, warn in writing, initiate probation or terminate employment, whichever it chooses and at any time. It is also your right as an employee to terminate your employment at any time for any reason.

It is the policy of Puppy Love that any conduct that in its view interferes with or adversely affects employment is sufficient for disciplinary action ranging from oral warnings to immediate discharge.

Depending on the conduct, disciplinary steps may be enforced by the following methods:

1. Verbal warning;

2. Written warning;

3. Probation;

4. Termination.

Factors that may be considered in determining the appropriate disciplinary procedure include:

1. The seriousness of the conduct.

2. The employee's employment record.

3. The employee's ability to correct the conduct.

4. Action taken in similar circumstances with other employees.

5. Improper handling of livestock.

Puppy Love continually updates and reviews its policies; its disciplinary procedures are subject to change.

Voluntary Termination:
Employees are expected to give notice two weeks before their last day of work.

Employee Pilferage:

Employee pilferage cannot be tolerated. STEALING FROM PUPPY LOVE IS STEALING FROM ALL OF US. IT IMPACTS ON THE PROFIT SHARING, ON THE ABILITY TO GIVE RAISES AND TO INCREASE BENEFITS. Any theft, no matter how small, will result in immediate termination and arrest. Employees having knowledge of employee theft can report it directly to Sherri or Mort, with the understanding that we have never violated that confidence. When a reported theft is substantiated, the employee who reported the theft will receive a $50.00 reward.

Actions which are considered dishonest and would result in termination include:

1. Any act which intentionally results in shortages of money or merchandise either from the store or from fellow employees.

2. Receiving pay for time not worked.

3. Favorable treatment in the form of discounts.

4. Abuse of employee discount privileges by providing discounted merchandise to those not entitled to it.

5. The issuing of false or improper refunds.

6. Personal use of company property or merchandise.

Employee Safety:

The safety of our staff and also our customers is a primary concern. We fully support and comply with all state and federal safety regulations. It's important we all do our share to prevent accidents—work safely at all times.

- Put equipment away after use and be sure not to leave it in the aisles—someone will eventually hurt themselves.

- If you're carrying boxes, be careful where you're going.

- If you're lifting heavy boxes, do it carefully so you don't hurt your back.

- If you feel any area is not safe or not well-lit, please bring it to our attention.

- If you use a ladder to get products, be sure that the ladder is firmly in place and that you can remove the products without a problem. If in doubt, call for help.

- Electricity can present a problem, particularly around water. Be extra cautious when it comes to power plugs.

- Avoid creating unsafe situations (e.g., water on the floor, boxes in the aisles, cords stretched across aisles). Our customers may have their minds on other things and not see the problem.

- If you are injured on the job, report the injury immediately.

Nondiscrimination Employer:

Our policy is not to discriminate against any employee or applicant on the basis of sex, race, color, creed, national origin, age, marital status, handicap or other factor as required by local, state or federal law.

We are committed to both diversity and equal opportunity in our business, in the way we treat members of our staff and our customers. We expect all employees to contribute to the nondiscriminatory environment at Puppy Love.

We are also an employment-at-will employer. In other words, we can terminate an employee if we feel that the person doesn't meet the requirements for continued service. Employees are also free to terminate their employment at their discretion.

Acknowledgments:

Please acknowledge that you have received a copy of the Personnel Guidelines for Puppy Love.

I understand that I am obligated to be familiar with and abide by the guidelines and procedures set forth in this document.

Employee Signature_____ Date_____

Store Manager Signature_____ Date_____

(TO BE SIGNED AND KEPT IN EMPLOYEE'S PERSONNEL FILE)

- We want to provide you with the training to make your job productive and enjoyable.

- We want to provide advancement to all employees based on their performance and our ability to provide the opportunities.

Our Objective:

We sincerely hope you find working for Puppy Love a rewarding and enjoyable experience. We will attempt to make your career with us as valuable as possible. Learn as much as you can about pets, pet products and people. The information and experience you gain with us will benefit you for years to come.

Thanks for becoming part of our team and best of success.

Appendix E

Cash Out Sheet

Puppy Love Pet & Aquarium Center

1805.06 CASH
325.02 CHARGES
$2130.00 Total

DATE: 12-12-96 WEATHER: _____ CUSTOMER COUNT: _____

	FIRST CASH OUT	SECOND CASH OUT
DOGS	94.34	615.00
DOGSUPPIES	274.86	170.01
FISH	97.11	12.98
FISHSUPPLIES	190.12	58.44
BIRDS & SUPPL.	118.78	30.88
SMALLANIMALS	235.73	164.35
SALTWATER	—	—
TAXFREE	—	—
TAX	60.67	63.11
GROSS SALES	1071.61	1114.77
PAID OUTS/ VOIDS	43.83	11.01
NETSALES	1027.78	1103.76
① CASH	795 43	⑤ 1009 63
② ALLCHARGES	233 01	⑥ 92.01
OVER/SHORT	.66 ↑	2.12 ↓ = 1.46 ↓

PAID OUTS

③ Store Credit Used   33.81

PAID OUTS

⑦ 3.17 TAPE - Store Supplies
1.26 Store Credit

VOIDS

④ VOID 8.35
VOID 1.67

VOIDS

⑧ 6.58 VOID

Cash Out Paper Trail

First Cash Out Paperwork

① First Cash Out Deposit Ticket

② First Cash Out Credit Card Sales

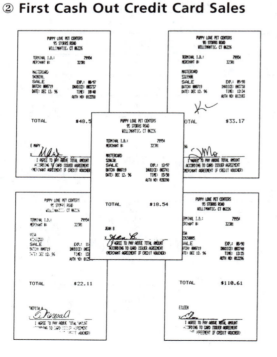

③ Store Credit Used During First Cash Out Period

④ First Cash Out Void Slips with Cash Register Receipts

Second Cash Out Paperwork

⑤ Second Cash Out Deposit Ticket

⑥ Second Cash Out Credit Card Sales

⑦ Paid Out for Store Supplies During Second Cash Out Period

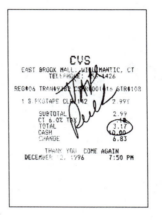

⑧ Second Cash Out Void Slips with Cash Register Receipts

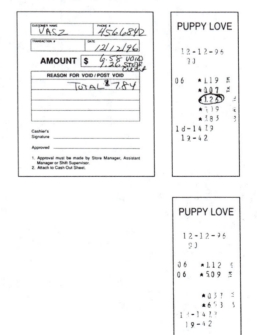

Cash Out Paper Trail

First Cash Out Paperwork

First Summary Register Tape by Department

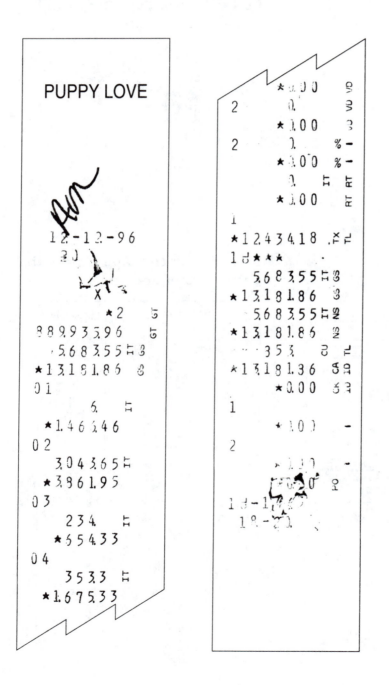

Second Cash Out Paperwork

Second Summary Register Tape by Department

PUPPY LOVE

pm

12-12-96
30

x

★2   5
891.05173   5
5.576.35 ± 3
★14.29.63   3
01
7   5
★218146
02
3.26.44.54
★4.031.96
03
242   5
★567.31
04
4533   5
★1.73377
5

★1.00   3
2
3   3
★100   3
2   1   % -
★100   % -
1   AT AT
★100   AT AT
1
★13.485.84 5 ±
10 ★★★
5.576.35 ± 3
★14.29.63   3
5.576.35 ± 3
★14.29.63   3
300   5 ±
★14.29.63 - 53
★100 5 ±
1
★400   -
2
★100   -
★400 2
10-151.6
21.-32

Cash Out Paper Trail

Day's End

Transaction Tape for Credit Cards at Day's End

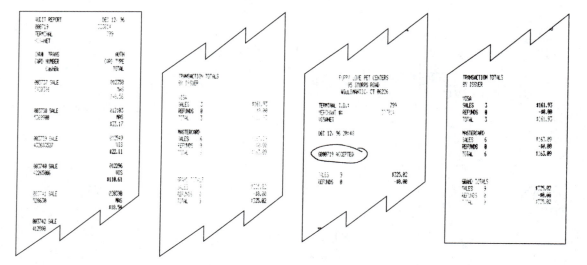

Transaction Tape for Day's End

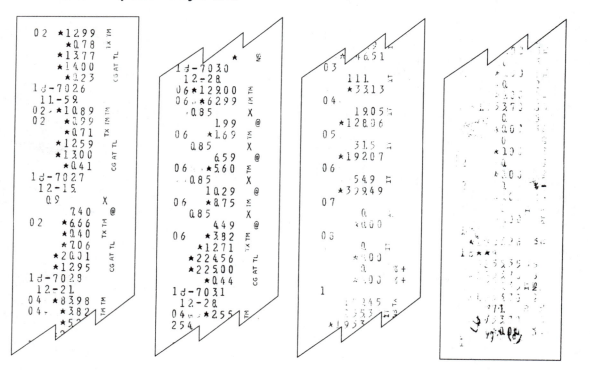

Glossary:
Speaking Retail

Above market pricing — Pricing above the normal market value. Trendy items such as Cabbage Patch dolls, Pogs, and Miatas have all, at one time or another, sold above their price. This flip side of the discount coin occurs where there is a scarcity of the particular item to sell.

Absentee ownership — Ownership by a distant proprietor. The term usually refers to a store, but may also be applied to a whole mall. A mall that is owned locally but managed from afar is usually more difficult to work with.

Anchor — The large chain store usually found at either end of a mall or a strip center.

Boilerplate

A preprinted document or one taken directly from the computer and handed to the client for signature. Boilerplate looks official but can always be changed by mutual consent.

Boutique department

A mini theme store within a larger store, such as the Armani Shop in a department store or the Yankee Dugout Store at Macy's.

Breadth

How extensive your line assortment is, how many different styles of, say, hair clips or bathing suits you carry.

Business plan

The detailed, often optimistic written road map of where a business is going and how it's going to get there.

Cash flow statement

A month-by-month projection of your income versus expenses. The biggest mistake beginners make is to have constant projections. In a gift business, for example, 35 percent of your yearly sales might be in December and 4 percent in July. Project a constant cash flow in such an instance and you'll be out of business within a year.

Circular

An advertising insert, also referred to as a flier or a tab, stuffed into mailboxes or newspapers. If you use circulars, use coupons with a key so that you can determine if these often cost-effective sales tools are working in your situation.

Consignment store

A store, reflecting a recent trend in retailing, in which the merchandise, new or used, is owned by the individual delivering it. The store does not pay for the inventory, but rather keeps a percentage of the receipts from each sale.

Current liabilities   Debts payable within one year.

Deep pockets   A reference to finances, not fashion, indicating someone with a large cash reserve that he or she is willing to commit to a business.

Depth   The quantity of merchandise you carry, as in "How deep is your stock?" Do you carry two or five or ten of each item? The higher the number, the greater your depth.

End cap   The display at the end of each store aisle. End caps stand out in the consumer's eyes and should always be well stocked. Change them frequently.

Facing   When you look at a store shelf, the row of merchandise you see, as opposed to the items behind the first row, is called the facing. The better an item is selling, the more facing it should have.

Flat   An answer to "How's business?" signifying that it's not up or down, but more or less the same.

FOB   A commercial term from the days of sailing ships standing for "free on board" and meaning that you pay the freight from the location specified in the sales agreement.

Gross sales   Total sales excluding sales tax.

Jobber   A supplier who stocks and services a display in your store. You sell the goods and pay the rack jobber. The jobber selects and maintains the merchandise for the display.

Key

An identifier such as *F129* (standing for Flier January 29th) in the corner of a clip-out coupon enabling you to measure the effectiveness of various print advertisements.

Leasehold

Everything you do to upgrade a location, as, for instance, putting in a bathroom, that remains the landlord's property once you move out.

Lease renewal

The right to renew a lease. A lease is written for a specific time period, say five, ten, or fifty years, at the end of which you may or may not have the right to renew it, depending on what you signed in the first place.

Logo

The symbol that defines your company. The degree of identity and recognizability of your store's logo is the measure of its success. Think Joe Camel or the Golden Arches. A jingle, as in "You deserve a break today," is the radio equivalent of a logo.

Ly

Last year (pronounced as two separate letters), as in last year's sales figures, last year's merchandise, and so on.

Mall

An enclosed shopping center with a large common space or a courtyard. In some consistent climate locations, such as San Diego, the common area may be an open garden.

Markdown or Md

Lowering the regular price of merchandise in order to help move it.

Mom and Pop

A retail establishment typically locally owned and operated by a family. A three- or four-store chain may be a Mom and Pop operation as well if the owners are involved on a daily basis at each store.

Net sales

Gross sales less any returns made to suppliers.

Prime rate

The lowest interest rate for loans that a bank will offer at any given time. The prime rate is for the crème de la crème of the bank's customers, and even they often pay 1/2 percent over prime. Typically, the small business borrows at 2 to 3 percent over prime.

SBA

The Small Business Adminstration, a government office available to help people starting small businesses. The SBA provides counseling and business plan evaluation. It does not lend money, but it will guarantee part of a bank loan, making the loan easier to get.

Sixties (also Thirties)

The number of seconds in a radio commercial. Local radio, particularly at drive time, 7:00 to 9:00 A.M. and 4:00 to 5:30 P.M., can be very effective in drawing customers.

Soft

An answer to "How's business?" indicating that it's inconsistent, not up, not down, but mixed, a bit of both. One line may be doing very well while another, inexplicably, isn't selling at all.

Spiff

A bonus paid by a manufacturer directly to sales associates or through the store owner to promote specific merchandise.

Strip

An outside shopping center with all the stores in a row or surrounding the parking lot horseshoe fashion.

Triple net lease

A lease under the terms of which you as a tenant pay your percentage, based on leased square feet, of all costs, maintenance charges, taxes, insurance, water, landscaping, and so on, pertaining to the landlord's premises.

Turn

The number of times you sell the equivalent of all the inventory in your store. If you stock $200,000 worth of inventory and your annual sales are $400,000, you're doing two turns.

Upscale

A retailer specializing in goods at the high end of both price and quality.

Variable expense

An expense that you control directly and can raise or lower in response to changes in sales volume. Variable expenses include such costs as advertising, payroll, and commissions.

Weak anchor

An anchor store that is not a draw in and of itself but, rather, depends as much on the traffic generated by the mall as does the smaller retailer.

Index